General Chennault's Secret Weapon

General Chennault's Secret Weapon

The B-24 in China

A. B. FEUER

Based on the Diary and Notes of Captain Elmer E. Haynes

Forewords by
ANNA C. CHENNAULT
and
COLONEL WILLIAM D. HOPSON

Westport, Connecticut
London

Library of Congress Cataloging-in-Publication Data

Haynes, Elmer E., 1917–
General Chennault's secret weapon : the B-24 in China : based on the diary and notes of Captain Elmer E. Haynes / [edited by] A. B. Feuer ; forewords by Anna C. Chennault and William D. Hopson.
p. cm.
Includes index.
ISBN 0–275–94353–4 (alk. paper)
1. Haynes, Elmer E., 1917– —Diaries. 2. World War, 1939–1945—Aerial operations, American. 3. World War, 1939–1945—Campaigns—China. 4. B-24 bomber. 5. World War, 1939–1945—Personal narratives, American. 6. Air pilots, Military—United States—Diaries. 7. China—History, Military. I. Feuer, A. B., 1925– .
II. Title.
D790.H389 1992
940.54'4973—dc20 92–14748

British Library Cataloguing in Publication Data is available.

Library of Congress Catalog Card Number: 92–14748
ISBN: 0–275–94353–4

First published in 1992

Praeger Publishers, 88 Post Road West, Westport, CT 06881
An imprint of Greenwood Publishing Group, Inc.

Printed in the United States of America

The paper used in this book complies with the Permanent Paper Standard issued by the National Information Standards Organization (Z39.48–1984).

10 9 8 7 6 5 4 3 2 1

This story of the 308th Bomb Group is dedicated
to the members of the Fourteenth Air Force
and to the memory of General Claire Lee Chennault.

Contents

Maps

Foreword

Anna C. Chennault

Generalissimo Chiang Kai-shek said of the Flying Tigers:

> The men of the American Volunteer Group [AVG] of the Chinese Air Force have acquired a worldwide reputation for great courage. The splendid victories the Volunteer Group has won in the air are a glory that belongs to the Chinese and the Americans alike. The record of what you have done shows that every one of you has been a match for thirty or more of the enemy. Your friends and relatives will undoubtedly have felt boundless pride and elation over your exploits. The blows you have struck at the Japanese have put you in the forefront of the Allied Forces fighting the aggressor. You have established a firm foundation for the campaign against lawlessness in which China and America are united. You have written in the history of this world war a remarkable page, the memory of which shall live in our minds forever.

For the younger American generation, 1941 was so very long ago. Yet, in 1937, the Japanese attacked China and we experienced the beginning of the Sino-Japanese War that lasted eight years. The Chinese had to cope with Japan's massive ground and air attacks on many coastal provinces, seaports, and cities. China needed help, and thanks to General Claire Lee Chennault, their call for help was answered.

The American Volunteer Group, better known as the Flying Tigers, was born thanks to and with the blessing of President Roosevelt. Chennault was able to obtain 100 planes and over 300 ex-military pilots and ground crew. For a critical period, from December 1941 to July 1942, the AVG was the only American combat unit fighting in East Asia—the "forgotten theater." The Chinese called its members "Angels with or without wings."

Captain Elmer E. "Bud" Haynes's story is the account of many men who fought in China during a very difficult time, faced with many unusual challenges, and yet who proved that "faith can move mountains and rivers." All these individuals took a leading part, big and small, in the struggle for the freedom of an ancient civilization alien to their own. Each of them in his own heart began to identify with the aspirations of these strange people who had become tired of believing the many so-called promises. However, these men fought on. Their creative imagination had to invent on-the-spot answers to the irregularly shaped realities for which there were no precedents. This group of men with courage, skill, and devotion did more with less than any American who fought in other World War II theaters. These young men, so far from home, with few supplies, and against fearful odds, won the war against the Japanese when victory was needed most. Courage is grace under pressure.

I am glad Captain Haynes kept a diary, and I am grateful that he was able to come home to share his "days in China" with us. He tells it the way it was, and his account is most moving.

We salute those who did not come home and those who were fortunate enough to return.

Foreword

Colonel William D. Hopson
United States Air Force (Ret.)

This is the true story of the air war conducted in an exotic theater—the China Sea—as seen through the eyes of a combat pilot. It narrates day-to-day episodes in the life of "Hainan Harry" Haynes, highly decorated as a bomber pilot and later highly commended for his operational and administrative skills.

His organization, the 308th Heavy Bomb Group, received a Presidential Unit citation that stated in part:

> This group preyed relentlessly on the Japanese Sea shipping lanes between the Japanese homeland and her conquests in Southern Asia and adjacent insular territories. During most of this period it was the only organization among all of the Allied Forces in a position to conduct interdiction operations against their vital supply lines. Operating from bases in China, the Group swept the East and South China Seas, the Straits of Formosa, and the Gulf of Tonkin, thru all kinds of weather, sinking and damaging nearly three quarters of a million tons of vital Japanese shipping.

The book is chock-full of human interest stories that make it as interesting reading as a novel—hard to put down once started.

Preface

In March 1943, the 308th Bomb Group (also called the Heavy Bomb Group), comprised of B-24 Liberator bombers, was sent to China and assigned to General Claire Lee Chennault's Fourteenth Air Force—more popularly known as the "Flying Tigers." The headquarters of the 308th was located at Kunming, China, and its squadrons were deployed at satellite airfields in the surrounding countryside and at forward bases established near Liuchow and Kweilin.

The B-24s were not equipped with radar and were used in daylight air strikes against Japanese troop concentrations and shipping operations. They also flew bombing missions against enemy-controlled rail centers and coastal cities. The Liberators, or "Flying Boxcars" as they were called, suffered heavy losses with marginal results.

About the end of April 1943, a conference was held in Washington, D.C., to discuss war strategy and how the conflict was being conducted. Generals Joseph Stilwell and Claire Chennault gave their respective reports on the status of the war in the China-Burma-India (CBI) theater of operations. Their information was anything but encouraging. It was evident that something had to be done to stem the Japanese tide in the Far East.

General Chennault stated emphatically that he had airfields within range of enemy shipping lanes, and, if given enough heavy bombers, his command could sink a million tons of Japanese ships—seriously hampering Japan's war effort. It was a conservative statement. (In actuality, by the end of the war, the Fourteenth Air Force had blasted nearly two and a half million tons of enemy vessels to the bottom of the South China Sea.)

Time was of the essence, and President Franklin Roosevelt promised Chennault that the required planes, crews, and supplies would be made available as soon as possible.

Research and development quickly came into play. Special electronic equipment was hurriedly designed and—out of necessity—high- and low-altitude radar bombing was born.

This untold story of General Chennault's secret weapon—the night-flying, radar-guided B-24—is based on the diary and papers of Captain Elmer E. "Bud" Haynes, who flew 40 combat missions with the 308th Bomb Group in China. Among his many decorations, Captain Haynes was awarded the Distinguished Flying Cross with oak leaf cluster, the Air Medal with oak leaf cluster, and the China Service Distinguished Unit Citation.

Acknowledgments

I would like to thank Elmer E. Haynes for his permission to use his diary and notes to compile this account of his experiences with the 308th Bomb Group in China during World War II.

I am also indebted to Anna C. Chennault for her kindness in writing a Foreword to the story and her permission to quote from General Claire Lee Chennault's book *Way of a Fighter*.

A special thanks to Colonel William D. Hopson, U.S. Air Force (Ret.), for his interest in this project and for writing an additional Foreword to the manuscript.

I would also like to recognize the members of the Fourteenth Air Force Association, the Hump Pilots Association, and the China-Burma-India Veterans Association.

Photographs are courtesy of Elmer E. Haynes, Anna C. Chennault, Colonel William D. Hopson, and the National Archives.

Introduction

Bud Haynes was born on June 25, 1917, in Kansas City, Missouri, and, in the mid-1920s, lived near Mines Airfield on the outskirts of El Segundo, California.

During the Depression, Bud earned his spending money by washing down aircraft on the flight line and sweeping out hangars. The Army Air Corps had based a squadron of Boeing pursuit planes at the base, and Haynes became enthralled with the pilots and their aircraft.

On March 10, 1941, Bud enlisted in the U.S. Army, and in 1942 he passed the entrance examination for the Aviation Cadet Program. In May 1943, Haynes graduated as a second lieutenant, with twin-engine expertise, from the Army Air Force Training Center, Columbus, Mississippi.

The following month, Lieutenant Haynes was assigned to the Second Sea-Search Squadron, First Sea-Search Attack Group, based at Langley Field, Virginia. By what Bud calls "a stroke of good fortune," he was now attached to the organization involved in the development of experimental electronic equipment and airborne radar. The sea-search squadrons were to be used in the perfecting of tactics and techniques in handling these new instruments while on antisubmarine patrols. Haynes remarked:

> Security in our job was extraordinarily tight. Everything we worked with was classified as "SECRET." It was even forbidden to mention the word "radar" except within the confines of squadron activity. The hangars—housing planes equipped with electronic gear—were guarded and patrolled day and night. No one was allowed in the classified area without special identification.

When the sea-search squadrons were first activated in July 1942, only one squadron had been fitted with radar. The device was of British manufacture and consisted of fork-like antennas that hung underneath the wing. The unit was called air-surface vessel (ASV). This radar equipment, together with another electronic apparatus named magnetic anomaly detection (MAD), enabled sea patrol aircraft to detect surface vessels at long distances—and even submerged submarines.

As the research and development of these new systems progressed, the Third Sea-Search Squadron began using B-24 Liberator four-engine bombers in test flights. The bombers were capable of long-range patrolling and were equipped with a new rotating antenna located in the plane's lower belly retractable turret. Crews were trained in the use of the radar rather than flying actual combat patrol missions.

In September 1943, the First Sea-Search Attack Group began intensive training and indoctrination of electronic crews for the low-altitude bombing (LAB) and the high-altitude bombing (H2X) systems. The LAB radar was installed in B-24s and designed for use against surface vessels. The H2X radar was placed aboard B-17 Flying Fortresses that were to be employed in attacks on land targets. (The H2X crews, also called "Mickeys," led the saturation bombing missions over Europe.)

Both the LAB and H2X radars were integrated with the Norden Bombsight, and both systems worked in conjunction to compute the actual moment of bomb release. This combination feature took the "drift factor" out of the bombing problem and became known as "blind bombing." Visual sighting of the target was now no longer necessary.

At first, the effective range of the LAB radar bombsight was 7,000 feet. However, as work progressed on the system, the altitude was gradually lowered to the 1,000-foot level for bombing runs.

In August 1943, ten radar aircraft, under what became known as the Wright Project, were sent to the South Pacific to test the electronic equipment under actual combat conditions. And in October, the Scott Project provided 12 more aircraft and crews to the Pacific war zone.

Bud Haynes was transferred to the Fourth Sea-Search Squadron in November and began flying B-17s equipped with H2X radar. Test flights were conducted, and the men were indoctrinated in the use of the apparatus.

By early December, the training sorties increased dramatically. Haynes's section was given the bulk of the new crews, and instruction missions were flown around the clock. It was exhausting work with no relief in sight.

However, about the end of the month, fate stepped in. Bud Haynes narrated:

> I was standing at the bar in the Officer's Club—having a drink to steady my nerves after a grueling, long-distance training flight—when my pal Milt

Wind tapped me on the shoulder. Wind was also a second lieutenant and had been flying LAB B-24s about the same length of time that I had been piloting B-17s. We had often discussed the tension and frustration of training new flight crews day after day. But, this time, Milt had hit on a way out of our predicament. He said that a unit was being formed—using highly trained LAB crews—for combat duty in the Far East.

At first, it didn't make sense to me, and I asked Wind, "What are you telling me this for, I'm a B-17 pilot and I don't know a damned thing about a B-24, except that it's the ugliest airplane I've ever seen." Milt agreed with me on that score but said that after he had flown them for quite some time, he found the Liberator to be a great aircraft—and, in comparison, the B-17 was like flying a kite.

Wind laid his proposition right on the line. If I wanted to get out of the rat race at Langley, he could arrange it—that is, if I wasn't too proud to fly as his copilot. Milt also stated that he would have me checked out as a B-24 first pilot. He figured that both of us, flying as a team, would have a better-than-average chance of survival. And possibly, we might be able to acquire quite a bit of combat experience before the air force discovered that both of us were first pilots and split us up.

The idea sounded pretty good to me—and if this was my only chance to get out of Langley, I was willing to go along with Wind and his scheme.

In the early part of January 1944, word was passed to all sea-search personnel that a secret meeting was to be held in a large hangar on the flight line. Interested people were told where and when to report and to fill out a form swearing them to secrecy as to anything said or discussed. Security would be tight, and no one would be admitted who had not signed the form nor volunteered to attend.

A couple of weeks later, the big night arrived. Bud Haynes, Milt Wind, and a few hundred other members of the sea-search squadrons presented their credentials and filed into the hangar. Haynes continued:

The entire floor of the building was covered with folding chairs. Several men were seated on a platform at the east end of the hangar. After the meeting was called to order, an officer from Air Force Headquarters introduced himself. The speaker put all his cards on the table, and the picture he painted was not a pretty one.

The objective of this secret project was to seek out and destroy Japanese surface vessels by using LAB radar equipment. Strikes against enemy shipping would be flown at night—under cover of darkness—to help escape detection and gain the element of surprise. The operation had the highest priority and, if successful, would break the back of the enemy war effort in the Pacific.

Attacks would usually be made by single sorties—each plane carrying a normal load of twelve 500-pound bombs to be dropped from an altitude of 1,000 feet or less. Three bombs would be released on each attack run. This method would give a covering pattern on almost any type of vessel.

The aircraft to be used in the project would be the latest model Liberator—the B-24J. We would be flying through some of the worst weather conditions in the world—and over the roughest terrain. The men chosen for this mission would be the best pilots, bombardiers, navigators, and enlisted personnel that could be assembled.

We would fly our own planes with hand-picked crews of ten men each. All training would be done within the framework of the First Sea-Search Attack Group and would be accomplished in about 90 days. A minimum of 30 LAB crews would be selected.

Upon leaving Langley Field, each pilot would be given sealed orders—to be opened in flight—giving the route to be flown and final destination. We had two weeks to sign up or decline. It was a very quiet and somber group of men that left the hangar after the meeting. Every one of us was absorbed in his own thoughts—trying to figure out what the chances of survival would be.

Bud Haynes, Milt Wind, and several of their friends—including George Pierpont, Tommy Tomenedale, Harry Marshall, and Carl Weitz—were selected for the secret project and assigned to Section E, 11th AAF Base Unit (Sea Attack and Staging). Haynes narrated:

Wind and I picked our crew and, about the end of March, began specialized training. I finished the written exams on the B-24, put in the necessary hours of dual transition, passed the cockpit tests, completed other requirements, and was checked out as a B-24 first pilot—just like Milt had promised.

The switch from the B-17 to a Liberator came easily to me as far as actual flying was concerned. However, the B-24 was more difficult to handle from a physical perspective. It was heavier then the Flying Fortress, and required more exertion to operate the dual rudders and aileron controls. But its Davis wing allowed the aircraft to cruise at a much higher speed than the B-17.

The overall visibility from a B-24 was much better than that of a Fortress. The Liberator's shoulder mounted wings permitted excellent observation under and around the plane—plus its tricycle gear afforded better frontal vision when taxiing, since it sat level on the ground.

On the minus side of the ledger was the fact that the Liberator needed longer airstrips than the B-17. A combination of the plane's long take off runs, higher landing speeds, and tricycle wheels, allowed the aircraft to roll for miles before it finally braked to a stop. In landing tests on the dry Utah lake beds, a B-24 rolled for more than five miles before coming to a halt.

April 1944 found the LAB crews on an intensive indoctrination schedule. The new B-24Js also began arriving—a few planes each week—and were assigned to various outfits. Each aircraft was equipped with the latest radar gear and bombsight—identification friend or foe (IFF), low altitude radio altimeters, with an accuracy of ten feet or less, and a newly developed drift meter for navigational purposes.

Near the end of May, the first section comprised of 20 LAB crews took off from Langley Field. The flight was commanded by Lieutenant Colonel William D. Hopson. Although their destination was secret, everybody had a good idea where they were headed.

It was not until June that enough planes arrived to equip the second section of what was now known as the "Hopson Project." This unit consisted of 25 aircraft and included Milt Wind, Bud Haynes, and their crew. Haynes recalled:

> Our section was called together for a meeting to hear Hopson's report of his group's flight to China. He related the pitfalls along their route—across central Africa, Pakistan, India, then over the "Hump" of the Himalaya Mountain Range to Kunming, China—headquarters of General Chennault's Fourteenth Air Force, the Flying Tigers.
>
> The B-24s of the first section were assigned to four squadrons of the 308th Bomb Group. Hopson stated that everything necessary for us to fight and work with had to be flown over the Hump—and, even then, only the bare essentials were available. We were also warned to guard our planes at all times and never leave them unattended—especially in Africa, or else the people working at the airfields would steal us blind. He suggested that a route across northern Africa would be more suitable—depending, of course, on the military situation, landing strips, and the availability of fuel.
>
> Hopson also described the conditions existing in China. As far as food was concerned, we would have to live off the land, so to speak, and it would be an entirely different fare than we were used to. Disease was endemic, and proper inoculation shots were absolutely necessary. In malaria districts, Atabrine tablets were a must.
>
> Weather would be a major problem at all times—especially during the monsoon season. More importantly, very few accurate navigational charts were available. Due to China's size and rugged terrain, many areas had never been properly mapped. We all agreed that our future looked bleak indeed.

By the middle of June, all crews of the second section had received their aircraft. Each new B-24 had to be checked out from nose to tail. Numerous test flights were conducted and fuel consumption noted. This factor could vary greatly from one plane to another due to its weight when fully loaded. An extra gasoline tank was installed in the bomb bay of each Liberator, thereby giving the B-24 enough fuel to keep it airborne for long periods—often more than 16 hours at a stretch.

Bud Haynes described the frantic activity in getting his aircraft, the *Innocence Abroad*, ready for its journey to the Far East: "Magnetic compasses had to be swung for varying deviation caused by equipment in the plane, radios checked for reception and transmission, radar tested for proper calibration detection capabilities, continuous day and night flying was conducted to familiarize our crew with the new electronic gear—day after day, training was maintained at a rapid clip."

Figure 1
Overseas Orders for Milton Wind and Bud Haynes

Special Orders Number 186, Headquarters Army Air Base, Langley Field, Virginia. Restricted Extract.

2 B-24J Electronic Trained Replacement Crews are hereby relieved from assignment to Section E, 111th AAF Base Unit, Langley Field, Virginia, and are assigned to Shipment No. FM-322-AP-8 (Crew Number), and FM-322-AP-9 (Crew Number), Project No. 90701-R, and will travel via military airplane on or about 11 July 1944 to Dow Field, Bangor, Me., and or any such stops as the CG ATC only may direct, reporting on arrival to the CO thereat for temporary duty, subsequent movement by air to an overseas destination for permanent change of station.

Crew No. FM-322-AP-8 Project No. 90701-R	AP No. 44-40786 B-24J
2nd Lt. (1092) Wind, Milton. 0-799909	Pilot
2nd Lt. (1022) Haynes, Elmer E. 0-803618	Copilot
1st Lt. (1034) McClure, Robinson C. 0-1577544	Navigator
2nd Lt. (1030) Miracle, James V. 0-688200	Bombardier
S/Sgt. (748) Armstrong, Jasper V. 1403665	Flight Engineer
T/Sgt. (757) George, Philip J. 35510959	Radio Operator
Sgt. (612) Thomas, Henry M. 14050877	Aerial Gunner
Pvt. (611) Carpenter, Fred A. 12154128	Waist Gunner
Cpl. (611) Cuva, James V., Jr. 32746584	Waist Gunner
Cpl. (866) Atkins, Milton 39041354	Radar Operator

Finally, on July 8, 1944, Milt Wind and Bud Haynes received their overseas orders (see Figure 1). And at 8:15 A.M. on August 11, the *Innocence Abroad* took off from Langley Field, Virginia, on the first leg of the arduous trip to China.

CHAPTER 1

Flight to Chabua, India

July 15, 1944

After stops at Bangor, Maine, and Gander, Newfoundland, we took off this morning for the long flight to Largen Field in the Azores—across 1,500 miles of nothing but water.

The Azores are farther from the U.S. mainland than any other group of islands in the Atlantic. When we received our briefing for this leg of the journey, I warned our navigator, Jim McClure, "Mac, if you miss that dot out there in the middle of the ocean, we'll all end up swimming." Needless to say, my remark made a serious impression on McClure—we hit the Azores right on the nose.

As we made our landing approach, I wondered how in the world this airstrip was ever constructed. The islands seemed to consist of nothing except volcanic peaks poking straight up from the sea. The field had been carved across the mountainous terrain and laid with a steel-grid runway. We made a perfect landing, but the noise and vibration, caused by our wheels rushing over the metal surface, was deafening. Despite the shaking, the plane stayed together in one piece and we finally rolled to a stop. What a flight—seven hours over the ocean. I was ready to kiss the ground when I climbed out of the aircraft.

Flying the B-24, on a long flight such as this, demanded constant attention to every detail. It was especially important to keep the airplane in correct trim. As our gasoline supply decreased, the center of balance of the ship changed. The high-speed Davis wing required a correct angle of attack through the air in order to be efficient. The B-24, when trimmed out properly, should fly with its nose slightly below the level position. If the angle of the plane is "tail down," the drag on the aircraft increases, the ship cruises at a slower speed, the engines have to work harder, and fuel consumption increases.

On the trip from Gander to the Azores, we flew at 8,000 feet—burned about 160 gallons of fuel per hour, and averaged 200 MPH ground speed. Due to the weight of radar gear equipment, LAB B-24s were heavier than the straight Liberators and consumed more gasoline.

July 17, 1944

We departed Largen Field at 0800 and Mac set a course for Marrakech, Morocco. The five-and-a-half-hour flight covered 1,000 miles. This was our first taste of desert country, and it was hot as hell.

July 18, 1944

In the early morning, our plane lifted off from Marrakech—destination Tunis. The route carried us across the Atlas Mountains and over the combat areas where many battles had raged during the North African Campaign. Several thousand feet below us, the seemingly endless ocean of sand revealed the grim and grisly evidence of warfare. The debris was strewn about like the broken toys of children—tanks, trucks, armored vehicles, jeeps, artillery pieces, and aircraft—the entire arsenal of military hardware was represented.

Half-buried in the scarred desert landscape were vestiges of burned-out, empty villages—mute testimony to the waste and senselessness of war—the tragic aftermath of all the bloodshed and killing.

As we cruised above mile after mile of this ethereal landscape—and the world's largest junkyard—I recalled news reports describing the battles and what had occurred on the blood-soaked sands. It was difficult to tell from our vantage point exactly who had won—and who had lost—the conflict.

We landed at Tunis about 1600 and parked our plane after a long taxi down the edge of the field. My first impression, upon leaving the aircraft, was the barnyard smell that permeated the air. The odor was overpowering at first, but after a few hours, I became used to it.

We spent the rest of the afternoon touring the city in a horse-drawn carriage—which they call a taxi around here. The most confusing aspect of our journey so far has been the exchange rate of American dollars for foreign currency. Since leaving the United States, we have had to deal with Canadian, Portuguese, and French money. (Before our trip was over, however, we would end up being totally confused. We still had the currency of Egypt, Iran, Pakistan, India, and finally China to contend with.)

July 19, 1944

We were airborne from Tunis at 1000. McClure plotted a course along the southern coastline of the Mediterranean—1,400 miles to Cairo, Egypt. On our approach to Payne Field, we flew over the Pyramids and Sphinx at Giza. It was a sight I shall never forget—wonders of the ancient world that I had read about but never expected to see. But now, there they were—before my eyes—standing, as they had for centuries, like taunting monoliths, defying the crudities of man, wind, and sand.

After an uneventful landing, Wind, Miracle, McClure, and I grabbed a ride to town and arranged for quarters at the Pension Trianon—an officer's hotel in downtown Cairo. The rooms were large and with all conveniences. We decided that after several thousand miles of tedious flying, we were entitled to a night on the town. We shaved, showered, dressed up in clean uniforms, and inquired where we could get a good meal and a few drinks. I was told that the International Club had everything a man could desire. We had no trouble finding the place. The four of us were greeted like war heroes and shown to a table down front where we could watch the stage show. One exotic course after another was brought to our table—each washed down with potent beer and liquor.

Throughout the evening, we were entertained by one sensuous, frolicking show girl after another—many of them belly dancers. We were so close to the action that I could almost reach out and touch them. McClure finally cracked under the pressure and had to be forcibly restrained from climbing up on the stage. The club was jammed with people, and they were getting a big kick out of Mac's antics. However, I must admit that the well-oiled movements of those voluptuous beauties could raise the blood pressure of a wooden Indian.

The management finally asked us to leave, but McClure refused to go without taking at least one girl with him. It took all of our persuasive power, plus some physical force to get him out of the club. The rest of the evening was spent walking around to sober up. We eventually returned to the hotel for a well-deserved rest. It had been a long, strenuous day.

July 20, 1944

We were back at Payne Field about noon and were briefed on the next leg of our journey—a 1,000-mile flight to Abadan, Iran. Because of the intense desert heat at Abadan, our departure was scheduled for after midnight.

Since we had the rest of the day to kill, the whole crew decided to go sightseeing and shopping. We had been told that the Cairo bazaar was the "must see" place to visit. It proved to be that and more.

The bazaar was really a city in itself—row after row of small shops, stalls, and open air markets. Beggars were everywhere. We were swamped by ragtag crowds of children with outstretched hands—all of them screaming for "buckshee" (money).

I was amazed by the limitless variety of items for sale—the swarm of hustling humanity—and the exotic dress of the people. The sights, sounds, and smells of the bazaar were unbelievable. There was a constant deafening uproar created by the noisy haggling between merchants and customers. The intense bargaining was conducted at the top of their lungs and accompanied by threatening arm waving and hand gestures. It was a real show. There were many times when I thought a fight was about to erupt—but, after much yelling and wailing, an agreement was usually reached between buyer and seller. I became exhausted just watching the carrying on.

We wound up the day with an excellent dinner at Shepheard's Hotel—which was an experience in itself—and then headed back to the airstrip to get some rest before our late-night flight to Abadan.

July 21, 1944

We lifted off from Payne Field at 0200. The weather was still warm in Cairo, even at this hour—but, before the morning was over, we would find out what *hot* really meant.

It was an eight-hour flight to Abadan over desolate desert that stretched for miles in all directions. We cruised at 8,000 feet, and it was even warm at that altitude. As we began our landing procedure, I could see the heat radiating from the ground. By the time we stopped rolling, and taxied to the parking area, the metal parts of our plane were scorching hot. We wasted no time unloading and taking a truck to our quarters. This is one of the hottest places in the world—130° in the shade during the day and near the century mark at night.

July 22, 1944

We departed Abadan about 0500. When we climbed aboard the plane, just before dawn, it was already hot as a firecracker. And all of us were dripping wet with perspiration by the time we were airborne. It was a welcome relief to get off the ground and start climbing to a cooler altitude. I would never want to be stationed in that godforsaken place.

Our next stop was Karachi, India [now Pakistan]—located on the north shore of the Arabian Sea at the Gulf of Oman. It was another long, boring flight—ten hours and 1,200 miles.

After landing and debriefing, we passed through quarantine and were directed to the supply building where we were issued additional equipment, including .45 caliber automatics and shoulder holsters. After chow we hit the sack dead tired—but now, we were officially in the CBI theater.

July 23, 1944

Our crew was awakened at 0500 to be briefed for the flight to northern India. We had just finished receiving our instructions when Jim Cuva burst into the operations office with news that one of the airfield's ground personnel had taxied our ship into another plane parked along the runway. Wind and I rushed to investigate the accident. We discovered that our aircraft's left wingtip had been badly damaged. We were grounded until repairs could be made.

The rest of the morning was spent trying to find somebody to give us information as to when our plane would be patched up—but to no avail. By this time, Milt Wind and I were disgusted, and returned to our quarters to wait out the delay.

But then, one resourceful crew member suggested that, instead of sitting around feeling sorry for ourselves, why not grab a ride to town? The idea sounded like a winner, and our whole gang piled into a bus bound for Karachi.

So far, this journey to the Far East had been across nothing but empty desert—and this region was no exception—hot as the devil day and night, and a countryside of barren rock and sand.

Despite the slow-moving traffic, created by stubborn camels, we finally reached the city. Karachi was anything but clean—and had a stench to match. We were forced to fend off the usual crowd of beggars—and pathetic children with shoeshine kits, their only means of survival.

As we pushed our way through the narrow, dusty streets, it seemed as if everyone in this part of the world was trying to buy or sell something or other. The people were fully aware that American soldiers had money to spend, and the natives were in there pitching for their share of the loot.

July 24, 1944

Wind and I were up bright and early this morning and hurried to the flight line to find out if our plane was ready—but no luck. Temporary repairs could be made; however, we would have to fly to Agra where sheet-metal experts were available to restore the battered wingtip to its original shape. Since the rest of the day was shot, Wind, Miracle, and I hopped the bus to Karachi to do some shopping.

Mosquitoes, in this part of the country, were especially ravenous, and delighted in feasting on ankles. I had noticed that most of the men stationed at the airfield wore a low-cut, nice-looking boot that frustrated the ankle biters. The shoes were called mosquito boots. While we were in town, I bought myself a pair. It was probably the best investment I made on the entire trip. Not only were they comfortable, but they were great for flying, and could easily be slipped on and off.

July 25, 1944

We departed Karachi at 0600 for the 750-mile flight to Agra. Our approach to the airfield took us over the Taj Mahal. In the bright morning sunlight, the white marble stonework of the mausoleum glistened like polished pearl. From the air, it was an unforgettable sight.

After landing and being debriefed, we inquired about our aircraft, and were told that it would not be ready until the following morning. The skin, on and around the damaged wingtip, would have to be replaced.

The extra day gave us an opportunity to tour the Taj Mahal and the old city of Agra. Our guide steered us to the city market place, which consisted of many small, uncovered stalls. It was here that I witnessed my first, and only, cobra-mongoose fight. It was a staged affair, and the combatants were separated as soon as the mongoose clamped his jaws near the snake's head. Both animals were then placed in their respective cages—to live and fight another day.

By the time we returned to the base, our whole gang was bushed. We hit the sack early. I slept like a log—not even dreaming about snakes.

July 26, 1944

Milt Wind and I were up bright and early in the morning. Our plane was ready—the mechanics had worked on it all night. About noon, we met with Major Hightower Smith and were briefed on the next 1,200-mile leg of our trip. The destination was Chabua, India, near Ledo, the eastern end of the Burma Road. At the other end of this one-way, narrow strip of highway was Kunming, China—1,000 torturous miles across the Himalayas.

We took off at 1430 and set an easterly course. Chabua was situated in a valley at the foot of the western slope of the huge mountain chain. Thus far, during our journey, I had viewed dozens of unforgettable wonders. But, about halfway to Chabua, I was treated to one of the most awe-inspiring sights I had ever seen. The Himalayan Mountains rise like a rugged wall of granite from the river plains of eastern India. And, towering above the rocky crags, the gigantic mass of Mount Everest—five miles high—thrusts its snow and ice-covered crest skyward.

Like a stone fortress, Everest stands as a protecting sentinel over the surrounding mountains—powerful winds battering its summit, leaving a trailing plume of ice crystals and snow, like the wake of a comet.

We flew parallel to the Himalayan Range and landed at Chabua at dusk.

CHINA-BURMA-INDIA THEATER

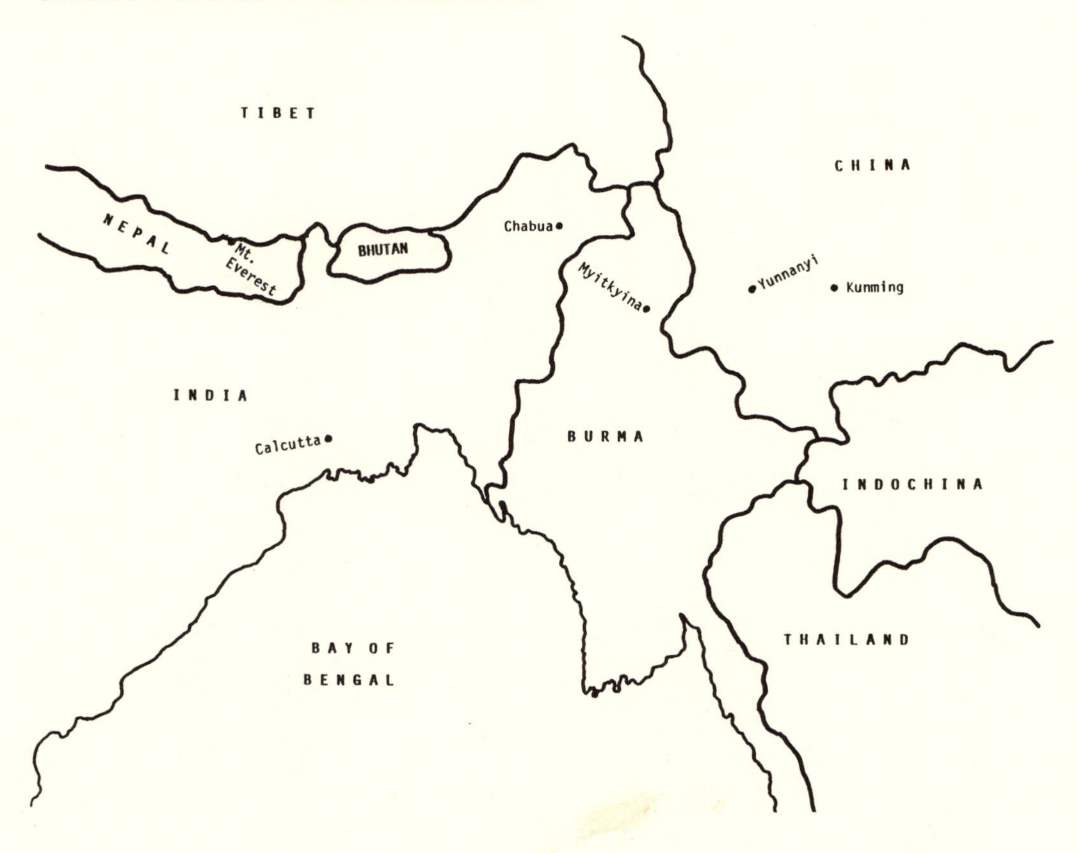

SOUTHEAST ASIA

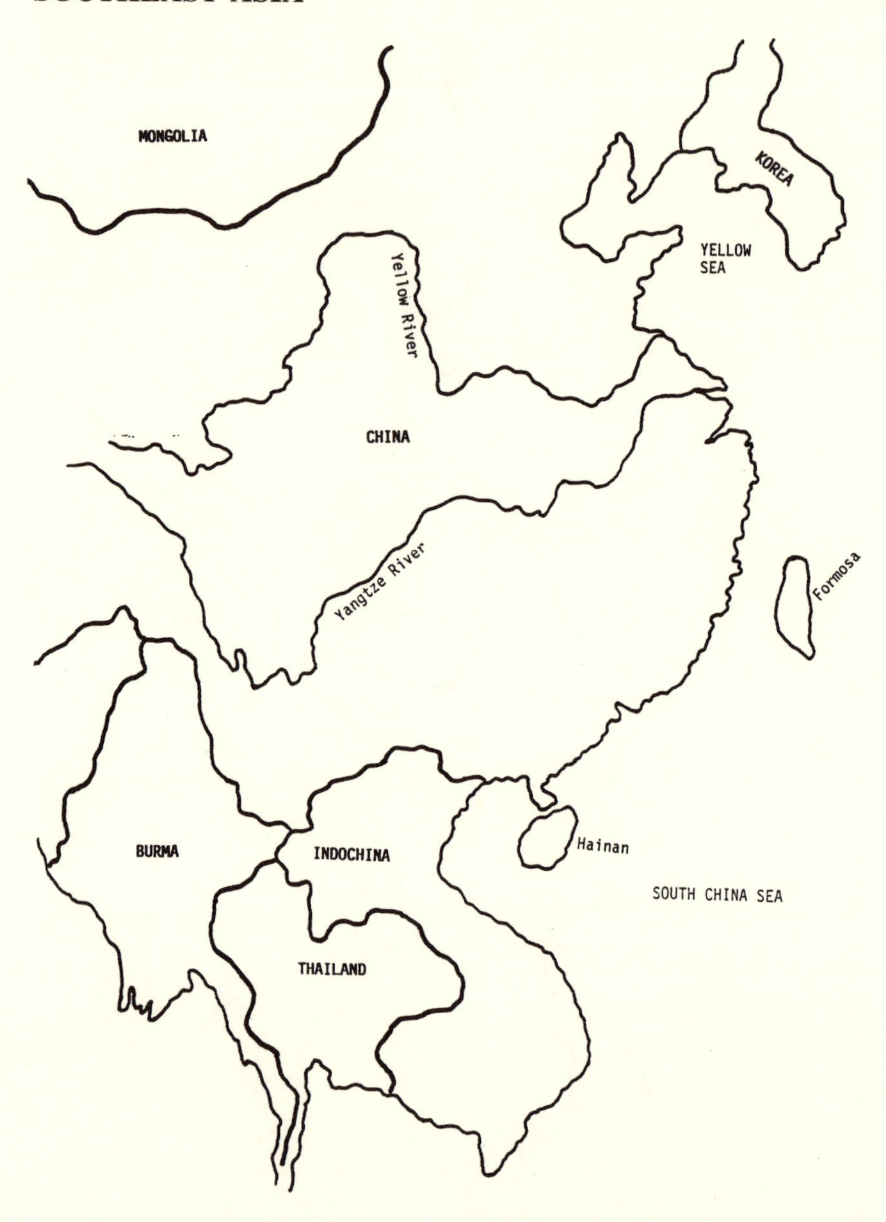

We had finally reached the rear detachment of the 308th Bomb Group, Fourteenth Air Force—the jumping-off place to China.

Milt Wind and I were shown to our quarters and then took a brief stroll around the airstrip. We located the PX [post exchange] and bought a few necessities. We were also introduced to the guide-pilot, who would navigate our route over the Hump. It was required that every new crew have an experienced aviator to direct its initial crossing of the Himalayas.

We were told that many planes had already been lost—not only because of enemy action—but also due to the weather, running out of gas, or crashing into cloud-covered mountain peaks. I asked the guide-pilot what was happening in China, but he was not current on the subject. He was stationed at a small field up on the Hump at Yunnanyi, and spent most of his time guiding new flight crews over the mountains.

After chow and a few beers, we hit the sack. I found it hard to sleep. My imagination was working overtime. The next day was going to be quite a day!

CHAPTER 2

Introduction to War in China

In April 1944, Lieutenant General Takahashi, Japan's chief of staff in China, opened an all-out offensive to cut China in half. The military operation, known as "Ichigo," was commanded by General Shunroku Hata, and comprised 15 divisions. One objective of this attack was to put an end to General Claire Chennault's Fourteenth Air Force strikes against Japanese shipping in the South China Sea, inland rail centers, and occupied coastal cities.

Takahashi's strategy was to overrun and destroy Chennault's forward air bases that stretched along the rail line from Hankow to the Kweilin-Liuchow area. By July 1—despite efforts by the Chinese Army to halt the enemy advance—the Fourteenth Air Force fighter base at Hengyang had fallen. The Chinese suffered heavy casualties and retreated south.

The Japanese assault along the railroad swept aside all opposition. Civilians were shot, businesses and homes destroyed. The panic-stricken refugees fled into the countryside, with nothing but the clothes on their backs and whatever they could carry. In the mass exodus, entire families perished. The dead were stripped of their clothing—cattle, horses, ponies, and dogs were killed and eaten.

The Fourteenth Air Force had complete superiority in the skies and pounded the Japanese Army day and night in an attempt to disrupt the enemy's progress south along the vital rail line.

July 27, 1944

The big day finally arrived. We were briefed early in the morning and told the hard facts about flying the Hump. The flight from Chabua, India

THE HUMP OF THE HIMALAYAS AND THE BURMA ROAD

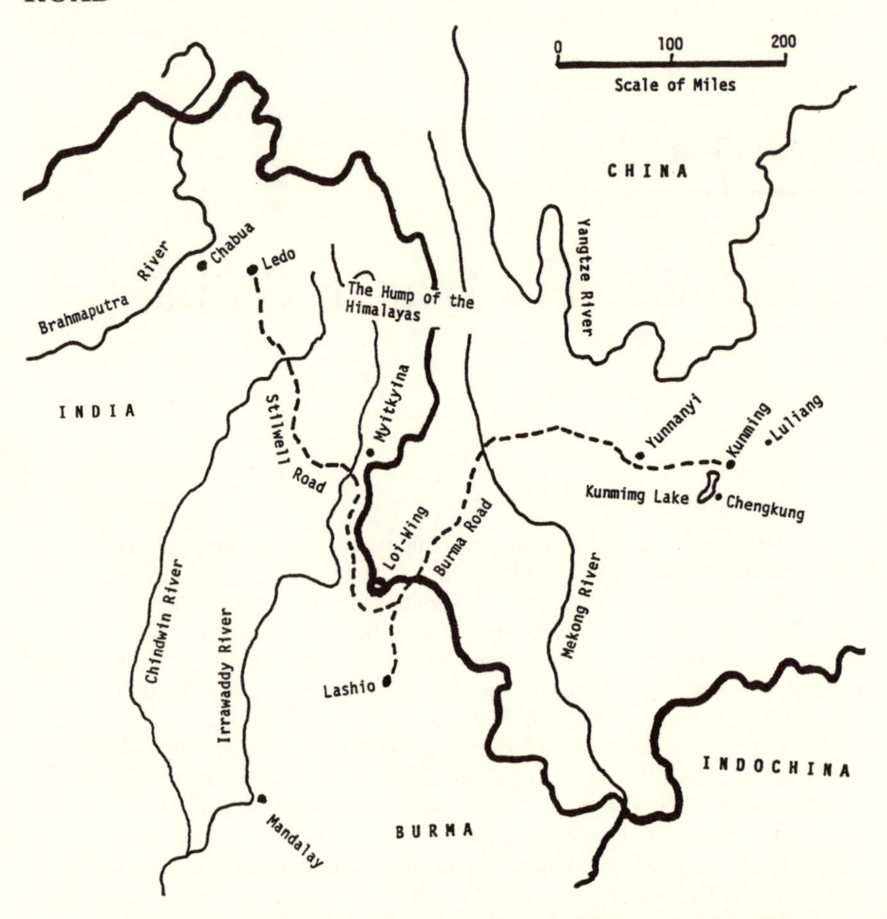

to Chengkung, China (our new home base) would be a 500-mile journey over some of the roughest terrain in the world. The monsoon season started about mid-May and would last until the middle of September. We would encounter violent storms with snow and icing conditions. Winds, at times, reached 200 miles per hour. Our route would require a minimum altitude of 16,000 feet—and we would be flying through every kind of lousy weather in the book.

With this "good news" still ringing in our ears, we took off with a guide-pilot at 1000. It was necessary to fly up and down the valley several times in order to reach the required altitude for the plane to make it over the nearest group of mountains. Immediately after crossing the first range, we ran into thick clouds, heavy turbulence, and driving rain. Upon breaking out of this mess, and into a fairly clear sky, everyone breathed a sigh of relief—but not for long. Suddenly, I felt a sharp jolt on our right wing. My first thought was that we had been struck by ack-ack fire. A moment later, one of the men in the waist called over the intercom that we had just hit a big bird. I shook my head in disbelief, "What the hell do you mean we hit a big bird?" The fellow replied that it had to be a large bird of some kind, because feathers were really flying when the "thing" bounced over the top of the wing and disappeared in the slipstream. It was at this point that our guide-pilot broke into the conversation and remarked that we must have struck a condor. He stated that it was not uncommon to find the birds flying at this height, and some of the condors were huge—with wingspans of more than 14 feet.

While all the excitement was going on, I had not realized that we were freezing. The sudden change to a much colder temperature was beginning to have a drastic effect. The crew in the waist section quickly distributed warm clothing to cover our shivering bodies.

In the meantime, our guide-pilot kept up a steady chatter about the rugged countryside below. He related many "comforting" facts concerning the hostile looking terrain. Besides jungles, swamps, wild-rushing rivers, and deep canyons, the territory was inhabited by tribes of head-hunters and cannibals.

We landed at Yunnanyi and dropped off our guide-pilot. I inspected the right wing of the aircraft. The condor had made quite a dent—about a foot deep and two feet long in the leading edge of the wing. The crumpled metal was covered with blood and feathers. It seemed incredible that a bird, even the size of a condor, could have caused this much damage.

We took off again, without mishap, and began the final leg of our flight to Chengkung. We followed the Burma Road. As I looked down, it was hard to believe that anyone could have built a highway over the mountains, gorges, and rivers far below us. From our altitude, the road appeared like a long, thin snake—winding here and there—and in some places, looping back on itself in a series of coils.

Scattered along the mountainsides, and in the jungle, could be seen the wreckage of American, British, and Japanese aircraft—pitiful victims to the harsh weather and fierce air battles. The Air Transport Command (ATC) named the route "The Aluminum Trail."

After flying for nearly four hours, we crossed the last range of mountains and Kunming Lake came into view. It would be the landmark for our base at Chengkung. With the radar equipment we carried on board, this lake could be picked up on our scope at high altitude and long distances—thus giving us a very valuable navigational aid.

The single runway at Chengkung ran north and south. It was 6,000 feet long and was constructed of crushed rock. The airstrip was laid out in a large valley with high mountains to the east and south. There was also a small range on the west side, between the runway and Kunming Lake. The north end of the strip opened into the valley and was free of obstacles.

We modern "Marco Polos" had arrived at our combat zone after a journey of more than 11,000 miles—almost halfway around the world. It had been 700 years since Marco Polo had visited this area (Yunnan Province) during his travels. Our trip had taken 16 days.

We were a tired and worn-out group of men by the time we landed, parked the plane, and unloaded our gear and luggage. Two trucks arrived to take us to our new homes. The enlisted men were quartered on the east side of the field in the squadron area, while we four officers were housed in temporary quarters on the west side of the runway. After unloading our baggage, we reported to the operations building where we were given a rundown on the field and told a few things about what our role was to be in this war. From the gist of this briefing, I got the impression that we would be doing just about everything—except what we had been trained for.

After chow, we were transported back to our quarters, a single room with double bunks and a large picnic type table. We unpacked and began to get acquainted with our new home and its surroundings. This was definitely going to be a life of no luxury whatsoever. The bunks had rope bedsprings, and our only light was a 12-volt electric bulb hanging over the table. The privies were outside and a considerable distance from our building, but that was OK because they smelled to high heaven. A Lister-bag supplied us with water for drinking, cooking, and washing.

We picked out our bunks, hung up mosquito nets, then sat around the picnic table—looking at one another with disbelief and bewilderment. We were all thinking the same question, "What the hell were we supposed to be doing over here anyway?" None of us could come up with any answers that made sense, and I was so pooped that I gave up trying to figure it out. I hit the sack and passed out immediately. The others followed suit.

July 28, 1944

Somehow things looked much brighter this morning than they had seemed the night before. We were strolling around the hostel area when a truck rolled up. The driver told us to climb in. He was to take us to the operations section for our orientation lecture on the China theater.

The speech was very interesting—we finally had numbers to go with our names. Our crew was assigned to the 375th Bomb Squadron, 308th Bombardment Group (Heavy), Fourteenth Air Force. Home base would be Chengkung, and we would receive our official orders as soon as they were printed at the airforce headquarters at Kunming.

We spent the rest of the day hanging around the squadron area and talking to some of the airmen. From the stories we heard, this assignment was going to be anything but a picnic. Losses of personnel and planes had been heavy. Most of the pilots were flying straight B-24s in high altitude formations against land targets during daylight hours. Some of their missions had P-40 and P-51 fighter escorts—others had no fighter protection at all. Aircraft losses were in proportion.

After returning to our room, we sat around the table to do some serious talking about the situation. We had acquired a great deal of bad news to go along with our grim faces. But the Japanese were not the only enemy—the weather would be just as deadly an adversary.

The monsoon season was beginning in this area, and we were warned of the terrible weather that we could expect. It would rain every day and, between showers, the sun would come out, turning the region into a steambath.

Wind and I were determined to stay together and keep our crew intact if possible. It was obvious that we needed all the experience we both possessed in order to survive. Our night-flying practice and instrument training would certainly be a valuable asset over here—and it was, saving our lives more than once.

From a vantage point on the steps of our barracks, I could see an army of coolies—comprised of men, women, and children—toiling up and down the runway. Like a colony of hard-working ants, they kept constantly busy—fixing taxi strips, repairing holes in the pavement with crushed rock, and building additional revetments on the eastern side of the field to protect the B-24s.

The laborers had no modern machinery. The work was done by hand, with only the help of water buffalo and small Chinese ponies pulling two-wheeled carts. The wagons were piled high with loads of rock that would kill an ordinary horse in the States.

The long lines of humanity were in continuous motion—moving methodically like links in a seemingly endless chain. Many of the workers carried rock and dirt-filled baskets on their heads. Others balanced long poles stretched across their shoulders—a heavily loaded basket at each end. One group could be seen straining their arms, backs, and legs, pushing and pulling cumbersome, stone-crushing rollers. Every person worked—from the very young to the very old. There were just as many women as men—perhaps more.

July 29, 1944

I spent part of the day trying to catch up on my letter writing but began to feel ill in the afternoon. I probably had caught a cold from getting chilled on the flight over the Hump. I decided to take life easy and played a few hands of gin rummy with Mac McClure.

The mess hall for our barracks was nearby. The food was cooked by Chinese men and served by male waiters. I was surprised by their flair for seasoning. They used liberal amounts of garlic and hot peppers in many of the dishes.

The Chinese idea of an edible chicken was to find the oldest, scrawniest bird running around and cook it until it became as hard to chew as leather. Meat was cooked the same way—well done and tough. Water buffalo was the animal used in this part of the country for beef. I have always suspected that the buffalo slaughtered for our meals were probably ready to die of old age.

The Chinese, except for the wealthy, ate very little beef since it was quite expensive. The principal meat dishes were pork and chicken. Puppies were considered a rare delicacy but were costly and out of reach for the average coolie.

Bread was made from rice flour, but the Chinese bakers did not use anything to make the bread rise. Each slice not only had a sour taste and smell, but weighed several ounces.

Because of resupply problems in the China theater, we ate whatever was available in our local area. However, we were cautioned not to eat raw vegetables nor drink water that had not been boiled first. Only about ten percent of our food came from scant provisions that were flown over the Hump.

July 31, 1944

Two of my Langley Field buddies, Captain Paul Brosious and First Lieutenant Ross Batchelor, flew in from our forward base at Liuchow. They were with the first section of twenty B-24s, under command of Lieutenant Colonel Hopson, which arrived here in May.

Liuchow was strictly a combat base—about 450 miles east of Chengkung—and dangerously near Japanese airdromes. The airstrip at Liuchow was encircled by needle-like rock formations that rose more than 100 feet above the valley. Because of their unusual shape, these jagged pinnacles were called "ice cream cones."

Hopson's crews had already been in action. Their first mission was a night attack against Samah Bay—a large enemy naval base on the southern tip of Hainan Island. Twelve B-24s went in, one behind the other. Ack-ack fire was fairly heavy. Although several planes were hit, there were no casualties and all aircraft made it safely back to the field.

The raid did very little damage to Japanese shipping, because surrounding high hills and mountains blocked out their radar. Therefore, most of the bombs were dropped on secondary targets, such as land installations around the harbor.

Shortly after the Samah Bay strike, 13 B-24s were sent out to hit a large enemy convoy between Hainan Island and Hong Kong. They sunk several ships and damaged a few others. However, they paid a heavy price. Four aircraft did not return from the mission.

Brosious told me that, after the first two strikes, the radar equipment was modified, and some sets were recalibrated to get a better image on the radarscopes.

On the night of July 27, Paul Brosious flew as copilot with Lieutenant Colonel Hopson on a sortie against a Japanese convoy. Paul said that instead of dropping their bombs from the usual 1,000 feet, Hopson made his runs at 400 feet—dropping three bombs on each run with a five-second delay set on the fuses. This delay enabled them to escape the blast area before the bombs exploded. The results of the attack were fantastic—three enemy ships were sunk.

I listened to Brosious's account with avid interest. His descriptions of their bombing passes were extremely exciting. I could feel the sweat on the palms of my hands, to say nothing of my quickened pulse. They picked up heavy antiaircraft fire, but most of it went over their heads. "Hell," I thought to myself, "anyone with a shotgun could hit a B-24 at 400 feet."

Paul remarked that, due to the excellent results of the low-level strikes, all radar crews would be advised of these latest tactics, and bombardiers trained for the attack run and the proper fusing of bombs. This sudden surge of new information gave me plenty to think about—and they were not exactly happy thoughts.

August 1, 1944

Father Steele, a Catholic priest, paid us a visit this morning. He has been a missionary in China for six years, and described the power struggle that has been going on since the late 1930s between Chiang Kai-shek's faction and the communists. While the Chinese were fighting among themselves, the Japanese had occupied principal coastal areas of China—virtually without opposition.

Steele further stated that the conflict between the nationalists and communists was causing Chiang Kai-shek problems within his own ranks. Several of Chiang's generals were more interested in using forces under their command to further personal gains rather than fighting the communists or Japanese.

Another dilemma was the Chinese economy. Inflation was running wild. The ratio to the American dollar was 200 to one and still climbing. I told Steele we had heard rumors that large quantities of paper money were being flown over the Hump—taking up valuable cargo space and making our supply problem that much more critical. The priest confirmed the rumor and also informed us that large numbers of the Chinese people were not friendly toward the Americans—nor any other foreigners for that matter. Steele also said that the Allies were paying exorbitant costs for the construction of runways, buildings, and other facilities.

The picture of China, presented by Father Steele, was very different from Stateside media reports. It became obvious that we would be fighting more than just the Japanese in this war.

I had been told that it was the policy of the 308th Bombardment Group for the pilot of each new crew to be checked out by a veteran flight leader for at least two combat missions. The purpose of this test was to acquaint the pilot and crew with various routines of flying under battle conditions. The pilot's proficiency would be closely monitored during these missions before he and his men were released with a valuable plane. It is hard to predict how people will react the first time under fire and the stress of combat. Therefore, this strategy proved very effective and undoubtedly saved many lives.

This afternoon, a messenger from the operations building showed up at the barracks. He reported that our plane's damaged wing had been repaired, and the aircraft was checked out and ready to go. We were also notified that our first mission was scheduled for the following day. This was the big moment we had been waiting for. We became so excited that everyone began talking at the same time. Our crew was finally getting its chance to go into combat—everyone but me, that is. A flight leader would be sitting in my seat as check-pilot.

August 2, 1944

Milt Wind and the crew were briefed at 0700. The two squadrons at our field—the 374th, and my squadron, the 375th—put a total of 16 planes in the air. The majority of the aircraft were straight B-24s—no radar. The only perceivable difference was that the underside of the radar planes were painted black, so that enemy searchlights could not easily locate them at night.

I waited around the airstrip several hours—sweating out the mission. The boys started returning late in the afternoon. It was a thrilling sight to watch all the aircraft return safely. After our plane was parked, I greeted the crew. They were a happy bunch of guys.

Milt Wind filled me in on the mission. The entire crew worked perfectly together. The check-pilot said that they had performed like seasoned veterans. Several Japanese Zeros were sighted, but they were kept out of range by our fighter escorts. Jim Miracle dropped his load of 500-pound bombs right on target. It was a job well done, and everyone went to sleep that night feeling self-satisfied, except me—I still hungered for my first taste of combat.

August 3, 1944

Not much doing today—bad weather. McClure and I went target shooting with our .45 caliber pistols. As usual, we could not hit a damn thing. Mac and I talked about the previous day's mission. He remarked that the navigational charts were so inaccurate that they were almost useless. During the briefing session, the squadron navigator worked with Mac and helped him in correcting the maps and pinpointing the target. Navigation was difficult in China due to inaccurate mapping of the country and the absence of navigational aids.

In the early years of the war—before enough missions had been flown to somewhat correct the charts—a number of planes and their crews had been lost. Many aircraft ran out of gas on the way home from their missions. The crews were forced to bail out, and the odds of men landing safely—without breaking arms and legs—were definitely against the flyers. But, even if a man landed unhurt, he would still have to traverse the rugged terrain and cross miles of hostile territory.

The Japanese posted large rewards for anyone capturing an airman and turning him in alive. A person would be shot if he was caught giving aid to a downed flyer. In our present situation, any mistake could be disastrous.

August 4, 1944

We were not scheduled for a mission this morning, so Wind, McClure, Miracle, and I decided to hop on a truck that was going to Kunming. The journey turned out to be a mission in itself—nearly 25 miles of solid bumps and jolts along one of the roughest roads I had ever traveled. The highway was constructed of rocks. The stones were from the size of a man's head to gravel. The path was ages old and, over the centuries, had been worn down to almost a foot below the surface of the ground.

Traffic along the road was heavy and included every kind of land transportation imaginable—two-wheeled carts, wagons, bicycles, rickshaws, automobiles, and charcoal-powered buses. Water buffalo, ponies, and long lines of shuffling, foot-weary Chinese also crowded the roadway.

Our truck slowly eased its way through this motley mixture of traffic, the driver continually honking the horn. There were numerous vehicle breakdowns along the route. On two occasions, we piled out of the truck and helped clear the road of traffic jams caused by these bottlenecks.

We passed three funeral processions and witnessed several burials, which were being conducted in the many cemeteries bordering the road. Not one piece of land in China was wasted. Every plot of earth was used in one way or another to grow whatever it could produce. This even included hillsides, and just about anyplace where a man could stand up.

Land that was not under cultivation became cemeteries. Father Steele had told me that, while building our airstrip at Chengkung, several hundred burial mounds were relocated, and now surround the entire base.

After a few hours of bone-jarring travel, we finally arrived at Kunming. The driver dropped us off near the Fourteenth Air Force Headquarters. The airfield was nearby. We wandered around the landing strip and saw what was left of the Chinese Air Force. It was not a pleasant sight—about ten beat-up, antique planes in various states of disrepair. We made arrangements for a night's lodging, had a good meal, and eased our aching bodies into bed. It had been a long, but very interesting day.

August 5, 1944

At breakfast, we renewed acquaintances with the Langley Field gang who had come over with Lieutenant Colonel Hopson. A few of the boys had the day free and volunteered to show us around Kunming.

The city was very filthy and had an obnoxious odor to boot. Most of the sickening smell came from raw sewage running in the gutters. We hired a few rickshaws and toured the points of interest—ending up at the main marketplace. I visited several booths and shops but found the prices to be out-of-sight. A pack of cigarettes from the United States cost $3 American money in Kunming. The prices of jewelry, silks, and other luxury items were outlandish. An ordinary, inexpensive watch was marked at U.S. $300. Good cameras ran as high as 6,000 bucks. The black market was flourishing. How the average Chinaman can exist under this inflation is beyond me.

During the tour of Kunming, our guides pointed out the scars from Japanese bombing raids. The city had been on the enemy's daily target list until General Chennault's American Volunteer Group (the Flying Tigers), piloting P-40 fighters, began knocking the Japs out of the sky. In the six-month period—from the end of 1941 to the middle of June 1942, the Tigers cost the Japanese practically every plane they sent over Kunming. The enemy finally got the message, and bombings of the city came to a halt.

Upon the return to headquarters, one of our guide-pals suggested we stop at the base hospital. A Japanese pilot had been shot down and taken prisoner. My buddy thought we might be interested in meeting the enemy face to face.

The captured airman had been wounded, and was also injured when he bailed out of his crippled plane. He had been recuperating in sickbay for the past few months. The Jap flyer had the look of a caged animal. He sat in a small tent, surrounded by a fence and guarded by two armed soldiers.

At the time of our visit, a doctor was busy treating the prisoner. When the medical officer had finished, I asked him how his patient was progressing. The doctor said that the fellow was improving, but that he was firmly convinced he would be executed. The doctor also revealed that Japanese prisoners were few and far between. The Chinese would butcher captured enemy pilots before they could be taken into custody and interrogated.

As I took another glance at the pathetic man in the cage, I wondered how I would feel if I was in his position—with people staring at me like an animal at the zoo—and if he had any relatives in the United States. I had grown up with the Japanese people in California, and now they were also being treated like prisoners in a camp near Big Pine.

August 6, 1944

We headed back to Chengkung in the afternoon. It was a repeat trip of the day before. We passed about 100 Chinese soldiers trudging along the roadside. They were a pitiful group—part of Chiang Kai-shek's ragtag army. Only one man in four carried a rifle. The others had no weapons of any kind. In case of a battle, the men without guns would advance alongside the armed troops and pick up the rifles of their dead or wounded comrades. It was not much of a future to look forward to.

It was late when we arrived back at the field and unloaded our sore and battered bodies. What a ride!

We reported to squadron headquarters and had a welcome surprise—our first mail from home. I received letters from my wife, parents, and relatives. It was almost like being back in the States again. I spent the evening writing letters and talking about the news from home. I hit the sack, a tired but very contented man.

August 7, 1944

Another rainy, cloudy, muddy, miserable day. This part of the country must have the lousiest flying weather in the world. We sat around the barracks and discussed what we had learned at Kunming. In the past three months, the 308th Bombardment Group had lost a considerable number of planes and men. The straight bombing crews had suffered the heaviest losses. They were the first units over here and, up to the time of Hopson's arrival, had been bearing the brunt of the fighting.

I also learned that my copilot status was in jeopardy. As soon as our crew's flight records arrived at squadron headquarters, the operation's chief would discover that both Milt Wind and I were qualified first pilots. In that event, we could count on being split up—especially since radar pilots were in short supply. I kept my fingers crossed that the two of us could get in as much combat experience as possible before we were found out.

Every few days, another plane from our section flew over the Hump to one of the 308th Bombardment Group bases in China. This afternoon, Tommy Tomenedale, George Pierpont, and their crew arrived at Chengkung. We had a backslapping reunion and stayed up until lights-out at nine o'clock. It was a great feeling to see more members of the Langley Field gang. An additional bit of good news—Tommy and his crew were assigned to our squadron.

August 9, 1944

At 0800, Milt Wind and the boys took off on their second mission. This would be the last flight before I replaced the check-pilot. I walked over to the operation's office to wait out the long, tense hours.

By nightfall, Wind's plane still had not returned. The men at squadron headquarters were sympathetic. They tried to console me with comforting remarks: "The weather's bad. They probably landed at one of the forward bases—Liuchow or Kweilin." I was instructed to go back to my barracks and get some sleep. It was one of the longest nights of my life.

August 10, 1944

I checked with operations about noon and learned that Wind had landed safely at Liuchow. He had run short of gasoline and could not make it home. The mission was a success. However, one plane had not been heard from. It carried a new crew, on their first flight, and they were flying our B-24 with the repaired wing. I suddenly felt a great loss—not only for the crew—but also for the aircraft, which did such a great job in getting us to China. Apparently she had made her last flight. But, at least she had seen combat, which was more than I could say for myself.

August 16, 1944

We have had six bad weather days in a row. Everyone is stir-crazy. There has been nothing to do except play cards, write letters, shoot the bull, and drink the local "moonshine." The main native alcoholic beverage in this part of the hills is called "Jing Bow Juice." The colorless liquid is made from rice, has the kick of a mule, and tastes like bad whiskey. This liquor, in its undiluted state, burns with a clear blue flame—like natural gas or pure alcohol. "Jing Bow Juice" was so powerful that we had to mix it half-and-half with water, and then add powdered lemon juice from our K-rations to kill the taste. A couple of good snorts of this "magic elixir" could make a man brave enough to take on the whole

Japanese Air Force. However, it also came with a built-in headache beyond belief. And smokers beware—doing both at the same time could turn a guy into a circus fire-eater.

Another Chinese fermented drink was their homemade mulberry wine. The wine had the color of old mahogany, was very sweet to the palate, and went down smooth. But, a couple of glasses of this stuff would make a man's legs feel like they belonged to somebody else.

Imported liquor was practically unheard of in China. A bottle of Stateside bourbon or Scotch cost from $50 to $100. All the good booze was on the India side of the Hump. With local grog the only alcoholic beverage available, it took a hardy soul to do much drinking around these parts.

August 17, 1944

The weather finally cleared enough for a bombing mission to be scheduled. Twenty planes from the two squadrons would participate. Time of departure was set at 0800. Our crew was not selected for the flight, so we hurried over to the revetments to watch the aircraft take off.

Each B-24 carried a full load of bombs and gasoline—adjusted to the field's elevation of 6,250 feet above sea level, and the runway length of 6,000 feet.

Because of thin air at this altitude, a short-field take off was necessary in order to get the heavy aircraft airborne. The procedure was both difficult and dangerous. The plane's brakes were locked and engines revved up until the wheels began to skid. The brakes were then released and engines pushed to full power. Vibrations aboard the aircraft rattled the rivets and the noise was deafening. Every pilot prayed that his plane would hold together. The tremendous surge of power on the take-off roll—with propellers biting the air at full RPM—strained the prop governors to the breaking point. If a governor failed to hold, the propeller blades on that particular engine would start running away. Power to the disabled engine then had to be cut back and the prop feathered.

There was no possibility of getting airborne on three engines. Therefore, when this type of emergency occurred, the safety measure was to shut down all engines, drop full flaps, hit the brakes, and start looking for an open area before racing out of runway. Within seconds, the plane's brakes burn out and all tires blow.

Bombs are never armed until the aircraft approaches the target so, theoretically, as long as the safety pins are in the fuses, the bombs will not detonate. If there is time to open the bomb bay doors, the bomb load can be dumped by yanking the salvo handle. But, there is no sure way of knowing whether they will explode or not. Therefore, the salvo handle is only pulled as a last resort.

If a pilot is too far down the runway when an engine fails, he has no

CHENGKUNG AIRFIELD

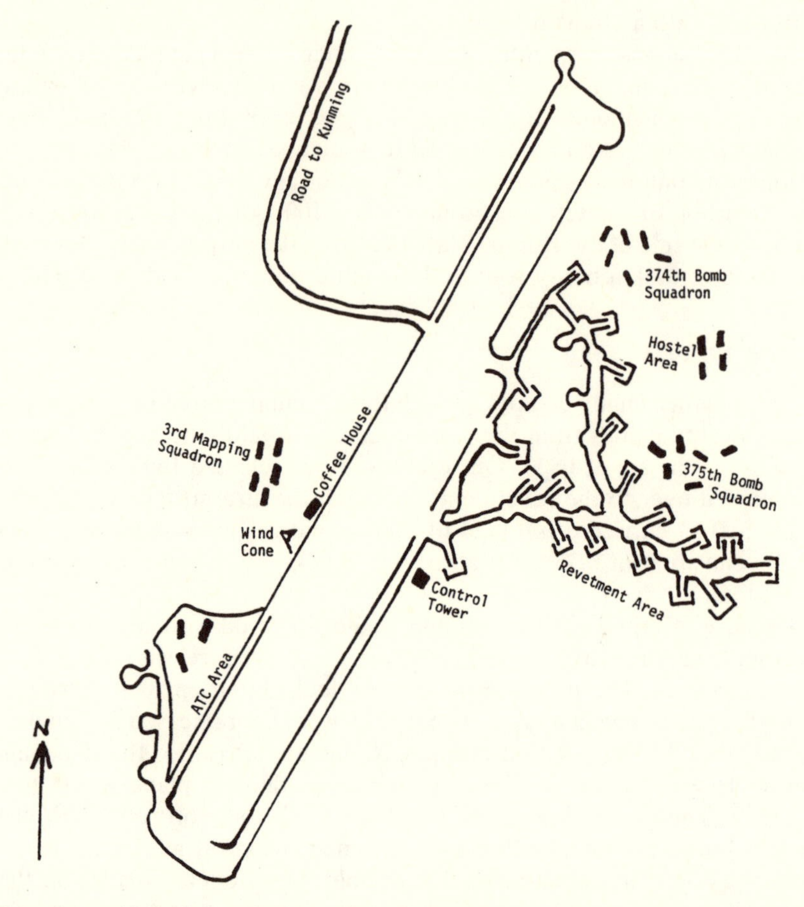

Chengkung Airfield was the home base for the 374th and 375th Squadrons, 308th Bomb Group (Heavy). Field elevation: 6,250 feet.

choice but to unload his bombs. The frightening prospect of a crash during take off—in an aircraft packed with explosives, and carrying full tanks of 100-octane gasoline—is too terrifying to contemplate.

We sat on the top ledge of the revetment and watched the planes dash down the airstrip. Three B-24s had taken off safely and were circling the field when the next pilot began his run. The aircraft had only traveled about 200 yards when the sound of its motors indicated trouble. I noticed a prop being feathered on the No. 3 engine. The bomb bay doors quickly opened and 500-pound bombs began bouncing down the runway like footballs.

Our location was very close to the flight line and several bombs were seen bouncing in our direction. There was no hesitation—we jumped into the revetment and hoped for the best. The drop down the revetment was at least 20 feet, and tumbling down the rock-filled slope was not exactly a joyride.

I dragged my aching body to where I had a clear view of the accident. The B-24 crashed off the end of the runway. Miraculously the plane did not catch fire and none of the bombs exploded. However, two crewmen were killed in the crash and the rampaging projectiles damaged several aircraft parked alongside the flight line.

We were a silent and somber group of men as we watched the rest of the planes take off. I could imagine the feelings of the crews as their aircraft became airborne over the crash site. I instinctively realized that an accident such as this could just as easily happen to us.

CHAPTER 3

Combat at Last

August 23, 1944

We received flying orders this morning. I would be riding in the copilot's seat. The briefing was held at noon, and an hour later we took off for Liuchow. Bad weather was forecast, but that was putting it mildly. We hit severe turbulence, and for the next four hours our plane was buffeted by heavy rain and strong headwinds. Despite being almost shaken to pieces, we managed to make a safe instrument landing.

The single runway at Liuchow had been carved through the "ice cream cone" formations. The surrounding terrain was somewhat level, and in prehistoric times was covered by the South China Sea. The rocky pillars gave the entire countryside the appearance of a Martian landscape.

This forward base had only the bare essentials for combat operations. The buildings were flimsily constructed and covered with tar paper. One of the men stationed at the airstrip stated: "There's nothing fancy here. We're so close to enemy territory that we never know when we'll have to burn everything down to keep the Japs from using the place."

Liuchow was within easy reach of Japanese bombers based at Hong Kong and Canton—a distance of 350 miles. We were told to expect enemy attacks on any clear night—especially if there was a full moon. Slit trenches, located near the barracks, were pointed out, and we were instructed to haul ass over there at the first air raid warning. It would probably be the only alarm signal we would get. Because of the close air proximity, there was also a good chance of being bombed without any warning at all.

There were no protective revetments for the B-24s. Therefore, the planes were scattered as far away from the landing strip as possible—so as not to provide the Japs with a clustered target.

We were assigned a day room that was lit by a 12-volt generator. Our sleeping quarters had peanut oil lamps and bunks covered with mosquito netting. Chow consisted of whatever could be obtained locally—the usual rice bread, plain rice, and a little chicken and pork. Occasionally we had beef or fresh eggs—a real treat.

What concerned me the most about the airfield was its vulnerability to attack by an enemy parachute force. The defensive setup was very inadequate. The only weapons at Liuchow consisted of Tommy guns and .50-caliber machine guns mounted on the planes and posted around the field. We were supposedly protected by a handful of Chinese soldiers, but their only duty was to guard the main road running through town.

However, my fears were unfounded. The only thing the Japanese dropped on us were bombs—and they were a nuisance more than anything else. The enemy bombers came over practically every night, and we would blast away at them from the cover of our slit trench. They were, of course, out of range from our small arms fire, but it helped to vent some of the frustration.

August 25, 1944

We had a pleasant surprise this morning. Ann Sheridan's USO tour stopped at Liuchow. The show was enjoyed by everyone—especially the sight of beautiful American girls. Captain Melvin Douglas was in charge of the troupe. Ben Blue was the comic. It felt great to laugh for a change. After the entertainment was over, we reported to operations for a combat mission briefing. Our assignment was to fly a specified search pattern and, as a secondary target, to hit the Kowloon Docks at Hong Kong.

We took off at 1700 and headed for the Chinese coast—about 250 miles to the south. We flew our assigned search pattern around Hainan Island, but no targets were sighted. A course was then set for Hong Kong. We came in over the Kowloon Docks at an altitude of 8,000 feet and dropped twelve 500-pound bombs. Jim Miracle, our bombardier, was right on target. The bombs landed with pinpoint accuracy—resulting in many fires and secondary explosions.

I felt a flood of exhilaration after my first taste of combat. But, the feeling was only momentary—our plane was suddenly trapped in the beams of two searchlights. After flying in darkness for several hours, the bright lights were blinding. Within seconds, deadly puffs of ack-ack fire began trailing us through the sky.

Milt Wind and I were caught by surprise. We had to escape the searchlights before we got our tails shot off. I jammed my seat as low as it would go and flipped my sunglasses down to cut the glare. Wind quickly threw

EASTERN CHINA AND FORMOSA

the ship into a steep diving turn. The abrupt dive and rapid change of course tossed our crew around like tenpins. We pulled out at 1,500 feet, evading the searchlights, and dashed north across the bay toward Canton.

Radar proved a godsend in this case. It gave Atkins, our radar operator, a clear picture of the entire area. He would be able to guide us in any direction. McClure set a new course. We banked northwest and climbed for altitude—landing safely at Liuchow about 0330.

I had often wondered how I would react the first time under enemy fire. I discovered that I was too busy flying the plane to be scared. It was not until we were in the clear that I experienced any reaction. Surprisingly, dodging antiaircraft bursts did not bother me in the least. However, the blinding searchlights—and the long plunge through the blackness of night—had an effect. After leveling off, I realized that I was trembling and covered with sweat. I glanced over at Wind. He was also sweating profusely.

Our entire crew had performed superbly, and everyone felt a great sense of satisfaction with a job well done. We certainly learned a lot about searchlights—and what to expect when caught in their beams.

August 29, 1944

A few days of monsoon weather almost flooded us out at Liuchow. We endured from one to three rains per day. Then the sun came out, and the countryside was turned into a giant steambath.

The torrential rains also made the mosquitoes raging mad, and they did their damndest to carry us off to their lairs. We discussed loading our .45s with birdshot and knocking them out of the air. But then we thought better of the idea. We were such "expert marksmen" with the weapon that we would probably end up shooting each other. The crappy weather, lousy chow, mosquitoes, and Japanese bombing raids kept us in a nasty fighting mood.

About noon, we received word to round up our crew for a briefing at 1430. The operation's officer gave us our mission instructions. We would be laying mines in the harbor at Shanghai. Milt Wind, McClure, and I studied maps of the target area to fully acquaint ourselves with antiaircraft locations. There was no doubt that this mission was going to be a hot potato to handle.

There were several small islands in the harbor, just north of Shanghai and not far from the mouth of the Hwangpu River. The Hwangpu flowed along the east side of the city. It was the major waterway servicing the area, and by placing mines across the entrance, we could seriously hamper water traffic on the river.

A thorough examination of aerial recon photos showed that there was no way to reach the target without flying directly over enemy antiaircraft positions. We decided that our best bet would be to approach the harbor from the ocean side and skim the water at 400 feet. After dropping the mines, we would escape to the southwest.

We were the last of four planes to take off. Each plane carried five large mines. We flew through thick clouds most of the way. But when we neared Shanghai, the heavy weather cleared, and the entire region was bathed in bright moonlight. Not only would our aircraft make excellent targets for ack-ack fire, but the enemy would already be alerted by the first three planes. There would be no element of surprise when we made our run.

Hundreds of tracers followed our approach to the target. From an altitude of only 400 feet, I could see the muzzle flashes of guns and searchlights swinging around in their efforts to locate us.

This time, Wind and I were both prepared for searchlight beams, but luckily we were not spotted. Apparently, the direction and low level of our attack must have surprised the Japs. Most of the gunfire was aimed above and behind us.

The harbor was packed with shipping of every kind, including merchant and naval vessels. Miracle dumped five mines in the middle of the river and McClure charted our escape course.

Evidently, from all the fireworks going on, we were not considered very welcome around these parts. So we pushed the throttles to full, put the props in high pitch, turned up the supercharger, and set emergency rich on the carburetor controls. With our plane bolting through the night sky, at top speed and under full power, the people on the ground must have thought a squadron of planes was racing over their heads. A B-24, wound up like this aircraft, makes one hell of a roar at low altitudes. Vibration from the sound waves can break windows and dishes. There must have been plenty of wet pants down below, because we undoubtedly scared the pee right out of the Chinese and Japs.

Wind and I fought lousy weather all the way home. In fact, it was so bad that we overshot the field at Liuchow—but finally made a safe landing at 0330. We rode a truck over to the debriefing room and reported the results of our mission. I learned that the other three planes had also returned safely. After a shot of "combat whiskey" and plenty of hot coffee, we hit the sack—a tired but happy group of airmen.

August 30, 1944

Throughout the day, planes from our squadron began arriving at Liuchow. It was like a Langley Field reunion—Pierpont, Tomenedale, Brosious, and Batchelor were among the incoming crews. Previously scheduled missions had been canceled. Something big was in the offing. Rumors were flying all over the place.

August 31, 1944

News was announced this morning that a group mission was slated to hit Takao, Formosa. Recon photos showed large numbers of Japanese naval vessels and support craft in the harbor area.

The attack force comprised two formations of radar-equipped B-24s. The first group of 12 planes would come in over the Takao docks at 5,000 feet and bomb ships at anchor and vessels tied up at piers. A second flight of four aircraft would dash across the port entrance at 400 feet—each B-24 dropping five mines. This tactic would serve to trap enemy ships inside the harbor—like putting a cork in a bottle.

Our crew would be flying the lead mine-laying plane. We would take off a half-hour after the last bomber was airborne. Milt Wind's assigned drop site was near the harbor inlet and adjacent to the beach.

Two types of mines would be employed—acoustic and magnetic. We carried the acoustic variety that floats a few feet below the surface. The sound from any nearby ship's propeller would set off the explosive.

At 1720, we left Liuchow for the 675-mile trip to Formosa. At about 50 miles from the target, I sighted fires lighting up the night sky. As we neared Takao, Atkins guided us parallel to the shoreline. I could easily see the havoc that the first wave of bombers created within the harbor. Flames were jumping hundreds of feet in the air, and secondary explosions echoed like thunder across the water. The fires were so bright and intense that Miracle reported he was able to see the drop zone visually.

Wind began our mine run at 400 feet on a northerly heading. As we raced across a spit of land between us and the inner harbor, the entire beach suddenly lit up from muzzle-flashes of guns and tracers. Shells were flying at us thick and fast—like being sprayed out of a garden hose. We ran this gauntlet of death for about five miles before making our drop. Miracle shouted "Bombs Away!" and closed the bomb bay doors. We immediately dove to the deck—skimming the water to avoid searchlights and tracers. The moonlight gave us an excellent view of the mountainous terrain surrounding the narrow neck of the harbor. Beams of light and streams of tracers continued to flood the sky, searching the night for the B-24s that were following directly behind us. Thomas and Carpenter, our waist gunners, called over the intercom that the other planes were catching hell.

We stayed on the deck until out of ack-ack range and then climbed for altitude. McClure charted a westerly course back to Liuchow. About the time we reached 5,000 feet, Atkins reported that his radarscope indicated we were flying over a small convoy. He had barely got the words out of his mouth, when the enemy ships opened fire with a heavy antiaircraft barrage. Flak began coming uncomfortably close. We pushed the throttles to full power and roared away from the danger zone.

At 0100, when we were 40 miles from Liuchow, our radio operator received a message that the base was under air attack and we should head to Kweilin. McClure quickly figured the course. But, by the time we changed to the new heading, heavy weather closed in. We began flying on instruments and tried reaching Kweilin on radio to get a compass fix—

no answer. Neither Wind nor I had ever flown this route before. Therefore, we were unfamiliar with the layout of the airdrome or the countryside. Consequently, even if we located the base, it would be almost impossible to make an instrument approach with the suspect information on our maps.

We had no choice but to keep circling and try to raise the field's radio operator. Finally, by sheer luck, we reached a directional finding station and were given a position fix.

It was daybreak by the time we located the Kweilin airstrip. The clouds had lifted and we made a visual landing. After parking our plane, I checked the fuel tanks—they were practically empty. What a night!

September 1, 1944

I awoke about nine o'clock in the morning from a deep sleep—got quickly dressed and began scrounging around the field, trying to find enough gasoline to get us back to Liuchow. Kweilin was being used as a fighter base and fuel was at a premium. I had to make all sorts of "pay-back" promises but was finally able to latch onto 800 gallons.

I was worn out from all the cat-and-mouse bickering and walked out to our plane to make a preflight inspection. The outside of the aircraft looked in good shape. We had picked up a bullet hole here and there, but that seemed to be the only damage. Then I climbed inside to check out the engines. They all turned over except number one. By this time, Jim Miracle showed up to see how I was doing. He found me sweating and cussing. I told Jim to get the rest of the crew out to the plane—we had problems.

After checking out the motor, it was the starter that proved to be defective. We borrowed tools from the field's ground personnel. Some of us worked to get the bad unit off, while others removed starters from an old B-24 that was being used for spare parts.

It took most of the day, but we were finally able to build a working starter from the pieces of two bad ones. It was nearly dark. We were all dirty, greasy, tired, and irritated. We walked slowly back to our quarters to get something to eat and then hit the sack. Tomorrow was another day.

September 2, 1944

We took off from Kweilin in the afternoon and arrived back at Liuchow without further mishap. We had no sooner walked into the debriefing room, than we were told that two planes were missing. Pierpont's and Clendenen's aircraft never returned from the Takao raid. Four members of the lost crews lived in our quarters—Pierpont, Tomenedale, Deming, and Ward. I had noticed that they were not around when we showed up. However, I presumed they were flying a mission.

Both missing planes were among the twelve that had bombed the inner harbor at Takao. Pierpont and Tomenedale were flying the eighth B-24 to take off. While Pierpont was over the target area, the crew of a plane behind him reported seeing an aircraft ahead take a direct hit from heavy ack-ack fire. Flames started pouring out from both starboard engines. The B-24 immediately began losing altitude and slammed into the side of a hill at the north end of the harbor.

This sense of tragedy and loss was compounded by the fact that this was Tommy Tomenedale's first combat mission as copilot. A check-pilot had flown with Pierpont on his two previous bombing flights.

Lieutenant Clendenen's plane was the last B-24 of the first section to take off on the Takao raid. Nothing has ever been heard from him or his crew.

Tomenedale and Pierpont were two of my best friends. I also knew Ward and Deming very well. Milt Wind and I discussed their chances of survival, but deep down inside, we knew they were gone. Even if they lived through the crash, the Japs would make short work of them.

All combat crews had been thoroughly briefed on what to expect if captured alive by the Japanese—especially those of us flying the radar planes, which were responsible for sinking their merchant shipping and naval vessels. Nightly broadcasts from Tokyo Rose made this message abundantly clear. We tuned her in every evening when we were on a mission, and well out to sea from land interference. Her transmissions came in loud and distinct on our large radio-command set. Rose played the sentimental music of the "Big Bands," while, at the same time, insisting that our girlfriends and wives were having the time of their lives shacking up with civilians. She also spread the old bullshit that the girls back home did not care whether we lived or died fighting for the Chinese.

The Japanese had a very efficient spy network in China. They had a list of our names—and Tokyo Rose told each of us personally that she knew we were preying on their shipping—and what the Japs would do to us if we were captured. I must admit, it gave me an eerie feeling to hear my name called out by a stranger broadcasting hundreds of miles away. Her propaganda was pure corn, but her choice of music was great. We enjoyed listening to the radio programs. They helped to pass the tedious and lonesome hours as our engines droned monotonously over the wide expanse of ocean.

We were ten lonely men in a plane suspended in space—either in the inky blackness of night or bathed in brilliant moonlight above the scattered clouds. Stars sparkled like jewels in the rarified atmosphere. It seemed hard to believe that, below all this quiet and serene beauty, people were busy killing one another.

The war had now become a personal vendetta. Up to this point, the killed and missing were merely acquaintances—names without faces. But now, the Angel of Death had entered my room and taken my friends. I made a solemn promise to myself that I would make the enemy pay dearly for the loss of Pierpont and Tomenedale. From this moment on, it would be kill or be killed—no quarter asked or given.

September 3, 1944

At 1400, we were briefed for a mission to bomb the railroad yards at Pukow-Nanking. This region—850 miles northeast of Liuchow—was a main hub of the Chinese northern railway system, and was vital to Japanese supply lines.

Ten B-24s were assigned to the strike and spaced at half-hour intervals. We took off at 1640, carrying twelve 500-pound bombs. Our automatic pilot system was not working, so Wind and I were forced to fly the entire mission manually.

We reached the target about 2130. Although the area was hidden by cloud cover, our radar picked up the marshalling yards bright and clear on the scopes. We had been instructed to drop our bombs from 7,500 feet. But, because of the overcast, we plunged down through a break in the clouds and leveled off at 1,500 feet to make our bombing run. By this time, however, the enemy had been alerted. As we raced across the railroad yards, our plane was rocked by the concussion of bursting ack-ack shells. Despite the heavy flak, Jim Miracle dropped his bombs "down the throat."

The bombs had instant fuse settings, and the resulting detonation, at this low altitude, bounced us about. The heat from the explosions shot up through the open bomb bay doors like a furnace blast at close range. It took the combined efforts of both Wind and I, wrestling with the controls, to keep the plane on a steady course. We finally managed to get the hell away from the area before being clobbered by flak, or the explosion of our own bombs blowing us out of the sky.

As we started to climb through the overcast, I glanced at the control panel and had a real scare—we were pulling full power with the carburetor mixture on auto-lean. Neither Wind nor I knew how long we had been flying with the mixture controls in this position—but we could have blown the cylinder heads completely off all four engines. I immediately switched to emergency-rich—the proper setting for a full-power run. However, I was not fast enough—two of our superchargers caught fire, making our ship an excellent target for antiaircraft gunners. Fortunately, we climbed for altitude so quickly that the Japs lost visual contact.

We broke out of the cloud cover at 9,000 feet. The fires in the superchargers eventually burned out without doing too much damage to the engines.

Wind and I had very little to say to each other during the flight home. Both of us realized how lucky we were to still have four motors running. This incident made us painfully aware that *any* mistake can be fatal. Despite the fact that we were both first pilots—with plenty of experience between us—we had goofed. It was a bitter pill to swallow, but a valuable one. We discovered how easily something like this can happen. The good Lord was watching over us on this mission—and Milt Wind and I knew it.

September 4, 1944

It rained most of the day and the field was socked in. Therefore, there was no flying and everyone was happy to get some rest. The last few days had been hectic. Ground crews worked day and night getting the planes back into operational condition and patching bullet and flak holes.

The weather cleared by late afternoon. After chow, we sat around the dayroom writing letters and playing cards. We also had a jackpot drawing as to what time the Japs would fly over and drop a few bombs. The moon would be up about 2200 and the enemy would never miss an opportunity of this kind.

Sure enough, as soon as the moon rose, the Jap Betty bombers arrived. We called them sewing machines because of the sound of their motors. The noise of the alert—beating on a sheet of armor plating—shattered our sleep. The alarm was loud enough to wake the dead. We had gone to bed fully clothed, so only had to put on boots, grab flak helmets, strap on our .45s and dash to the slit trench. We no sooner reached the trenches, than the Bettys were sighted coming in from the southeast. There were 12 bombers in the enemy formation. Eight of the planes turned toward the runway and our parked aircraft. The other four headed for our barracks area to drop antipersonnel bombs.

These fragmentation bombs were nasty little fellows. They were about the size of hand grenades and were tied together in large cluster bundles. At approximately 1,000 feet above the target, the packets would blow apart—throwing the deadly missiles over a large area. The bombs would explode on impact and spray shrapnel in all directions. Usually, they did very little damage—unless, of course, one happened to land in a slit trench.

However, the little monsters played hell with our planes parked out in the open. We lost several aircraft to fragmentation bombs. The heavier explosives succeeded in tearing up our runway. But, every day, a small army of coolies patched the airstrip and filled in the bomb craters.

The most frightening aspect of the Japanese air raids was the shrill shriek of the bombs as they tumbled down from the sky. We could tell when a missile was going to hit near us by the variation in sound. It was very unnerving to be pinned down in a slit trench while bombs were exploding on all sides. But, eventually, I reached a point where I could sleep in a ditch almost as well as in my own bunk.

Since this was the monsoon season, the excavations were always muddy and filled with puddles of water. To make matters worse, the Chinese were using the trenches as latrines. Although they were severely reprimanded, the coolies continued to use the ditches for this purpose.

Every now and then a lone Japanese aircraft would sneak over the field, drop a few bombs, and do a little random strafing. We were usually caught by surprise whenever this occurred, and did not have time to inspect the nearest trench. We dove in and hoped for the best. Most of the raids took place at night, and chances were pretty good that somebody would land in a coolie's deposit. It was just another one of the war's occupational hazards.

Another enemy tactic was to send a flight of bombers over Liuchow—one at a time and spaced a half-hour apart. Although very little damage was done, the raids accomplished one objective—ruining a good night's sleep.

Perils of combat lurked in the most unsuspecting places. Besides the Japanese, the weather, and equipment failure, we had C- and K-rations to contend with.

The long hours we spent in the slit trenches made us hungry and thirsty. Therefore, we started carrying our canteens and a package of C- or K-rations with us when the alarm sounded. These "delicious" gourmet meals had been packed in thick, waxed cardboard cartons to keep them moisture proof. Often, when faced with the prospect of staying hungry or eating one of the rations, I felt like throwing away the contents and munching on the cardboard.

Among the items in some of the packages were plastic eating utensils, a neat little can opener, toilet paper, and a small packet containing several cigarettes. One brand of smokes in particular was packaged in a small paper box printed to look like genuine wood. The name of this cigarette was Edgewood. Anyone finding these beauties in their box of rations would automatically cuss up a storm. If there was ever one cigarette in the world that would cure a person of smoking, this was it! One deep drag off an Edgewood would gag a Camel smoker. It was our contention that this death-meat cigarette was made from pure horse manure. One of our boys was positive that he could tell what kind of food the contributing horse had been eating—hay, oats, or corn.

All ration cartons contained a packet of powdered lemon juice. It was the most useful item in the box. We mixed the powdered citrus with water to kill the taste of the "Jing Bow Juice."

September 6, 1944

We were placed on standby status tonight—ready to fly a bombing strike should any of the sea-sweep radar planes spot enemy targets. Our aircraft was fueled and loaded with nine 500-pound bombs. We had a briefing at 1500 and then went back to the barracks to sit and wait.

We had a good poker game going late in the evening, when Milt Wind received word that a small convoy had been sighted near the Chinese coast. We scrambled to our ready aircraft, made a quick check of instruments, and took off at 2200.

As a rule, Atkins guided us to within eight miles of our objective. At this distance, the blips showed up clearly on Miracle's radarscope and he would begin to adjust his bombsight.

The blips on the radarscope only gave us the target location. We were unable to tell the type of vessel until it was sighted visually. We always hoped for merchant ships instead of naval vessels—but even many of the merchantmen were armed. Every bombing run was a new adventure.

As soon as Jim Miracle picked his target, he would notify the radar operator. Atkins would then start calling the target's range at half-mile intervals.

From this point on, our attack was the bombardiers' baby. Miracle would order the bomb bay doors opened, check them visually, and direct the plane to its target by adjusting the bombsight. If our airspeed and altitude were steady—the wings level, radar properly calibrated, and the bombardier did not have to make any last-second adjustments—then WHAM! A direct hit. Any variations in our approach pattern would mean a miss—and jeopardize the lives of ten men along with a costly radar-equipped B-24.

However, even if we hit the bull's eye, there was no guarantee that our aircraft would escape damage from flak—and possibly not make it back to base. The worse scenario, of course, would be a crash landing in the sea. The B-24 was noted for breaking up when it hit the water, and would usually sink in about one minute. Capture by the Japs, or becoming shark bait, were other unpleasant prospects to look forward to.

But, getting back to the mission—our sea-search altitude was 7,500 feet. It was not long before Atkins picked up three blips on the radar screen. We rapidly descended to 400 feet. Miracle immediately set up his bombsight and checked the autopilot to make sure it was functioning properly. Any directional changes would automatically alter the course of the aircraft. However, it was up to the pilot and copilot to maintain the designated altitude until the bombs were dropped.

(Later on, after a few frightening experiences with the autopilot, Wind and I decided to fly all bombing runs manually, and make course changes as directed by the bombardier.)

As we began our initial attack run, I made a final cockpit check of instruments and power settings. Everything seemed to be operating smoothly. Then, just when Miracle made his drop, I gained visual contact. Our targets turned out to be three large junks. Not only were these vessels a waste of explosives, but a malfunction in one of the bomb bay switches dropped all nine bombs at the same time. However, even with all our "heavy artillery" going off in a single barrage, the best we could do was two near misses.

Milt and I were more than disgusted. This job of flying combat missions was tough enough without having to contend with equipment failures. We were staking our lives on every bomb run. A faulty attack could get us killed just as easily as a successful one.

With nothing left to drop, except a few C- and K-rations, we headed home. But we were not out of the woods yet. Our radio operator received word that the Japs had launched another air attack on Liuchow. Wind was ordered to steer clear of the area until notified. After circling for about an hour, we were finally signaled to land. The time was 0400. We had been flying for seven hours and had accomplished absolutely zero. What a night!

September 7, 1944

On standby again today. The monsoon season is still upon us. The weather is wet, hot, and sticky. I feel like I am living in a sauna with a horde of bloodthirsty mosquitoes for company. The land elevation in this part of China is practically sea level—with no cooling breezes.

We were called to the briefing room at 2000, received reports of a five-ship convoy, and took off at 2130. We would be flying into a heavy weather front with towering cumulus thunderheads along the squall line. Air turbulence would be strong. Under normal conditions, a pilot would never dream of flying an airplane of this size through this kind of weather system. It was impossible to know what to expect in the wake of violent and tumultuous wind, rain, and lightning. But if we could cross the front in one piece, the cooling night air would dissipate the storm clouds by the time we had completed the mission and were heading back to Liuchow.

As we entered the squall line, the crew were alerted to tie everything down and secure themselves for a rough ride. Milt and I tried to keep the wings level and the altitude steady. Nothing else could be done except pray, and hope that our B-24 would hold together and not flip over on its back. A plane could be ripped to pieces in the rampaging storms of a thunderhead, with its vicious, wind-shearing currents acting like giant scissors on the body and wings of an aircraft.

The stress on a plane, traversing a weather system of this kind, was so great that rivets would pop, warping the fuselage. Many B-24s were so badly mangled that, once safely on the ground, they never flew again.

Fortunately, this was a narrow front. We passed through it quickly and into bright moonlight. Everyone was shaken by the strong turbulence, but no injuries were reported.

When we reached the target position, we made our low-level run only to discover that the ships were sampans. Bombs were too precious to waste on these small craft. We climbed to our sea-search altitude of 7,500 feet and made radar sweeps until daylight. No further contacts were made and we returned to Liuchow with our full bomb load. For the second night in a row we ended up with nothing to show for our efforts.

September 8, 1944

This afternoon, Major Hightower Smith visited our dayroom. He had the latest news—and it was not good. Smith said he had been informed that the enemy advance south down the railroad from Hengyang was picking up speed. The Japs were boasting that they would open a corridor from the Yellow River, move south across China, and end up at Hanoi.

Since the railroad ran through Kweilin and Liuchow, General Chennault was in danger of losing both forward bases. The Fourteenth Air Force was the only deterrent facing the Japs. Fighter and bomber strikes hampered the Japanese push, but the enemy continued to move rapidly south, repairing damaged tracks as they advanced.

Major Smith told us that Chennault's plan of action called for our personnel to abandon Kweilin and proceed by rail to Liuchow. We would then evacuate Liuchow by air—taking with us whatever supplies we could carry. Everything left behind would be destroyed. The airstrip would be blown up by planting bombs in the runway and detonating them with timing devices. The Chinese Army would take up positions about 50 miles north of Kweilin, and attempt to hold the enemy as long as possible.

The loss of Kweilin and Liuchow would transfer the main operation of the Fourteenth Air Force to Kunming and our other airfields in western China. We would have our backs against the Himalayas—with no place to go except over the Hump to India.

However, the Japanese forces were also desperate. They had to capture our forward bases in order to protect the vital shipping and overland supply routes to their troops in Indochina.

Jim Miracle and I discussed the seriousness of the situation on the way back to our quarters. We were feeling pretty glum and decided that writing a few letters home might help our morale. While we were busy trying to figure out what to write—that would not be censored—a large, lean, mean-looking rat scampered across the floor. Miracle relieved the anxiety of the day by remarking: "Being surrounded by the local wildlife makes for a nice homey atmosphere around this place!"

September 11, 1944

During the past few days, a steady stream of military personnel have been arriving at Liuchow from Kweilin. They are a tired, dirty, and hungry gang. The 100-mile bumpy train ride was anything but a picnic.

This place is beginning to look like a refugee camp. The ATC has its hands full airlifting the Kweilin evacuees to our bases farther west. I talked to some of the boys. They all said that the Japanese were much closer to Kweilin than we had been told.

We also received unsettling news from B-24 crews returning from recent missions. Our new M-64, RDX 500-pound bombs were detonating on impact regardless of their fuse settings. At the authorized 400-foot attack level against enemy shipping, the concussion from premature explosions almost blew the planes out of the sky.

Although the RDX bomb is supposed to be one and a half times more powerful than the 500-pounders we had been using, it has presented many difficulties in low-altitude attack runs. It was frightening enough to be shot down by the Japs—let alone being torn to pieces by our own bombs. Never a dull moment in this man's war!

CHAPTER 4

The Air War Heats Up

As the Chinese Army attempted to regroup and make a stand north of Kweilin, refugees from the vicious Japanese onslaught continued to flee south. In Kweilin itself, masses of people camped in the rail-yards. Men, women, and children swamped every train available in their frantic frenzy to escape the invader. Hundreds of refugees were killed when a locomotive ploughed into a mob attempting to climb aboard rail cars that were already filled to capacity.

It quickly became apparent that the poorly equipped and demoralized Chinese soldiers would only be able to fight a delaying action against the superior enemy forces.

But, to make matters even worse, General Chennault's B-24s, based at Liuchow, were in desperate need of fuel, bombs, and other war materials in order to fly counterattack missions against the advancing Japanese Army.

Liuchow was 450 air miles from its base of supply at Kunming. There was no connecting rail line, only ancient gravel roads. Everything necessary to maintain the operation of the Fourteenth Air Force had to be flown across the Hump by Liberators or ATC transports. However, despite the shortages, intensive air strikes were mounted against the main enemy rail centers and marshalling yards.

September 12, 1944

Terrible weather today—no missions scheduled. News sifting in from Kweilin states that the Japanese are mounting an intensive drive and are now practically at the gates of the city. The Chinese Army has been unable to slow the enemy advance.

A few of us decided to hop a ride into the town of Liuchow to see what was going on and get some different food for a change. The city was crammed with civilians fleeing the Kweilin area—men, women, children, babies—many of them with no belongings except the ragged clothes on their backs. The frantic refugees were flooding into Liuchow by any means of transportation they could find—on foot, horseback, carts, bikes, motor vehicles, and by rail. Anything that could move was being used. It was an experience I will never forget. This war is pure hell for innocent civilians. After witnessing the sight, I developed a very personal feeling about my own efforts to help them fight the Japanese invader.

We took rickshaws back to the field, more determined than ever to make the enemy pay for this insult on humanity. We were a somber group of men when we hit the sack. It was not easy to fall asleep.

September 14, 1944

I was notified this morning that we would be leaving Liuchow about noon. We loaded our plane with gear, equipment, and all the people we could jam on board, and took off for Kunming. After landing, a few hours later, and unloading the passengers, we were instructed to leave our B-24 at the airfield and climb on a truck bound for Chengkung.

By the time we arrived at our old quarters, we were pretty well bushed. The barracks seemed very lonely without Pierpont, Tommy, and the others who had roomed next door to us.

The weather at Chengkung was much colder than Liuchow, and the boys stationed at the base said that it had been raining practically every day for the past two weeks. However, there was also good news—we were paid and drew rations owed us during our stay at Liuchow. Wind, Miracle, and I were also notified that we had been advanced in rank to first lieutenants. This promotion had been a long time in coming. It meant an additional 50 bucks a month. We got together with some friends and threw a "Jing Bow Juice" party. We had plenty to celebrate—and did we ever!

September 17, 1944

This was a red-letter day. We were scheduled for our first daylight mission. It was to be a high-altitude attack and all four squadrons of the 308th would be represented. The target was Changsha—approximately 700 miles northeast of Kunming. Changsha was an important rail center, with marshalling yards, a motor pool, and military storage area.

Our aircraft was packed to the hilt—twenty 100-pound incendiaries, the same number of 100-pound general-purpose bombs, and 2,500 gallons of fuel. The gross weight of the plane at take off would be about 57,000 pounds. The maximum gross weight for B-24s was 65,000 pounds at sea level—Chengkung was 6,000 feet higher than that. It would be a tough job just to get our ship airborne—if we did not rip the engines to pieces in the process.

But, luckily, every bomber from our two squadrons lifted off safely, and we proceeded to the rendezvous point. The group formation, consisting of 27 aircraft, reached Changsha at 1700. Heavy flak was encountered over the target, but no enemy fighters appeared. Our squadron, the 375th, achieved the best bombing results—all bull's eyes—right on the button.

Four aircraft were hit by flak, but all planes made it back to their home base safely. We touched down at 2145, completing the nine-hour mission.

We were happy with the results of our squadron's efforts. However, it seemed strange flying in formation and bombing during daylight hours—especially after becoming used to night missions and low-level attacks. Flying midnight sorties was a lonesome business.

September 20, 1944

Three days of monsoon rains and sloppy mud have kept us grounded. We broke the monotony by writing letters, playing cards, and the usual bull sessions.

I knew that the time was fast approaching when I would be getting a crew of my own. I was not looking forward to it. Milt Wind and I had been flying together as a smooth operating unit. We had an excellent record to date, and had good reason to be proud of our men and team efforts.

I now had ten missions and a hundred combat hours under my belt. Every flight that Wind and I made together meant one less attack we would have to sweat through.

Just before we had left Liuchow, the engineer of Lieutenant Throgmartin's crew suffered an appendicitis attack. Throgmartin asked if he might borrow our engineer, Jasper Armstrong, for a scheduled mission. Wind and I agreed, and Armstrong said he would be glad to help out.

I never thought anything more about the incident until late this afternoon, when our squadron commander, Major Crawford, showed up at our barracks. His face was drawn and grim as he related the bad news. Throgmartin's plane was missing. The last message received at Liuchow was that they were heading in to attack a three-ship convoy.

Wind and I were shocked. Armstrong was one of the best flight engineers in the entire 308th Bomb Group. He knew the B-24 inside and out, and could fix practically any problem that came up.

As the implications of Major Crawford's report began to sink in, I thought about what this loss would mean to our crew. Besides being a first-class engineer, Armstrong was also the leader of the enlisted personnel. I could not help thinking about how he had willingly volunteered to go out on the mission. Jasper could have declined, and no one would have thought anything more about it. Instead, he put his life on the line attempting to assist another crew.

We were a sad and silent group of men when we finally turned out the light and hit the sack. I had already lost several good friends, but Armstrong's death was even more personal. The damn war had really picked our pocket this time.

September 22, 1944

Another high-altitude group mission was scheduled today. Our target, the railroad yards and warehouse complex at Hankow, about 850 miles northeast of Kunming. We carried nine 500-pound clusters of fragmentation bombs.

After taking off at 1330, we rendezvoused over Luliang with planes from the 373rd Squadron. Our bombing formation consisted of 24 aircraft. We were the lead squadron.

By the time we reached Chihkiang, the weather was heavily overcast. According to briefing instructions, our attack force was supposed to be joined by a fighter escort and several B-25s. We circled the area twice, but no aircraft were sighted, so we proceeded to Hankow without fighter protection.

At dusk, the group was split into small flights of three planes each. Bombing runs were to be made in single sorties. We approached Hankow at 1930. Weather conditions were still overcast, and ground fog made visibility very poor. Flak was heavy, and searchlights tried unsuccessfully to pick us up through the haze. As Miracle shouted "Bombs Away," I spotted fires already burning, and explosions from what appeared to be gasoline and ammunition dumps.

However, as we banked away from the attack, I suddenly spotted another B-24—looming out of the haze—and racing straight toward us on a collision course. We were still in a loose three-plane formation. There was no room for evasive turns—or time to execute them. Both Wind and I instinctively jammed the control columns forward, throwing our plane into a steep dive. The fast, oncoming Liberator skimmed directly over our heads. Evidently, the pilot never sighted us—he made no attempt whatsoever to try and evade a certain crash.

We never did figure out where the phantom aircraft came from—or what he was doing operating in our bombing sector. The crew, in the rear of our plane, took some nasty knocks when we dived, but nobody was seriously injured. Everything happened so quickly that there was no time to sound a warning. It was another close call, and the identity of the

KWEILIN-LIUCHOW AREA AND RAILROAD

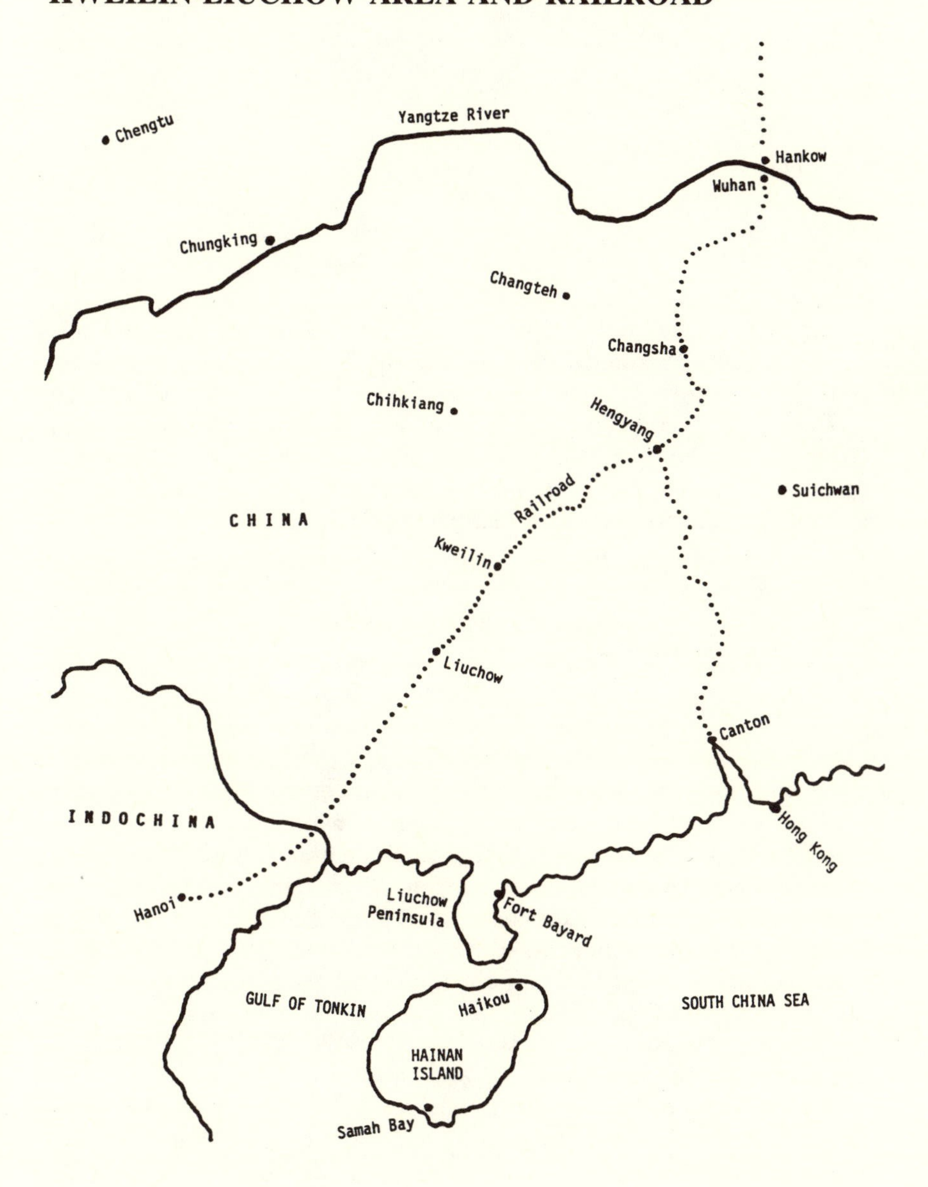

"mystery" B-24 was never solved. Our squadron returned to Kunming safely. We had survived another mission—just barely!

September 24, 1944

We were up before dawn, loaded twelve 500-pound bombs, and took off for Liuchow, arriving at 0930. I was not feeling well and, after fueling, found a bunk and sacked out, hoping to get some rest before another mission briefing and scheduled departure at 1730. I felt sick as hell but was determined not to lose any combat time. I climbed into the cockpit with Milt Wind just prior to take off.

The target was the Nanking-Pukow area—the same place we had bombed earlier in the month. I had a hunch that we would receive a very warm welcome this time around.

Our flight started out with ten planes, but one had to turn back after losing a couple of engines. We ran into rough weather and, as darkness settled in, the formation broke up and everyone proceeded on his own.

About 2230, we made our first pass over the target. However, cloud cover was too thick for visual observation, and radar was used to pinpoint the drop zone. We picked up quite a bit of ack-ack, but none too close. Enemy searchlights were also ineffective due to the overcast.

After the bombing run, we headed back to Liuchow through the same heavy weather—hail, snow, rain, and severe turbulence. We landed at 0355, went to debriefing, then collapsed on our bunks. We had been up for nearly 24 hours straight.

September 26, 1944

I awoke early this morning, and hoped to get away from Liuchow as soon as possible. This place had nothing but bad memories for all of us. Wind, McClure, Miracle, and I ate a quick breakfast, then headed out to the flight line. We had the usual problem of scrounging up fuel but, after more promises and IOUs, I managed to barter enough gas to get us back to our home base at Chengkung.

By the time we landed, late in the afternoon, the entire crew was worn out. And our disposition did not improve when we found out that no mail had arrived. Wind, Miracle, Mac, and I were plenty disgusted as we headed for the barracks area.

Our building was located on the side of a hill that separated the airstrip from the southeast shore of Kunming Lake. We were located on the west side of the field—about a quarter-mile from the north-south runway. The barracks were practically isolated from the rest of the compound since they were the last unit in the row of buildings. As a result, we became very friendly with the boys from the 3rd Mapping Squadron who occupied four of the eight rooms.

September 27, 1944

After spending most of the morning trying to straighten up our quarters, I borrowed a jeep and drove across the field to check on the mail situation. Imagine my surprise—after two weeks without any word from the outside world, we had finally been remembered by the Army Postal Service. My share was 16 letters. I certainly hope that mail delivery will be better after this war is over. The rest of the day was spent in reading letters and exchanging news from home. After chow, we relaxed with a poker game. I lost—as usual.

We hit the sack about eight o'clock. However, I had no sooner turned out the light, when I discovered we had a problem. Rats! Dozens of rats! They were holding a convention in our room—galloping across the floor and squeaking and carrying on like they were having an election.

Under these conditions, sleep was impossible. The only remedy was an all-out assault against our unwelcome guests. Because of "lights out" we were forced to rely upon flashlights and candles for illumination. Wind, Miracle, McClure, and I entered the combat zone armed with shoes, machetes from our survival kits, and an old saber that one of the guys had picked up somewhere.

After several minutes of shouting, cursing, and knife-swinging warfare, we managed to kill a couple of rodents, but almost did ourselves in as well. Somebody stomped on a rat—spreading its slippery innards all over the floor.

Our sudden attack scared away the intruders, and we finally managed to get back to our bunks after wading through the debris. The following morning was spent in cleaning up the mess, and thanking our lucky stars that one of us had not grabbed his .45 during the riot. But the idea did cross my mind.

It was apparent that we had to devise a better method of exterminating the beasts. Shoes, boots, and knives were definitely not going to do the trick. At the rate these critters were multiplying, we would soon be up to our asses in rats. There were too many of them and too few of us. And they were rapidly eating us out of house and home—literally and figuratively. The damn rats devoured anything that stood still long enough for them to gnaw on—especially if it had the scent of meat. Even wood floors were not safe if food was spilled on them. Candles, and anything made of leather, were delicacies.

At this rate—with Japanese air attacks on moonlit nights, and "Genghis Khan and his Rat Raiders" holding track meets in our room—we never would get any sleep. Something had to be done. Severe measures were called for.

September 28, 1944

Lousy weather this morning and no missions scheduled. However, the day off gave us an opportunity to discuss the problem of rodents using our room for a recreation hall. At breakfast, we formulated a plan of action. I sneaked a few pieces of bread back to the barracks with me, and scattered the crumbs in front of a large rat hole at a rear corner of our quarters. We then loaded .45s with bird shot and set up a watch. Mac and I took the first shift.

Sure enough, within a short time, two large rats—probably scouts for the rest of the pack—poked their heads through the opening and grabbed for the bread. McClure and I opened fire at the same time—three shots apiece from a distance of 12 feet. The rodents were blasted to rat heaven, but we nearly ripped out the wall. Blood, guts, and slivers of wood whizzed everywhere. At this point-blank range, the steel pellets did not have a chance to spread. They smashed into the side of the building like solid shot—blowing the wooden boards to pieces.

The sudden noise and commotion brought the boys of the 3rd Mapping Squadron charging into our room. They figured that it was too early for a ''Jing Bow Juice'' party, and demanded to know what the devil was going on.

Mac and I explained the trouble we had the night before, and that we were only trying to run off the rats. The guys next door were not very sympathetic. They chewed us out and said that the rodent problem was comparatively simple to solve. But our raising hell practically all last night, and then again this morning, was disturbing the entire barracks area. There was even a rumor that the Japs had parachuted into camp.

The mapping squadron boys had been at Chengkung longer than us. They knew all the angles and supplied a solution to our difficulty. By chipping in a few bucks apiece, we could hire the building's ''Number One Boy'' to patch the rat holes with tin can sheeting from the mess hall.

We followed their professional advice and located the fellow. After a long, frustrating session of sign language—compounded with our pathetic conversational Chinese—we managed to explain the rat dilemma, and the holes Mac and I had blasted in the wall.

The ''Number One Boy'' assured us that he would take care of our problem for only ten bucks—American money. I thought the price was a little steep, but this guy was a real businessman. We coughed up the dough and the lad took off like a shot. Minutes later, we heard the sounds and chatter of a repair crew hard at work on our quarters—despite pouring rain.

This had been a long, busy day and I was bushed. I told my gunslinging pals that after our unsuccessful war against the animal kingdom, I could not help wondering if we had enough sense to be let loose by ourselves. Wind, McClure, and Miracle all agreed that I might have a point.

It was plain to see that another menace had been added to our list of enemies. Survival now meant not only fighting the Japanese, the weather, and the mosquitoes but also the cunning, despicable, and hungry rat!

September 30, 1944

Finally a clear day and another group mission scheduled. Our target was the Tien Ho Airdrome near Canton. After briefing, our plane was loaded with fragmentation bombs and we took off at 1730. A total of 31 aircraft made up the strike force.

About halfway to the target we hit violent weather—heavy rain and thunderstorms. It was impossible to keep the formation together, so each plane proceeded on its own. McClure set a southerly course and we managed to skirt the worst part of the storm.

Upon breaking into the clear, we spotted another B-24 and the two of us headed to the drop zone together. At 2115, we were 12,000 feet over Tien Ho. The area stood out sharply in the bright moonlight. Miracle shouted "Bombs Away" and we immediately began evasive action to dodge heavy ack-ack fire and searchlight beams. Puffs of deadly flak mushroomed around us, but we were able to escape the searchlights and get the hell out of there. I had expected to be jumped by enemy fighters, but none showed up.

On our return to Chengkung, we avoided most of the bad weather and landed safely at 0100. At debriefing, I learned that eight planes had been forced to turn back because of mechanical trouble and the storm. Overall, the strike was not very successful. But, at least our crew had survived one more mission.

October 1, 1944

Our barracks had no sooner been repaired than we received orders to move to new quarters on the other side of the field. Personally, I would just as soon have remained where we were. But Major Crawford wanted the officers of the 375th Squadron to be together as one unit—and probably to keep his "big bad boys" out of any more trouble.

The four of us were split up. McClure and I were assigned to a room by ourselves. It was nicer than "Rat Hotel," but the building was also noisier. Every room was occupied and there was a lot of traffic up and down the hallway. Our new lodgings were better furnished and cleaner than what we had been used to. These were first-class accommodations.

We even had a "Number One Boy" to look after our laundry and keep the room tidy. Our fellow officers told us that there were no rats in the barracks. McClure and I wondered if we would know how to act among all the luxuries that had suddenly been thrust upon us.

We spent most of the day putting our belongings away and organizing the room. In the evening, we ambled over to the Officer's Club for a few drinks to celebrate our new-found opulence. I joined a craps game and won a few bucks, for a change.

October 5, 1944

Bad weather over target areas has kept us grounded for the past several days. Nothing to do but play cards and shoot the bull. Eventually our discussions usually get around to girls. But fraternizing with the local women can be as dangerous as fighting the Japs. The venereal disease rate in this part of the country is out of sight. Some cases were incurable even with modern medicine.

A few of us borrowed a jeep this afternoon to visit a member of the 3rd Mapping Squadron who was in the isolation ward of the Station Hospital at Kunming. He had contracted a venereal infection that was gradually eating away the flesh from his bones. The poor fellow was a shocking sight and told us that he was as good as dead because the doctors were unable to cure him. What a hell of a way to die!

I drove the jeep on our return trip to Chengkung. And, believe it or not, we were stopped by the Military Police and I was ticketed for speeding—32 miles per hour in a 20-mile zone. Imagine! Getting a speeding ticket in China—out in the middle of nowhere! A man's not safe anywhere these days. My punishment was even more ludicrous. I was instructed to write a letter to the provost marshal in Kunming—telling him how sorry I was, and that it would not happen again. What kind of crazy war is this anyhow? Are the Japs obeying the speed limit? I would give my eyeteeth to see their first traffic ticket.

Of course, when word got around the squadron about my criminal behavior, the boys had a field day. Old "heavy-foot" Haynes became the main topic of conversation. However, I failed to see any humor in their snide remarks.

October 13, 1944

The monsoon season is working overtime, with heavy rains every day, stirring the ground into thick, tenacious mud. The weather has served to give us plenty of rest, but it was cutting into our combat time. None of us was eager to get shot at, but we would never get in our required mission hours at this rate.

Replacement crews began arriving from Langley Field. They flew over the Hump with their own planes just as we had. Along with the arrival of new personnel came an unexpected treat—beer! One of the incoming crews packed several cases of brew in with their load of supplies. The occasion called for a celebration, so we threw a beer-bust. After all, today was Friday the 13th, and we were still alive and kicking. What more could a person ask for over here?

The Hopson Project had taken a considerable beating to date. Most of us had lost friends—and all of us were ready to fight like hell to avenge them. Although we seldom discussed the subject, it was there, constantly in the back of our minds—the realization that the next flight might very well be our last. The odds against surviving this war were looming larger on every mission.

October 15, 1944

Finally a break in the weather, and a group bombing strike was scheduled against the White Cloud Airdrome near Tien Ho. We took off about noon, loaded with 100-pound fragmentation bombs fused for instantaneous detonation. The group's rendezvous point was over Luliang. Our squadron led the formation of 28 planes. At 1330, 50 escorting fighters joined the flight. They were to be our cover when we reached the target.

We were over White Cloud at 1450 and made our drop from 17,000 feet. I spotted several Jap Zeros, but the P-40s and P-51s fought them off. It was a beautiful sight as I watched our fighters shoot down two of the enemy aircraft.

We encountered heavy ack-ack fire, but all the bombers returned safely to base. Many Japanese planes were destroyed on the ground and the airfield sustained considerable damage.

October 17, 1944

A welcome break in the routine today. We received orders to fly back across the Hump to pick up supplies and a load of gasoline. It was a rough flight over the mountains and it was about noon when we landed at Chabua. We had lunch at the mess hall near the flight line. It was a delicious meal compared to what we had been eating. The boys stationed on this side of the Hump really live a good life. Plenty of food, beer, and booze—and nobody shooting at them or dropping bombs on their heads every moonlit night.

After stuffing our stomachs, we made a beeline to the PX and picked up a beer ration for our crew and the rest of the squadron. After that was taken care of, we arranged for the supplies and gasoline. First things first, I always say.

We took off from Chabua at 1610, flew up and down the valley until reaching an altitude of 12,000 feet, and then started across the Hump. Our plane immediately began picking up ice. We climbed to 18,000 feet before breaking out into the clear.

When we landed at Chengkung and reported to debriefing, I learned that a Liberator from the 374th Squadron had crashed while flying the Hump. The entire crew was killed. They had not escaped the sleet fast enough.

Icing conditions and sudden wind shifts over the mountains can easily blow an aircraft off course and into a mountainside. Becoming lost and running out of gas were the two great dangers in Hump-flying. The minimum safe altitude was 12,000 feet. There was no way to escape icing except to keep climbing and hope to get above the cloud cover. If the ice buildup was too rapid, the plane gradually slowed down because of the increased weight and drag. A flight crew's only salvation in this situation was to bail out before their ship stalled. But parachuting into the jungles or mountains was also usually fatal.

After hearing this depressing news, I strolled over to the operations section to check on my flying time records. I found that I had racked up 150 combat hours. According to existing regulations, in order to finish my tour, I would need a total of 350 hours as copilot or 400 hours as first pilot. Slowly but surely my combat time was beginning to build up.

October 20, 1944

We were briefed at 0730 for an emergency flight to Chabua. Because of bad weather over the Hump for the past several days, General Chennault's supply of fuel and bombs was dwindling rapidly. The Fourteenth Air Force fighters and B-25 Mitchell bombers had been kept continually busy flying low-level attacks against enemy facilities and troop concentrations.

The increasing pace of the war was making our squadrons more and more dependent upon the highway of aircraft flying the Hump. Chennault's thin lifeline was stretched to the breaking point. Each unit of the Fourteenth Air Force became responsible for its own survival. It was up to the men of the 308th Bomb Group to haul their own gasoline and supplies over the mountains from India.

We landed at Chabua at 1230 and made a dash for the mess hall and that delicious Stateside food. On the way to fill our bellies, we ran into more of the Langley Field gang. They were on this side of the Hump for the same reason we were—trying to scrounge up fuel and supplies. They were from the 425th and 373rd Squadrons, stationed at Kunming and Luliang respectively, and were also having their share of bad luck with the weather and accidents.

We had a long gab session and learned that the USO was putting on a show in the late afternoon—Pat O'Brien, Jinx Falkenberg, and the usual troupe of Hollywood girls.

After the performance, we met the Langley bunch at the PX to have a few beers and talk about old times and our experiences in combat. I realized, after comparing notes, that all of us had lost good friends. The facts were cold and hard to take. But it was very possible that we might never see each other again after tonight. A very sobering thought!

October 21, 1944

We were up early, had breakfast, and loaded our plane to the hilt with 3,400 gallons of gasoline and supplies. Take off was at 0900 for the trip back to Chengkung. We had been flying for about two hours when I noticed that the oil pressure on the No. 4 engine was beginning to fluctuate. Wind and I crossed our fingers that the gauge was faulty. But, suddenly, the needle dropped to zero and oil began flooding across the motor cowling and wing. The engine was gone. We feathered it and shut down the controls. I yelled at McClure that there was trouble and to check our position. Mac quickly figured our location—about 30 minutes from Yunnanyi.

There were two emergency airstrips on the Hump—Myitkyina and Yunnanyi. Myitkyina was 150 miles east of Chabua and was carved out of a mountain crest. Yunnanyi was another 185 miles and half way to Chengkung. It had been hacked out of the jungle on the gentle slope of a mountain. Neither of these fields had anything to offer except the basic needs for survival and minimum repair service. However, in this part of the world, they were lifesavers to countless planes and their crews.

We lost our engine at 16,000 feet, and were flying over mountains almost as high. In order to maintain a safe altitude, we were forced to run the remaining three engines at maximum power—which meant emergency-rich fuel mixture, full supercharger boost, and 2,500 RPM on the props. After the adjustments were made, all we could do was pray that we had enough power to reach Yunnanyi without having to pitch any of our load.

Phil George managed to raise the field on his radio, advised them of our trouble, and that we were coming in on only three engines and with full tanks of high-octane gasoline. We received immediate instructions to land in an uphill direction so as not to burn out the brakes—hopefully!

The runway at Yunnanyi soon came into view. But it was not very consoling to watch ambulances, fire trucks, jeeps, and the ground crew—all dashing madly about waiting for our plane to touch down—in one piece or many.

But God was on our side. We made a perfect three-engine landing and rolled to an easy stop, barely touching the brakes. Wind and I looked at each other and breathed big sighs of relief. Anything could have happened on the final approach, such as loss of power in another engine. In that case, we would have crashed—and with all that fuel on board, everyone would have been burned to a crisp.

We taxied to the parking area and shut everything down. A group of men from the field's engineering section quickly drove up in a truck. While they removed the oil-covered cowling and checked the motor, we were taken to the operations office to make our report.

About a half hour later, I was notified that the engine was beyond repair and would have to be replaced. I sent a message to Chengkung advising them of the situation. Arrangements were made to billet our crew until another engine could be flown in from Chabua or Chengkung. After chow, Wind, McClure, Miracle, and I went to our quarters and played poker until lights-out. Never a dull moment in this man's war.

October 23, 1944

At 1100 hours, Captain Paul Brosious flew in from Chengkung with another engine. Several members of our squadron's ground crew came along with him. With all of us working like the devil, we had the new motor installed by 1530.

Captain Brosious continued on the Chabua to pick up a load of gasoline. Fortunately he left the repair party with us to help check out the engine. We had trouble adjusting the prop governor, but eventually had it working fairly well. However, just as we were racing down the strip for take off, the propeller began running away. It came as no surprise to me, and I was ready with the feathering button. I managed to hold the prop steady until we gained sufficient altitude. By the time we leveled off, and throttled back to cruising speed, the prop governor was holding a moderately consistent RPM.

The rest of the flight was without incident and we landed safely at Chengkung. It was a happy crew that climbed out of that plane and put their feet on home ground again.

October 24, 1944

There is no rest for the weary in this war. Immediately after finishing breakfast, Wind and I received orders to take off in the afternoon for Liuchow. Besides our crew and their gear, we would also be carrying 22 passengers and baggage.

At 1530, while taxiing to the runway, our wheels ran over a mud puddle that concealed a deep sink hole. It took two tractors to pull us out. I checked the landing gear, but there was no apparent damage. We finally lifted off the ground about an hour later.

The weather began to deteriorate rapidly. We climbed through heavy overcast and broke into the clear at 12,000 feet. Wind and I stayed on top of the clouds all the way to Liuchow. We made an instrument approach to the field. Dropping down through the dense mist, and narrowly missing the rugged cones of rock, we quickly located the runway and landed without incident.

After parking the aircraft and unloading the passengers, we were about to take a jeep to the operations office, when Harry Marshall and Carl Weitz drove up in a truck. We had not seen each other since Langley Field. What a reunion! It was great to see the guys again, but the absence of Tommy Tomenedale and George Pierpont dampened our spirits to some extent. However, there was a war to fight so, like it or not, we had to face reality and take our losses in stride. Any one of us could be flying the next plane to be shot down in flames.

We threw a "Jing Bow Juice" party in the evening, and talked about our adventures to date. The continual thought of survival was uppermost in the minds of us all. We still had plenty of combat hours to put in, and the missions were becoming more and more dangerous with every air strike.

The bull session broke up when we ran out of booze, and it was late by the time we hit our bunks. I had a difficult time falling asleep. For some unknown reason, a premonition of disaster kept invading my thoughts.

CHAPTER 5

The Quick and the Dead

In early October 1944, a long-standing feud between General Joseph Stilwell (commanding general of the CBI) and General Claire Chennault finally boiled over. Stilwell firmly believed that the vast areas of China that were under Japanese domination could only be won back by the foot soldier and that air strikes alone would not be sufficient to win the war against Japan.

General Chennault disagreed. He felt that the salvation of China hinged on airpower and insisted that the bulk of supplies coming from India over the Hump should go to the Fourteenth Air Force. Stilwell, on the other hand, wanted a large quantity of arms and ammunition in order to equip 26 Chinese divisions.

Although Stilwell was Chiang Kai-shek's chief of staff, Chennault had known the leader of China for many years prior to World War II. Both Chennault and Chiang were convinced that bombing attacks against Japanese land and sea targets would eventually defeat the enemy.

Since the trickle of supplies being flown over the Hump could not begin to support both a land and air operation, Chiang Kai-shek opted for the Fourteenth Air Force. General Stilwell was replaced by Lieutenant General Albert C. Wedemeyer as chief of staff to Chiang Kai-shek.

But, while all this bickering was going on at the high command level, the Japanese Army continued its advance. On November 10, 1944, Liuchow and Kweilin were abandoned to enemy forces. With the loss of these two forward bases of the Fourteenth Air Force, the situation in China seemed very glum indeed. Morale of the Chinese

Army was at an all-time low and the battle for the railroads had taken an enormous toll on Chiang's resources.

October 26, 1944

Late this morning, the officers of our squadron were summoned to the briefing room and notified that two large Japanese convoys had been sighted in the South China Sea. We were told to have our planes ready as soon as possible for a strike. All crews were ordered to the flight line to check over their aircraft and supervise the loading of gasoline, bombs, and machine gun ammunition.

At 1600, Wind and I reported to operations for the latest information concerning the position of the enemy vessels. The attack would be flown in single sorties, with planes taking off at half-hour intervals.

We were airborne at 1730, and McClure charted an intercept course. We had no sooner left the China coastline than Atkins reported he had picked up the targets at a distance of 40 miles. A couple of minutes later, we dropped down to 400 feet and made our first run on a Japanese freighter. The enemy spotted us at a mile and a half and opened fire.

Tracers coming our way looked like a Fourth of July fireworks display. I would have enjoyed the spectacle if I did not know how deadly those little fellows were. This was a lethal show—survival of the fittest—kill or be killed.

As we roared directly over the target, Jim Miracle dropped three 500-pound bombs. Wind immediately dove to the deck to avoid tracer fire from other ships in the convoy. While skimming the waves, I called for a station-to-station report from the crew. Everyone checked in okay. We had no apparent serious damage. Jim Cuva stated that the freighter was now in flames. Wind climbed for altitude, headed out and away from the enemy, and set up for another attack. We quickly turned back toward the convoy, swooped to low level, and raced across the water. Our target was a cargo carrier on the other side of the flotilla. I shouted for Miracle to take over and we began the bomb run.

This time, however, the Japs were ready. Every ship in the convoy seemed to be firing at us. As we crossed the deck of the vessel, Jim sent three more bombs plunging from the bomb bay. Milt immediately scooted for the water. When we pulled up, I thought I could feel the ocean froth tickling the belly of our B-24.

Another bull's eye, but heat from the exploding bombs and resulting flames made us an excellent visual target for Japanese gunners. Columns of tracers were so thick that they lit up the cockpit as we pulled away from the convoy.

A station-to-station check found all crew members uninjured. Reports from men in the waist section stated that our second target was burning

FOURTEENTH AIR FORCE BASES AND TARGET CENTERS

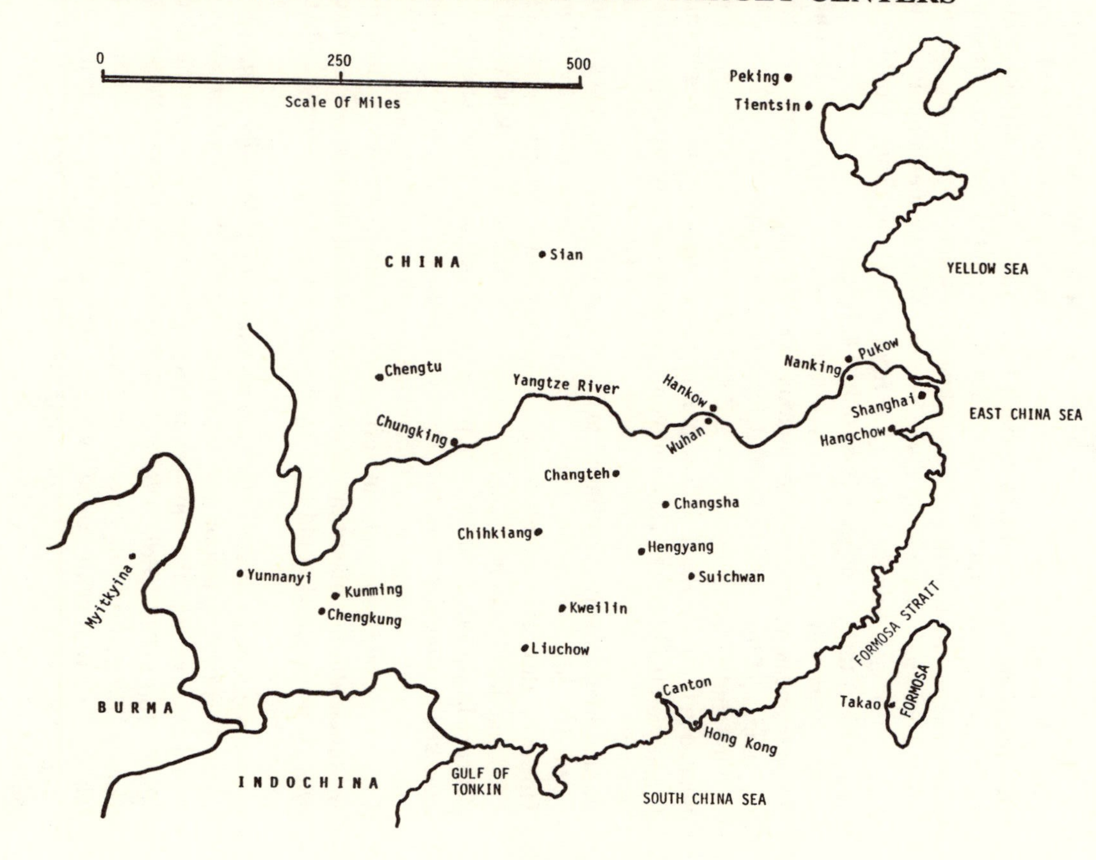

and dead in the water. But, we also received unsettling news—many holes could be seen in the wings and fuselage. Cuva, in the tail turret, reported that the aft part of the plane looked like a sieve. However, so far so good. No external gasoline leaks were visible on the wings, and the control cables were still in good working order.

Before making a third run at the convoy, additional time was taken for a more thorough inspection of the aircraft. Wind and I wanted to be sure that our plane was airworthy enough to try another pass without falling apart in midair. We still had six bombs left. The entire crew was consulted about attempting a further attack. I knew we would be pressing our luck to head back into that inferno again. The Japs were unquestionably waiting for a return visit, and the bright glow from their flaming ships would make us a perfect target—especially at only 400 feet.

But, even with the odds heavy in the enemy's favor, the decision to hit them one more time was unanimous. We were out here to sink Japanese shipping, and by God, we were determined to do just that!

Wind and I set up our plane and turned back to the convoy. As we headed in for the strike, I noticed fires from the previous bombings burning brightly on the horizon. This run would be the most dangerous yet. There was no way to tell on the radarscope exactly what type of ship we would be attacking. Positive identification could only be made by visual sighting.

We dashed low over the water, aiming at the target selected by Atkins. However, this time he had picked a destroyer and the warship was ready. We immediately ran into a hailstorm of every kind of ack-ack imaginable. Tracers lit up the inside of our plane from cockpit to tail. The aircraft bounced continually from the impact of large and small shells. I turned and looked aft down the aisle. Glancing through the open bomb bay doors,, I could see bullets ricocheting off the remaining six bombs. I knew that if Miracle did not blast that destroyer, we would be dead ducks. There was no way a B-24 could keep taking this kind of punishment and stay in one piece.

Our run took us directly over the man-of-war—practically at mast-high level. In a fleeting instant, as we zoomed across the destroyer's deck, I had a clear view of the ship—guns blazing away and men rushing madly about. Jim yelled "Bombs Away." In less than a second, Wind and I jammed the controls forward—raced clear of the convoy, and climbed for altitude. Cuva quickly called over the intercom that Miracle had scored a direct hit with his third bomb and there had been a tremendous explosion.

As soon as we had time to take our eyes off the flight panel and engine gauges, Wind and I looked at each other and took a deep breath. Not a word was spoken. After finding the plane and ourselves still in one piece, we were too stunned to talk.

Once again, a station-to-station report indicated no casualties. And, for the moment, our aircraft seemed to be operational. However, I could see large tears in the wings. Then Miracle reported that the bombardier's compartment was shot all to hell. The men in the waist also called in that their section was full of holes.

Cranton Terrall, who had replaced Jasper Armstrong as flight engineer, examined the ship to check the actual damage. He returned to the cockpit with bad news. Our wing tank fuel cells were leaking and 100-octane gasoline was sloshing back and forth along the bomb bay catwalk. Gas was flowing from inside the wing skin into the bomb bay. Although the fuel cells were supposed to be self-sealing, they had been ripped apart. Terrall also reported that the plane was leaking hydraulic fluid.

We had a very dangerous situation on our hands. The slightest spark could blow the aircraft into oblivion, and scatter us in bits and pieces all over the South China Sea. Although we still carried three bombs, the damage we had sustained prevented any possibility of making another run at the enemy. With raw gasoline flooding the plane, a hot bullet striking our ship would turn it into a fireball.

I told Miracle to jettison the remaining bombs and come up to the cockpit. After dropping the missiles, Jim made his way forward and stood between Wind and me. Miracle said he was amazed that we had not been shot out of the sky. Phil George leaned around the partition separating his radio compartment from my side of the cockpit and handed me several machine gun bullets. He found them on the floor under his seat. McClure also picked up bullets on his side of the compartment behind Milt Wind.

Besides wearing their flak suits and helmets, both men had also been sitting on extra flak suits. Mac said that he was determined to save the "family jewels" at any price. Those suits certainly did their job.

Remarkably our radio equipment was undamaged and in working order. I told George to call Liuchow and tell operations that we had been shot up, but were on our way back to base.

In the meantime, Wind and I were busy checking out the engines, and the plane itself, to see if we stood any chance of making it home. As we discussed the problem with leaking gasoline and hydraulic fluid, George reported he had contacted Liuchow, but the airfield was socked in by bad weather—visibility was zero. We were advised to try and make Cheng-kung. This was ominous news. The battered condition of our aircraft—plus loss of fuel and hydraulic fluid—made us a prime candidate for "one-of-our-aircraft-is-missing" reports.

Wind, McClure, and I held an emergency conference regarding the distance we still had to fly and the time involved. We then told Terrall to check on the fuel situation, determine which cells were leaking the most, and to transfer that fuel to other tanks in order to conserve as much gasoline as possible.

After accumulating all the facts, it was decided that we could reach

Chengkung—providing the plane held together and did not spring any additional fuel leaks.

Our next step was to lighten the weight of the aircraft. I instructed the crew to start throwing everything overboard that was loose or could be unbolted. This meant tossing out the .50-caliber machine guns in the waist windows, ammunition, flak suits, helmets, and any other items not essential to the safe operation of the plane. Terrall rounded up all liquids, including our water supply, and poured them into the hydraulic reservoir tank. Any kind of fluid was better than none.

Wind and I reviewed emergency landing procedures for hand-cranking the main gear and nose wheel down, and locking them in position for landing. Flaps would also have to be lowered manually.

The crew was informed exactly what to expect when we touched down, and that we would probably be without brakes. The men were instructed to rig a parachute in each waist window and tie the chute harnesses to the machine gun mounts. As soon as our wheels hit the ground, they were to pull the ripcords.

Since the entire plane was drenched with fuel and gas fumes, everyone had to be especially careful when moving about the aircraft. We were a flying bomb—any spark and we would all be playing harps. The boys got that message loud and clear.

Wind and I were also keenly aware that a B-24 could roll for miles without brakes. And we would be landing on a 6,000-foot runway—with raw gasoline flowing unchecked in the ship, a ruptured hydraulic system, and, perhaps, shot-up tires. Chances were very good that our plane would explode as soon as we hit the gravel strip. I thought to myself, how ironic it would be to come this far and end up in a ball of flame.

We were over Chengkung at 0100, but still carried 900 gallons of gas in the tanks. Apparently we had not been losing as much fuel as we thought. Getting rid of the excess weight must have helped. But now we had another problem. We could not risk a landing attempt with that much gasoline on board. There was only one choice—to keep circling the field and use up the fuel.

George contacted the tower—told them of our situation and described the condition of the aircraft. We were instructed to crack the bomb bay doors in order to suck out the fumes. Operations also advised us to circle in close proximity to the field so that, in case of an emergency, we could bail out over level terrain. I told George to radio the tower that we would try and stay aloft until dawn. We would stand a better chance of survival at daylight.

Wind and I circled Chengkung for nearly four hours, steadily watching the fuel gauge needle dip toward empty. About 0500, the sky began to lighten on the eastern horizon. We had just enough gas in our tanks for one landing attempt.

During the tense hours circling the field, we had ample time to discuss every eventuality. A poll was taken among the crew members to see if anyone wished to bail out. It was their lives at stake, and if any man thought his chances were better hitting the silk, it was his choice to make. The decision of the crew was unanimous—they would stay with the plane no matter what.

With this final word of assurance, we began the turn for our approach. I called the tower and told them we were coming in. I notified operations to give us plenty of leeway along the runway. We had no idea in which direction the plane would veer when it struck the runway.

The main gear and nose wheel were cranked down and locked. Tires were visually inspected and appeared to be inflated. Flaps were lowered. I reminded the boys in the waist section to yank the ripcords the moment we touched down, and to hit the ground running as soon as the ship came to a halt.

We slipped over the mountains and dipped toward the airstrip. Our wheels kissed the runway. Wind slammed on the brakes. Nothing happened. The brake line on the left main gear had ruptured. We swerved right. I jammed the starboard engine throttles to full power, hoping to straighten us out. No luck, they did not rev up fast enough, but only added to our forward speed. I quickly began cutting off every switch I could get my hands on, shut down the engines, and assisted Wind with the rudders.

We were now 200 yards down the runway and several feet to the right of the strip. Chinese workers had stacked large mounds of rock, for patching holes, about every hundred yards along the length of the runway. Our right wheels plowed into the center of a rock pile. The main gear collapsed upon impact, dropping the starboard wing and engines to the ground. The three-bladed props bent like limp spaghetti.

In a cloud of dirt and stone, our plane skidded out of control. The noise was deafening. The aircraft bounced, lunged and chewed up the ground for another 300 yards before it came to a grinding stop—almost to the front door of the ATC coffee shop.

An ethereal silence permeated the ship. The only noise I heard was the rapid pounding of my own heart. Then it suddenly dawned on me that the plane might go up in a ball of flame. I shouted at Wind. He quickly revived, reached up and jerked open the escape hatch above the cockpit. Wind hoisted himself through the opening and yelled for me to follow. I started to stand, but my left leg gave way. Milt grabbed my right hand and helped me climb through the hatch. I crawled forward along the top of the fuselage until I reached the front turret of the nose section. Grabbing hold of the twin .50 caliber machine gun barrels, I swung to the ground. My leg collapsed again. Two crewmen rushed to my aid and carried me away from the smoking wreck.

We huddled together a safe distance from the aircraft, and stood looking in disbelief at our fatally wounded bird. Even though shot to pieces, she had brought us home safely before she died. All of us were in a state of shock, wondering why we were still alive. It was miraculous that the plane did not catch fire. The boys in the waist said that after we struck the rocks, all they could see were clouds of dirt and showers of sparks as the props dug furrows in the hard ground.

Many of the ATC personnel had gathered in the coffee shop listening to a radio that was tuned to the tower frequency and sweating out our landing. One of the transport crews told what happened when they saw the plane skid off the runway and careen toward them. There was an immediate stampede of bodies trying to get out of the building. They could not escape fast enough. Doors were ripped off hinges and windows were smashed. One of the pilots wisecracked that our crash-landing sure scared the crap out of a bunch of guys. I told him in no uncertain terms, "What the hell do you think it did to us!"

The most amazing part of the mission was that not a single member of our crew was hurt, except for me—I banged my left knee on something during the landing. A squadron truck took us to operations for debriefing. I reported that we had sunk at least two ships, and possibly three. Wind and I also learned, to our dismay, that the time spent circling the field did not count toward combat hours. As far as I was concerned, it was a battle just keeping that hunk of Swiss cheese in the air.

We were a disgusted, but thankful, group of airmen as we walked to our quarters and hit the sack—completely and totally exhausted.

Later in the day, after a refreshing sleep, I heard about other casualties that occurred during the mission. Major Carswell and his crew hit the same convoy about an hour after our strike. The Japs were waiting for him. Carswell's plane sustained major flak damage, but he managed to guide his aircraft back to the Chinese coast. Carswell ordered his men to bail out while he searched for a crash-landing site. Eight crew members hit the silk. Major Carswell, Lieutenant O'Neal, and Lieutenant Hillier stayed with the ship. However, before they were able to set their plane down, it slammed into a mountainside and burned. Lieutenant Rinker and Sergeant Steinman were killed when they bailed out.

[Major Horace S. Carswell, Jr., was posthumously awarded the Medal of Honor for his action on the night of October 26, 1944, while attacking a Japanese convoy in spite of intense antiaircraft fire.]

October 31, 1944

On October 30, we were ordered to return to Liuchow. We had decent weather for a change and arrived in late morning. I ran into Harry Marshall and a few others of the Langley Field gang. It was the consensus of opinion that we were going to be stuck here for awhile—whether we liked it or not.

Wind, McClure, Miracle, and I had no sooner hit the sack that night than an operations officer rushed into our quarters with news that the Navy had received information concerning a Japanese convoy steaming somewhere in the vicinity of the Formosa Strait and South China Sea. They requested help from the Fourteenth Air Force in locating the enemy vessels and the number and types of ships. Our crew had been picked to make a daylight reconnaissance of the area to try and spot the flotilla.

We were awakened at 0330, dressed by the light of a peanut oil lamp, had a quick breakfast, and went to briefing at 0430. On this mission, we would not be carrying bombs—only ammunition for our .50-caliber machine guns and full tanks of gasoline.

A half hour later we were airborne, banked south 250 miles to the coast, then turned east on the first leg of our scouting assignment, the Formosa Strait. Search altitude was 7,500 feet.

After flying three hours on this heading, Atkins called excitedly over the intercom. He had picked up blips at 125 miles and 30° to starboard. We immediately swung right on an intercept course. The sky was bright and sunny, with hardly a trace of clouds and unlimited visibility—a perfect day for visual identification.

About 30 miles from the target, Atkins informed Milt and me that we should be able to see the ships through binoculars. I quickly grabbed my pair and began to scout the horizon. Moments later, I sighted them—eleven vessels, three destroyers and eight freighters, steaming on a southwest course toward the Indochina coast.

We closed to within nine miles when our plane was spotted. The destroyers broke away from the convoy and raced in our direction. They opened fire, but Wind circled just beyond the range of their guns. As soon as we made a positive identification, George radioed the convoy's location and types of ships. The waist gunners took photographs.

A few minutes later our radar malfunctioned and then went out completely. There was no reason to continue the search pattern since we had accomplished our objective. I told Mac to plot a route home and we turned to the new course.

Within an hour, we sighted a Navy submarine running at top speed on the surface—and in the direction of the convoy. Wind and I had a good look at the sub before it submerged for its attack.

We landed safely at Liuchow and learned that our contact sighting had been immediately relayed to the Navy, and submarines in the area were alerted. The boat we sighted was undoubtedly heading in for the kill.

[On October 31, 1944, the submarine *U.S.S. Guitarro*, captained by

Commander E. D. Haskins, sunk two Japanese merchant vessels—the *Komei Maru*, a freighter of 2,857 tons, and the *Pacific Maru*, a 5,782-ton passenger-cargo ship.]

While being debriefed, we were told that the Japs were making headway in their advance toward Kweilin and Liuchow. However, the enemy was feeling the effects of the Fourteenth Air Force bombing assaults. We were definitely a knife in their side.

November 4, 1944

Rain and fog have kept us socked in solid—no flying for the past few days. The Japanese are closing in fast—only 40 miles north of us. This bad weather is great for their army's progress. They can make good gains without our fighters and B-24s working them over.

November 5, 1944

An all-out evacuation of Liuchow began today. The military withdrawal was orderly. Baggage and equipment were packed and loaded aboard planes, along with ground crews and operations personnel. Engineers buried bombs under the runway and taxi strips. Drums of gasoline were placed in position around the buildings. When the last aircraft was off the ground, the engineers would detonate the explosives, set the gas drums on fire, and then hop on trucks for the trip to Kunming.

Continual streams of refugees fled like flood waters past our airstrip. They were a pitiful sight. Most of the people had escaped Kweilin just a few days before—and now they were fleeing for their lives again. Many of them trudged along the road with everything they owned on their backs. None of them knew where they were going or how they would survive. Among the slow moving mass of civilians were small groups of Chinese soldiers in tattered uniforms—most of them barefoot and without weapons. They would have stood and fought if they had been armed. I wondered how many of these refugees would still be alive a month from now. There was one thing for certain—if the Japs caught them, they would all be killed. What a futile existence!

November 6, 1944

There was a break in the weather this morning, and everyone was up at sunrise to finish loading the planes. The first B-24 took off at 0800. Our aircraft would be the last ship to leave Liuchow. Major Crawford and 21 others would be flying with us.

We anxiously watched as each B-24 became safely airborne. About 1130, it was our turn to depart Liuchow. We had just started our take off roll when the No. 2 prop began running away. I tried to hold the RPM steady until we reached a safe altitude, but was unable to get full power out of the engine. We were high enough to be out of danger for the moment, but with our heavy load, we could not risk flying on three engines. There was no choice—we had to return to Liuchow. George radioed the field not to set off the bombs—we were coming in.

After landing, everybody piled out of the plane and began working on the faulty governor. Luckily, most of our passengers were ground crew personnel, and the prop governor was changed in record time. By the time we were loaded and ready to go, the Japs were really breathing down our necks. But we had so sooner started to take off than the damned propeller ran away again. We braked the plane to a stop, taxied back to the flight line and unloaded.

Fortunately, the ATC flew in two C-47s and had them standing by in case of such an emergency. The passengers, along with Jim Miracle and three other members of our crew, quickly boarded the transports and were airborne within minutes.

Wind and I, and the rest of our crew remained behind. We had decided to try and fly the stubborn B-24 to Chengkung. Japanese troops were reported to be less than 20 miles from Liuchow. We had to get off the ground fast. It was going to be a close call.

We taxied the plane to the end of the runway, and once more started our take-off roll. Since we had lightened the aircraft, the engines did not surge as much, and I managed to control the No. 2 prop without too much difficulty. We climbed to cruising altitude and spotted the C-47s dead ahead of us. I looked down toward the airstrip. Bombs were exploding in the runway, and flaming gasoline engulfed the wooden buildings. A minute later, there was nothing to see but clouds of dust and smoke. I wiped the sweat from my brow, and heaved a big sigh of relief. This escape was too close for comfort.

We nursed the plane all the way to Chengkung, landing at 1730. It was a relief to be home safe again, but we had lost our forward bases at Liuchow and Kweilin. The Japanese now had our backs to the wall. But there was still 450 air miles between the Kunming area and Liuchow. And, before the enemy could reach us, they would have to move their land army over some of the worst roads and rugged terrain in the world. There were no railroads for them to use, and we controlled the air. From now on, the enemy would pay dearly for every mile.

November 7, 1944

Bad weather and no missions scheduled. I checked my combat time at operations—almost 200 hours.

For some unknown reason, I am beginning to feel detached from reality—as if I am watching another person, who looks like me, acting out this nightmare. The monotonous death-defying routine goes on and on—flying, eating, sleeping, and flying again. I watch men come and go in this dream game of war. Only it is not a dream—and the game is played for keeps. Our boys fly and die without a whimper. We are all human out here—with emotions of fear and hate. But the instinct for survival is the strongest of all.

Chapter 6

Suichwan: Outpost in Hell

The arrival of General Wedemeyer in the CBI and his ability to advise Chiang Kai-shek resulted in a complete turnaround in the training and equipping of Chinese forces.

Wedemeyer's mission was to safeguard the construction of the Burma Road and open this vital supply route to China. He advised Chiang to move more divisions into the Kweilin-Liuchow sector to stem the Japanese "Ichigo" drive toward Kunming—the final destination of the Burma Road.

The Fourteenth Air Force, with complete control of the skies, struck boldly, and virtually unopposed, wherever it so desired.

The U.S. Navy requested General Chennault's aid in pounding the final nail in the coffin of Japan's maritime and naval forces. The 308th Bomb Group became the eyes of the U.S. Pacific Fleet—conducting around-the-clock reconnaissance missions in the South China Sea, along the Indochina coast, and in Philippine waters.

November 10, 1944

Marginal flying weather today. Rain and fog have kept us grounded for the past 72 hours. Official word was passed that the Japanese have occupied Kweilin and Liuchow.

We were briefed at 1430 for a recon patrol and took off an hour later with a full load of gasoline (including bomb bay fuel tanks) but no bombs. We climbed through heavy overcast. Because of the loss of our forward bases, the distance from Chengkung to the coast was now 500 air miles—almost twice as far as operating out of Liuchow.

Just before departure, Phil George was notified that his father had passed away. Although George was entitled to return to the States for the funeral, he opted to fly the mission. There was no way he could remedy the situation, and combat hours were more important. Phil wanted to get his time in so that he could return home "permanently."

The B-24 assigned to us for this patrol was brand new. It had just been flown over the Hump. Wind and I did not relish the idea of flying a new plane on a long mission—especially over water—without having had a chance to check out the aircraft. But, as usual, our crew was picked for the job.

In a situation such as this, we were directed to run a cruise-control flight to learn exactly how much gasoline the plane would use. Cranton Terrall had his work cut out for him. It was his responsibility to take fuel readings every hour, while Milt and I experimented with different power settings in order to obtain the most efficient cruising speed using the least amount of gasoline.

According to existing figures on B-24s, each engine used an average of 50 gallons of gas per hour. Any airplane guzzling more than that was operating on the edge of disaster. Fuel consumption was different on every plane—depending on the load and airspeed at cruising altitude. The more miles nursed out of the gasoline supply, the better chance a pilot had of returning home safely.

Both Wind and I were well versed in the art of getting the most out of our aircraft when it came to gas consumption. The trick was to keep the plane properly trimmed at all times—flying "on the step" at its best performance level. This tactic required the constant adjustment of trim tabs, throttle settings, prop speed, mixture controls, and supercharger settings.

Other factors also entered into decision making. The center of gravity on a B-24 was very delicate. Practically any shifting of weight, fore or aft, would affect the operation of the aircraft and use additional gasoline.

After a bomb drop, the weight of the plane would be dramatically reduced. However, an experienced pilot could immediately feel any change in the altitude of his plane. Thus, the constant adjustment of trim tabs and other settings became reflex actions.

During our test flight, we ran into a considerable amount of bad weather and were forced to do most of the flying by instruments. Atkins reported that the new search radar was excellent. He was even able to pick up large rocks along the coastline of Hainan Island.

No enemy targets were sighted, but the mission went off quite smoothly with no major problems. When we returned to Chengkung at 0400 and made our final calculations on the cruise control chart, we discovered that the aircraft engines averaged 45 gallons of fuel per hour. These statistics were excellent, especially since the plane was a slightly heavier model than what we had been flying.

November 11, 1944

After debriefing from the long, 12-hour mission, Mac and I grabbed something to eat, and then stumbled like a couple of burned-out zombies to our quarters. Mail had been delivered during our absence. I received a letter from my wife, Dottie, but was too tired to read by flashlight, so I hit the sack.

I awakened about noon, and the first thing I grabbed for was Dottie's letter. My wife had sent a few pictures of herself in a nightgown. Well, after seeing how good she looked, I was ready to hop the next plane out of here heading for Virginia.

But I made one mistake. I showed the photos to McClure. What a wolf! He slobbered all over them! If we ever get home again, I will have to keep my eyes on that guy. I tacked Dottie's pictures up on the wall next to my bed and threatened Mac that if he ever so much as put his dirty paws near them, I would shoot him on the spot—and not with one of those damn .45s either.

November 17, 1944

Rumors are flying through our squadron that crew members' records are being checked for qualifications. When it is discovered that Milt Wind and I are both first pilots, all hell is liable to burst loose around here.

Another reconnaissance mission was scheduled. We went through the usual briefing and took off at 1530. The flight would cover more than 1,000 miles and take us to within 50 miles of the Philippine Islands.

The boredom that occurred on long flights such as this was broken by playing cards or chess. If our plane had a reliable automatic pilot, that equipment would also help to ease the monotony of the journey. But, few autopilots worked efficiently. They usually required constant attention and adjustment. In fact, it was easier to fly the ship manually than fool with the autopilot. Whether we used the apparatus or not, somebody had to be always on the alert to keep the aircraft running smoothly.

Wind and I were constantly busy scanning the instrument panel and gauges. We had become so accustomed to this procedure that we did it subconsciously. A fluctuation on any gauge was a cause for instant reaction. Even the slightest change in engine noise was important.

During the past few months, Milt and I had developed an efficient system to handle almost any eventuality. As soon as our plane reached the desired altitude, and was properly trimmed out, we alternated every half hour piloting the aircraft. By using this method, each of us could either take a nap or wander about the ship.

While we were cruising, and it was Wind's turn at the controls, the steady hum of the engines had a hypnotic effect on me. I would usually fall asleep. However, the slightest change in the pitch or rhythm of the engines, and I would be wide awake staring at the flight panel and instrument board.

We flew our search pattern, but no sightings, and turned back to the coast. Heavy weather and turbulence bounced us about. At 0430, we finally landed safely at Chengkung. After 14 hours in the air, it took me several minutes to get my ground legs working normally.

While undergoing debriefing, we learned that a Colonel Smith, from the Inspector General's Office, would be arriving to inspect our squadron. This nonsense meant rolling out of our sacks after only four hours of sleep.

I awoke early and, as usual, it was raining. I shaved, showered, managed to get a haircut, straightened up our room, cleaned my .45, polished my boots, put on my dress uniform, slipped on my shoulder-holster, and hurried out in the rain with my fellow officers.

However, this was only to be a practice drill. We formed ranks for inspection while Captain Beale demonstrated the proper method of presenting a .45 to the colonel for examination. As Beale was handling one of the pesky weapons—and attempting to explain the proper procedure for "present .45s"—the damn thing went off. The entire formation broke ranks, and every combat-skittish man made a mad dash for the nearest ditch. But all the trenches were filled with water, so nobody dove in.

Captain Beale was noticeably shaken and embarrassed by his goof, and several choice remarks were made about what he could do with the .45 automatic. Everyone ran grumbling back to their barracks to get out of the rain.

I had no sooner toweled myself off, than word was passed that the official inspection would be held immediately—so back out into the rain we went. Once again we formed ranks. Colonel Smith was waiting for us. As he strutted down the lines of our formation, each man briskly handed his .45 to the inspecting officer. The colonel looked at the automatic, then handed it back to the owner who would jam it smartly into the holster.

The inspection was proceeding smoothly—like we had been rehearsing it for a week. That is, until Smith approached Lieutenant Adam DeRocca. Adam presented his .45 but, upon receiving his gun back, he pointed it at the ground. And, to make sure the chamber was empty, he pulled the trigger. BANG! The gun went off! It was loaded! The powerful, high-velocity bullet splashed like an exploding bomb into the watery mud. A massive spray of brown rain blanketed everybody.

Our gun-shy, jittery squadron jumped about three feet, and I expected a stampede at any moment. But the colonel did not budge. He stood like a statue, paralyzed, and in open-mouth amazement. Our "brave" boys soon settled down and the inspection continued—but at a much faster tempo. Miraculously, Colonel Smith finished his assignment without getting shot. However, there was many a trembling hand turning over .45s for examination.

When the inspection concluded, and we marched back to barracks, the whole episode seemed funny as hell. I commented that the colonel must have had plenty of guts to stand out in the rain and mess around with guns from the guys in this outfit. Knowing the men, and their marksmanship at target practice, I would not have felt safe even on the other side of the field.

The oddest part of the affair though, was the lack of any remarks by Colonel Smith. I believe that he was still in a state of shock from almost having his foot shot off. I fully expected DeRocca to be hanged or drawn and quartered.

The way I have it figured, the Japs do not have to worry about shooting us down. If they wait long enough, we will eventually do the job for them. There are not many things to chuckle about around here, but you can bet we had plenty of laughs over our so-called "inspection" that day in the rain.

November 20, 1944

A search-and-strike mission over the South China Sea was scheduled for tonight. We would be carrying 2,750 gallons of fuel and twelve 500-pound bombs. With this load, the gross weight of our aircraft would be 60,000 pounds.

There was beginning to be a real nip in the air. And, at cruising altitude, it would be extremely cold. We dressed in winter flying gear to keep warm.

Wind and I took off at 1630, but, an hour out of Chengkung, we ran into turbulence and ice. The wings of the plane were not equipped with deicing boots and Wind climbed until clear of the storm front. We hit warmer air upon reaching the coast. The icing conditions stopped, and we dropped down to 7,500 feet.

The search sweep netted no enemy sightings, so Mac set a course for our secondary target—Fort Bayard. This was a Japanese harbor installation about 500 miles southeast of Kunming. We went in at 9,000 feet, and Miracle laid a spread of bombs right on target. We must have caught the Japs by surprise. There was no flak or other resistance.

Mac gave us a heading home. But, a few miles inland, we began picking up ice again. We immediately climbed upstairs and broke out into the moonlight at 20,000 feet.

Wind and I had discussed the possibility of this happening on the return trip, and made plans accordingly. We cut our search pattern short in order to make sure that we had enough fuel to climb above the heavy weather front, and to make a possible instrument approach at Chengkung.

The outside air temperature at this altitude was 30° below zero—and we began to feel the numbing cold. As we neared our field and began a gradual descent, the air became warmer. But at 12,000 feet, George reported that Chengkung was socked in with a solid overcast. We would have to make an instrument landing.

Kunming Lake was 35 miles long, 15 miles wide, and nearly parallel to the airstrip. Its location was principally used for instrument approaches, holding patterns, and turns. By the time we began our drop down over the lake, we had already been in the air more than ten hours—and most of that time flying on instruments. Wind and I had been taking regular shifts piloting the plane. But, even so, after sitting in the cockpit and staring at gauges and panels for long periods of time, vision becomes distorted and blurred. Instrument flying, such as this, was far from fun, and we had been doing it mission after mission.

While we were descending, I could see that Milt Wind was not feeling well. He continually blinked his eyes, shook his head, and cupped his hands over his ears to relieve the air pressure. Although it was bitter cold in the cockpit, he looked pale, and sweat was dripping down his face. I asked Milt if he was OK. But he answered in the affirmative, and thought he was just catching a cold.

The tower directed us to land to the north, so that our downwind leg would begin over Kunming Lake. We were then instructed to make a left turn and drop to 800 feet and to make another left turn for the final approach.

I set up the power settings for landing. We continued our letdown, and were nearing the airstrip, when I suddenly noticed that the plane was drifting to the left of the runway. We were seconds away from plowing into a line of parked aircraft. I yelled at Wind to push up the power—get back on the runway. Milt appeared paralyzed—acted like he did not hear me. I shoved the throttles up to their stops and grabbed the controls. We were almost at stalling speed and about to crash. I screamed at Terrall to hit the landing gear switch—retract the wheels and dump full flaps. We were barely moving—and only a few feet above a flight line of C-47s—when our ship staggered into a shallow climb.

I had my hands full—trying to keep the plane in the air and set up for another approach. The fellows manning the tower were shocked as they watched us narrowly miss the ATC aircraft. They kept calling excitedly over the radio, asking what the hell was going on. I finally managed to get the situation stabilized and informed operations that everything was under control and we were coming around for another landing attempt.

By the time we reached the required altitude and were back over the lake, Wind began returning to normal. I asked him if he realized what had happened—that we had drifted off the airstrip and almost smashed into a line of parked C-47s. He replied that, according to his eyes, we were perfectly centered on the runway. But, as far as I was concerned, he had suffered a clear case of vertigo.

I tried to convince Milt to let me land the ship, but he said that he was feeling better and could bring the plane in. I turned the controls back over, with the stipulation that I would take charge if any problems developed. Sure enough, he became disoriented when we began our approach. I took command and finished the landing without further incident.

Shortly after we parked our plane, Lieutenant Harold Rush radioed an emergency. He had lost one engine and was about out of fuel. Rush informed his crew that if any of them wanted to bail out—rather than risk landing with three engines and a thimbleful of gasoline—they could go ahead and jump. Four men bailed out. But, in the confusion, the flight engineer jumped without turning on the auxiliary valve for the aircraft's hydraulic system. Consequently, the wheels did not come down and lock. Rush made a picture-perfect landing. Fortunately nobody was injured, but his B-24 ended up in the "spare-parts" department.

Milt Wind and I learned a very important lesson that night. A pilot never flies a plane if he has a head cold. Wind told me that, according to his field of vision, we were coming in perfectly on both approaches. But the runway seemed to be moving to his left, and he kept correcting the alignment of our aircraft.

Harold Rush and I knew one thing for sure—that without an experienced crew, the likelihood of surviving this war was very slim indeed.

November 23, 1944

Thanksgiving Day and no flying. Everyone had the day off. We had our holiday dinner about noon—canned turkey, dressing, cranberry sauce, and all the trimmings.

Shortly after the meal, I stopped back at our quarters for a moment before going to meet McClure at the Officer's Club. Fred Carpenter, one of our waist gunners, came by the room and asked if he could talk to me. I invited him in to hear what was on his mind. We had a close-knit crew. All of us were good friends, officers and enlisted men alike. We were a smooth working bunch and proud of it.

After a couple of minutes of small talk, Fred finally got around to the subject of his visit. "Lieutenant Haynes," he said, "If I ever have to travel across the world again to be in combat, I want to be on your crew, and so do the rest of the boys."

I was not expecting anything like this. And to say I was caught completely off guard would be putting it mildly. Carpenter's words gave me a feeling of well-being and lifted my spirits more than any other incident on my tour of duty in China. The impact of his remarks must have shown on my face. At first, I was too surprised to speak. But, with a voice choked with emotion, I finally managed to answer. "Carpenter," I said, "as you can see, I'm at a loss for words. I really don't know what to say, except to thank you and the rest of the boys for this wonderful compliment. Coming from you fellows, this is the greatest show of confidence and trust that I could ever hope for."

We shook hands, and I believe that both of us were too embarrassed to say anything more. All things considered, it was a very good day. One that I will always remember. I kept my conversation with Carpenter private. I felt it was a confidential matter between me and the enlisted members of my crew.

November 24, 1944

A strike mission was called for 1500. Because of his head cold, Wind was grounded, and Lieutenant Rush took Milt's place in the pilot's seat. However, on take off, the No. 1 prop ran away. I managed to keep power on the engine by using the feathering button. We made our climb to a safe altitude and trimmed the ship for cruising. But the propeller would not hold a steady RPM at the lower power setting. We were forced to abort the mission and returned to base.

The continual failure of prop governors happened despite everyone's best efforts, but it was hard on our patience and nerves. Rush was still rattled from his crash landing a few nights before—and now this!

There was no way that the ground crew could get the plane operational again in time to fly the mission, so we had some free time on our hands. McClure and I decided to borrow a jeep and visit our 3rd Mapping Squadron buddies on the other side of the field. We had just crossed the runway and started up the slope to the barracks area, when we heard a plane racing toward us at high speed. We both remarked out loud, "What the hell is that guy doing buzzing the field?" I could tell it was a fighter by the sound of its single engine. We glanced back, and got the answer in a hurry. Darting down the middle of the runway was a Japanese Zero—laying bombs along the strip. Somehow he slipped through our alert system—probably at low level—and caught everybody with their pants down.

The concussion from exploding bombs rocked the jeep and showered us with rocks and dirt. Both Mac and I ducked and escaped injury, but that Jap sure scared the hell out of us. If we had been 50 yards closer to the runway, we would have been blown sky-high.

By the time we recovered our senses, the field was a madhouse—people running in every direction. Air raid alarms were sounded, but that only added to the confusion. The Zero was long gone by this time, but we had no way of knowing how many others might be sneaking in behind him or if the Jap pilot would turn around and come back for a strafing attack.

Mac and I hustled up the hill to the slit trenches. They were already filled, but we located the mapping squadron boys and had our visit right there in the ditches.

Additional enemy planes never showed up, and the field quickly returned to normal. More than 30 casualties were reported, but fortunately no deaths. Bombs dropped by the Japanese "Lone Ranger" damaged a number of aircraft and blasted deep holes in the runway. I remarked that we were lucky the Zero did not strafe the field. One of the comedians around here joked, "He was probably out of silver bullets!"

However, the sudden attack taught every one of us a lesson. There is no safe haven in a combat zone. We had to be alert at all times. I figured that the Zero sneaked into Chengkung from one of several enemy airfields around Hanoi, Indochina. But, I have to give that Jap pilot credit. He certainly had guts. He did the job on his own.

November 25, 1944

The entire native work force was out this morning, repairing bomb craters in the runway. A lot of questions were being asked about how the enemy plane managed to slip past our alerting outposts. Most of the damaged aircraft were ATC C-47s that were parked on the west side of the field. Practically all our B-24s were located in revetments on the east side of the runway and were not even scratched.

I strolled over to operations this afternoon when the commanding officer, Major James Edney, walked in. He inquired as to how Milt was feeling, and then casually asked if I had been checked out as first pilot in a B-24. I knew he must have seen my records or he would not have asked the question. I told Edney the whole story—how Wind and I planned the scheme to fly together, since we thought our chances of survival would be greater operating as a team.

The major listened intently to my explanation. And, when I had finished, he gave me a long stare, scratched his head, and said he could not argue with my logic. But, on the other hand, he could not waste manpower by having two first pilots flying on the same aircraft. I could see that Edney was not very happy upon learning that Wind and I had flown together for this length of time.

While Major Edney and I were talking, the operations crew had been listening in on our conversation. After the major left the building, they told me that they were afraid I might try and evade his questions. It seems Edney had been reviewing flight records and was damn angry when he discovered I was a first pilot. He told the boys in operations that he could not understand why I wanted to fly as copilot, and he was going to find out just what in hell was going on.

Of course, I knew the facts would come out sooner or later. But there was nothing in regulations stating that two first pilots could not fly as a team. The only thing Edney could do was split us up. The moment that Wind and I were dreading had finally arrived.

I hurried back to quarters and informed Milt what had happened—just in case Major Edney questioned him. We realized that both of us would soon be flying with a new copilot—and one of us with a new crew. Under combat conditions this would pose many real and dangerous problems. But there was nothing we could do about the situation. We were lucky to have made it this far without being caught.

November 29, 1944

Rumors are spreading around the base that headquarters is considering making McClure the squadron navigator, and there is also talk about a new crew being formed for me. As a first pilot, I would now have to fly the required 400 hours of combat time, which meant an additional month or so before I finished my tour.

Wind stopped by operations and learned that our crew was one of several that had been picked to operate from a new forward location at Suichwan. This base was about 300 miles northeast of Liuchow and, according to Intelligence, was 85 miles behind Japanese lines. I remembered our problems evacuating Liuchow—and now this. I can hardly wait!

November 30, 1944

Wind is still grounded with his cold, and I was scheduled to make the flight to Suichwan with our crew and a new copilot. However, at briefing, we were informed that there was a storm front to the east of us, and take off was postponed until the weather breaks. We will be on standby until then. I did get one surprise today. Orders were received awarding our entire crew the Air Medal.

December 3, 1944

The weather finally cleared and our departure was set for 0900. Milt's cold was better and he would be flying with us. Phil George needed to complete only one more mission before heading Stateside. He was instructed to remain at Chengkung to finish his tour. Phil walked down to the plane with us. We bid him farewell and Godspeed. He will be the first of our crew to go home. There was many a tearful eye as we moved out to the runway, leaving George standing alone on the taxi strip. Our new radioman is T/Sergeant Thomas L. Crouch.

We flew the entire trip unescorted and came within sight of two Japanese airfields. But, for some unknown reason, no enemy fighters showed up to intercept us. We landed at Suichwan about 1400. Talk about being stuck in the middle of nowhere!

Milt and I were greeted by our old buddy, Captain Harry Marshall. He had been appointed commanding officer at this outpost of civilization. Other friends from the Langley Field gang were also here—Carl Weitz, James Otis, and Seymour Richmond.

We had a bang-up, back-slapping reunion, and then the guys gave us the lowdown on this godforsaken place. Flying combat missions out of here was not going to be any cakewalk. We were completely surrounded by Japanese forces—some less than 80 miles away. Enemy air raids occurred every clear night—moon or no moon. The barracks area had just been completed, and only minimum essentials were available. But, worst of all, we learned that the food was terrible.

Sure enough, the night of our arrival was clear, and about a dozen Jap bombers paid us a visit. They destroyed one B-24 and damaged another. This place was definitely going to be the pits—worse than Liuchow if that is possible!

December 4, 1944

We were not scheduled for a mission today, so Cornelius Buckley, Captain Marshall's bombardier, offered to take Wind, Miracle, McClure, and I sightseeing. The town of Suichwan was only three miles from the field, therefore we decided to walk instead of taking a jeep. The road was packed with the usual traffic of carts, bicycles, and people on foot. The path followed a wide river, which was also crowded with small boats and sampans. I noticed many cormorant fishermen. It was a fascinating experience, watching these men and their webfooted friends. Each bird had a tight ring around its neck. The ring was attached to a heavy string and, whenever the cormorant grabbed a fish, the fisherman would drag his bird back to the boat. A brief struggle then ensued for the rights to the catch. The man usually won the argument—taking the fish away from the cormorant, and sending the bird out to hunt for another fish. We enjoyed watching the antics taking place on the water. But I do not think it would play on the Roanoke River.

The people we met on our way to the city were very friendly—bowing and greeting us with the expression "Ding How" and an upraised thumb. In other words, "Everything is OK." We replied in a similar manner.

We soon came to an open marketplace and watched the Chinese women shopping among the crowded booths and stalls. The commercial center of the town was boisterous and noisy with the sounds of squealing pigs, squawking chickens, howling puppies, and the haranguing chatter of merchants and customers. The intense shoppers thought nothing of forcibly dragging a frightened puppy from a cage and pinching its stomach to check the animal's fat. The thought alone of having one of those cute little puppies for dinner made me nauseous. But I had learned, over the past several months, never to ask the cooks what we were eating. They might actually tell us.

We strolled around the town until we found a few shops to buy gifts to send home. The prices of merchandise in Suichwan were very reasonable compared with Kunming and Liuchow, probably because not many Americans had passed through this area to bring on the usual inflation.

While on our "shopping spree" we ran across the rest of our crew. They told us about a nearby eatery that was owned by a local Chinese man who had lived several years in New York City. This news was like a breath of fresh air from home, and the gang of us hightailed it to the restaurant.

The owner of the establishment spoke fairly good English, and we spent an interesting afternoon exchanging information. The Chinese gentleman had left New York about ten years ago. He was anxious to learn what was happening in the States and gave us the lowdown on the military situation in the Suichwan region. He also told us where the Japanese were located. He hated them with a passion.

The food was excellent, and we were treated like celebrities. The best mulberry wine in the house was served in our honor. We kept drinking the "home brew," talking with our host, and having a grand old time until it was time to leave.

When we got up from our chairs, our legs were like rubber bands. It was quite a struggle, but, somehow, we managed to walk by propping one another upright. By the time we had stumbled the three miles back to base, we had pretty much sobered up. It was late afternoon when we returned, and the weather had turned biting cold. A coating of ice covered the rice paddies, and a brisk wind was blowing.

The barracks were unheated and without lights, except for peanut oil lamps. It was a good thing we wore warm clothing. We also had been issued sleeping bags. The sky was clear, so we did not undress. We figured the Japs would call on us before the night was over.

At 2100, we were roused by an air raid alarm and dashed for the slit trenches. This was a real nuisance sortie—only three planes. They dropped their payload and took off. The all clear signal sounded and we plodded back to our quarters. It had been quite a day!

December 7, 1944

The anniversary of the Japanese attack on Pearl Harbor. Bad weather had kept us grounded until today. A strike mission was scheduled. We were airborne at 1610, with nine 500-pound bombs and full tanks of gasoline.

We had no sooner passed the Hong Kong coast and were on a 90° heading toward Formosa than Atkins picked up a blip on his scope at about 20 miles. A heavy storm front was moving along the China coastline. Visibility was poor, and we encountered considerable turbulence.

Because of the weather, Wind and I decided to make our first attack run at 1,000 feet. As we roared over the target, I noticed that the ship was a small cargo vessel. Miracle dropped three bombs right on the nose. Our men in the tail section reported seeing secondary explosions. We swung out to sea, and then turned about for a second attack on the target. Miracle unloaded three more bombs, and the blip disappeared from the scope. Wind made one more pass over the site, but the ship had vanished. We still carried three bombs and continued our sweep. However, there were no additional sightings. Our crew was jubilant though—they had avenged Pearl Harbor.

We climbed to 10,000 feet. The night was very cold—with an outside temperature of about zero. We had been flying on instruments through a solid overcast but soon broke into the clear between two cloud layers. Snow and freezing rain smothered the aircraft. Suddenly, without warning, our plane was completely engulfed in an eerie, fluorescent glow.

The leading edge of the wings, the nose, and tips of the propellers, lit up in various colors that gradually increased in brightness. Our entire plane appeared to be outlined with luminous neon tubing.

The wings acted as a bowling alley for small, brilliantly hued balls of fire that danced in a continuous stream toward the fuselage. I automatically ducked as several flaming spheres rolled straight for my window—but they bounced off into space like tennis balls. Multicolored fiery globes whipped off the prop tips and catapulted into the black night. The interior of our plane was bathed in a ghostly glow of greenish-grey.

I glanced over at Milt. He seemed to be frozen in the pilot's seat. He was absolutely motionless—his face pale like a cadaver's. Because of static electricity in the air, any exposed hair stood on end. And I could feel a tingling sensation on the bare skin of my hands and face.

The parade of colors kept constantly changing and pulsating in intensity. Not a word had been spoken. The entire crew was speechless.

But then, almost as quickly as it began, the lights started dimming, the fire balls became smaller, and the night returned to normal, although it appeared darker than before.

Wind and I slowly recovered from this shock to our senses. I immediately called for a station check. The boys in the waist reported that the tail section looked to be on fire. And balls of flame, zooming off the wings, shot past the waist windows like streams of tracers.

The tense moments soon passed, and everyone began talking at the same time. The intercom sounded like a school yard at recess. I had read stories about the phenomenon of Saint Elmo's fire, and the panic it caused among men at sea. Our crew was no exception. We had been paralyzed by the wondrous display of celestial fireworks.

I have no idea how long we watched the awesome show, but everyone agreed that the whole experience was over in less than five minutes. There was one fact for sure—any person who is fortunate enough to witness Saint Elmo's fire will never forget it!

After nearly a nine-hour flight, we landed at Suichwan about 2300, debriefed, and hit the sack.

However, I had barely fallen asleep when we were awakened by several sharp jolts. I thought it was an earthquake at first. But then my sluggish brain became aware of thunderous explosions and of heavy concussions rocking the barracks. We sure as hell had been caught with our pants down again.

I squinted at the fluorescent dial on my watch. The time was 0300. Wind, Miracle, McClure, and I galvanized into immediate action. We attempted to dress by flashlight, but then heard explosions coming closer and closer. Another string of bombs began bracketing the area. There was no hesitation—we dove under our bunks—and just in time. Flying shrapnel and rocks ripped through the wooden walls of our quarters.

We did not hang around after the last blast but grabbed whatever clothes we could find and ran for the slit trenches. I probably set a world's record for the hundred-yard dash. We no sooner dived into a ditch than another wave of Japanese aircraft plowed up the ground with sticks of antipersonnel bombs.

The four of us were thankful that we were able to reach the trench while still in one piece. The latest explosions were practically on top of us, and we could hear steel shrapnel whizzing over our heads as we ducked.

After we had returned from the air strike, the weather began to clear. But nobody thought the Japs would pay us a visit this late in the morning. The enemy raid lasted until about 0500. Luckily, despite the number of bombs dropped, there were no deaths or injuries.

By the time we returned to our damaged quarters, we were shell-shocked, half-frozen, filthy dirty, and mad as hell. Such was life at a forward air base in China!

December 8, 1944

It was late in the morning when I crawled out of my sleeping bag and surveyed the wreckage of our room. The place was a shambles, but we all pitched in to make it livable again. We worked fast to keep from freezing.

It was about noon when we finally finished, then cleaned ourselves up, and headed for the mess hall. The fellows we shared the slit trench with were already having lunch. They complimented us on our bitter tirade of language, which, they claimed, warmed the air in the ditch. There were also snide remarks about my race to the trench. One smart ass said that he had never seen such speed from a guy with legs as short as mine. They were a solid blur—like Superman's. These characters are a real bunch of comedians. I told them they should have their own radio show.

We listened to Tokyo Rose in the evening. Her voice comes in very clear at Suichwan. According to her broadcast, the Allies are losing the war everywhere—especially in China. We had some good laughs over the corny propaganda. But she played good music, and we appreciated her efforts to entertain us.

December 15, 1944

Lousy, overcast weather. No flying for the past week. Enemy bombers have even been grounded. We have been stuck at this dangerous location for 11 days and have only flown one mission.

Captain Marshall and I discussed the possibility of being forced to evacuate the base in a hurry. There would be no advance warning like we had at Liuchow. We were sitting in the enemy's backyard—completely surrounded, and also at the very end of our own supply line. Both of us wondered why the Japs had not yet made a move to capture Suichwan. We knew they were determined to keep our aircraft as far away from their shipping lanes as possible. Talk about living on borrowed time!

However, in one respect the winter weather was a blessing. With every short break in the cloud cover, gasoline, bombs, and supplies were flown in from Kunming. Christmas packages and mail were included in one shipment. I received four boxes of goodies and seemed to have fared better than the rest of our crew. My roommates drooled as they gazed upon my "treasures" from home. But I informed the guys, in no uncertain terms, that I had taken an accurate inventory—and if anything turned up missing, I would shoot the gang of them, just to make sure I got the right culprit.

December 17, 1944

McClure was ordered back to Chengkung as squadron navigator. He will be promoted to captain and will not have to put up with these trips to forward bases anymore. But Mac will still be my roommate—if I ever make it back to Chengkung again.

Because of heavy weather along the coast, no missions have been authorized. Most of our time is spent in bull sessions, writing letters, reading, and playing cards. Letter writing is the most difficult. Anything that might be of interest, we are not permitted to write about.

The long intervals between mail deliveries have not helped our dispositions. I also learned from the crew of a supply plane that missions are being flown out of Chengkung on a regular basis. This news did not help our temperaments either. We have been sitting here, like ducks in a pond, with the Japanese calling the shots—and we cannot do a damn thing about it.

After dinner, I stepped outside the mess hall and actually saw stars in the sky. The climate in this part of China has become very cold. The rice paddies are frozen solid, and snow can be seen on the mountains.

The last enemy air raid destroyed several barracks, and now each room has to be shared by about a dozen men. There are charcoal stoves in the buildings, but charcoal is in short supply. We burn whatever we can find and try to keep a fire going day and night. One of the enlisted men's barracks burned to the ground. It went up like kindling. The guys were lucky to escape with the clothes on their backs.

December 20, 1944

The weather cleared long enough for a single mission. Lieutenant Folke Johnson and his crew were ordered out on a strike. They never returned—no word as to what happened.

I noticed that my men were beginning to show signs of hostility brought on by their frustration. Everyone's nerves seemed on edge. I finally decided to take the bull by the horns, and collared Marshall and Otis at operations. I lambasted both of them. I criticized why they were not taking advantage of occasional breaks in the weather to fly more missions. Then Marshall retorted about our combat experience. He dropped a bag of candy in my lap that time. I gave both of them a broadside. I reminded Marshall and Otis that my crew had more combat hours than either one of them. I knew what a mission entailed, and also how to get home alive.

My tongue lashing did not set too well with the base commander, but

I did not give a damn. We had been stuck in this hole for three weeks and had only flown one sortie. At this rate, I would be an old man with a beard before my China tour was completed.

I was just about to storm out of the office and slam the door behind me when a messenger rushed in with news that one of our squadron planes had landed. It was already late in the afternoon, and no aircraft arrivals were expected.

Captain Marshall asked me to accompany him to the flight line to see who came in. We hopped in a jeep and drove out to the plane. Surprise of surprises, I was greeted by Lieutenant George Turpyn. He had brought mail and supplies, and then dropped the bombshell—he had orders to relieve our crew. I was so damn happy that I slapped Turpyn on the back and told the guy that I would have kissed him if he was not so ugly.

George jumped in the jeep and we had a slam-bang reunion on the ride back to operations. While Turpyn was being debriefed, I ran all the way to the barracks and told Wind and the others the good news. We had opened our "fortune cookie" and it said we would be back at Chengkung in time for Christmas.

Our crew joined Turpyn and his men at the mess hall. I spotted Marshall and Otis having dinner and went over and apologized. We shook hands. All was forgiven. That is the way it is during wartime. A good commander realizes the tension his men are under and makes allowances. I only hope that if I am ever confronted with a similar situation, I will be as understanding.

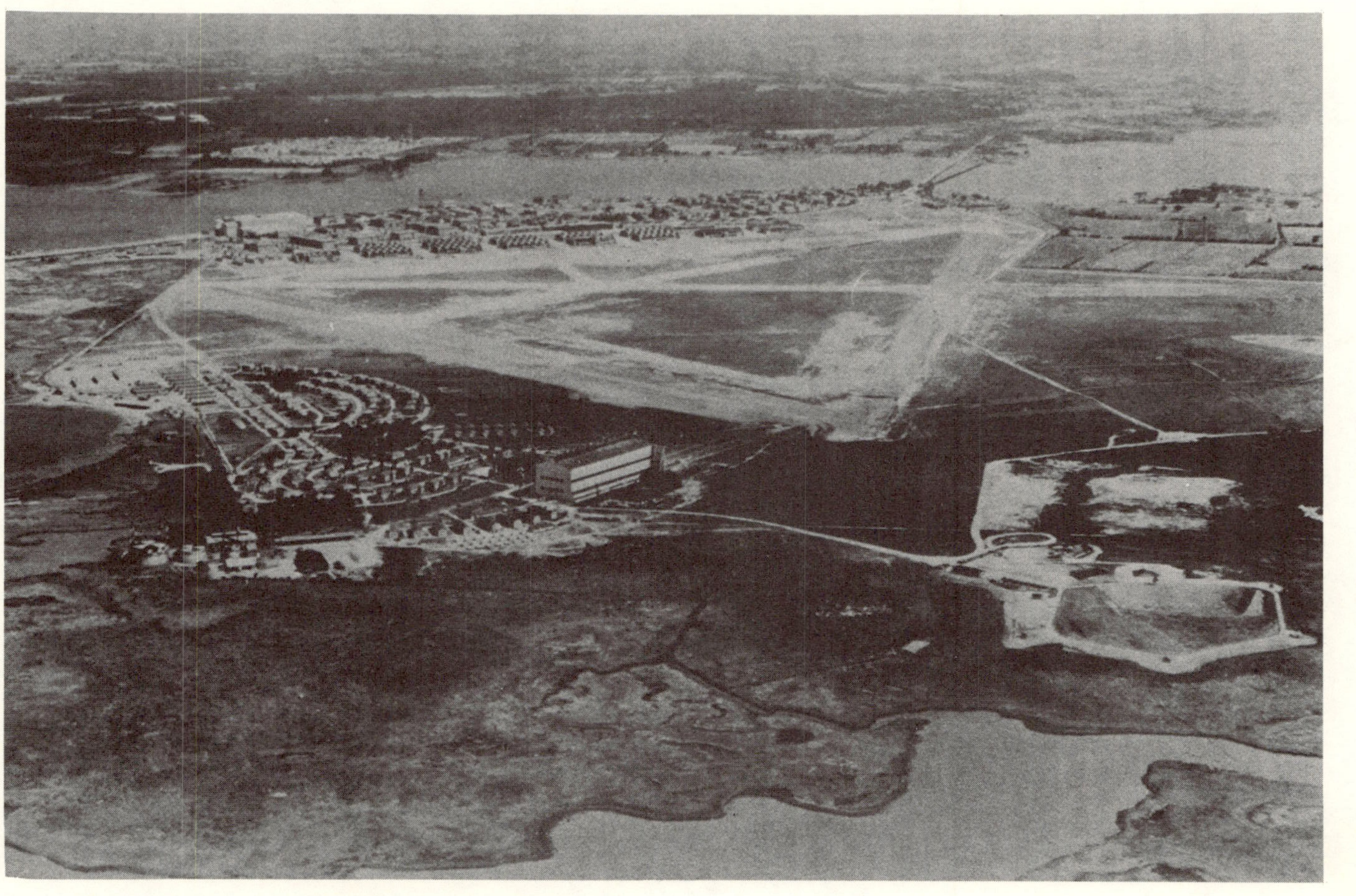

Langley Field, Virginia, circa 1942. *Courtesy Elmer E. Haynes*

Typical LAB radar B-24 flown by the 308th Bomb Group in China. Note the shark teeth and black underbelly. *Courtesy Elmer E. Haynes.*

Crew of the *Innocence Abroad*. Top row, left to right: Thomas, George, Atkins, Armstrong, Cuva, and Carpenter. Bottom row, left to right: Miracle, Haynes, Wind, and McClure. *Courtesy Elmer E. Haynes*

Standing alongside the *Willie Maker* at Chengkung. Left to right: Haynes, Miracle, Wind, and McClure. Note the black bottom of the radar plane. *Courtesy Elmer E. Haynes.*

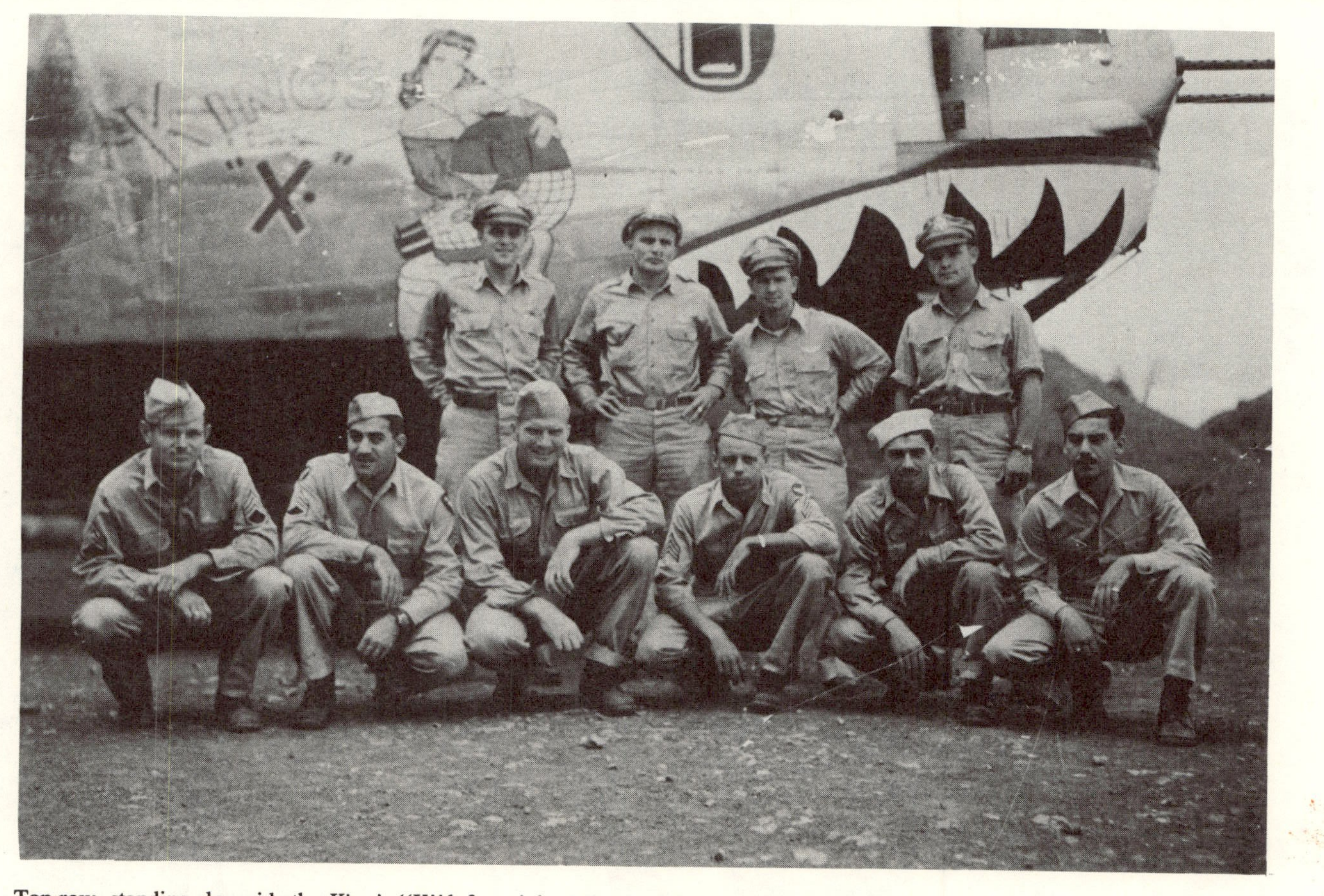

Top row, standing alongside the *King's "X"* left to right: Miracle, McClure, Haynes, and Wind. Bottom row, left to right: Armstrong, George, Atkins, Thomas, Cuva, and Carpenter. Note the Flying Tiger, shark teeth, and black underbelly. *Courtesy Elmer E. Haynes*

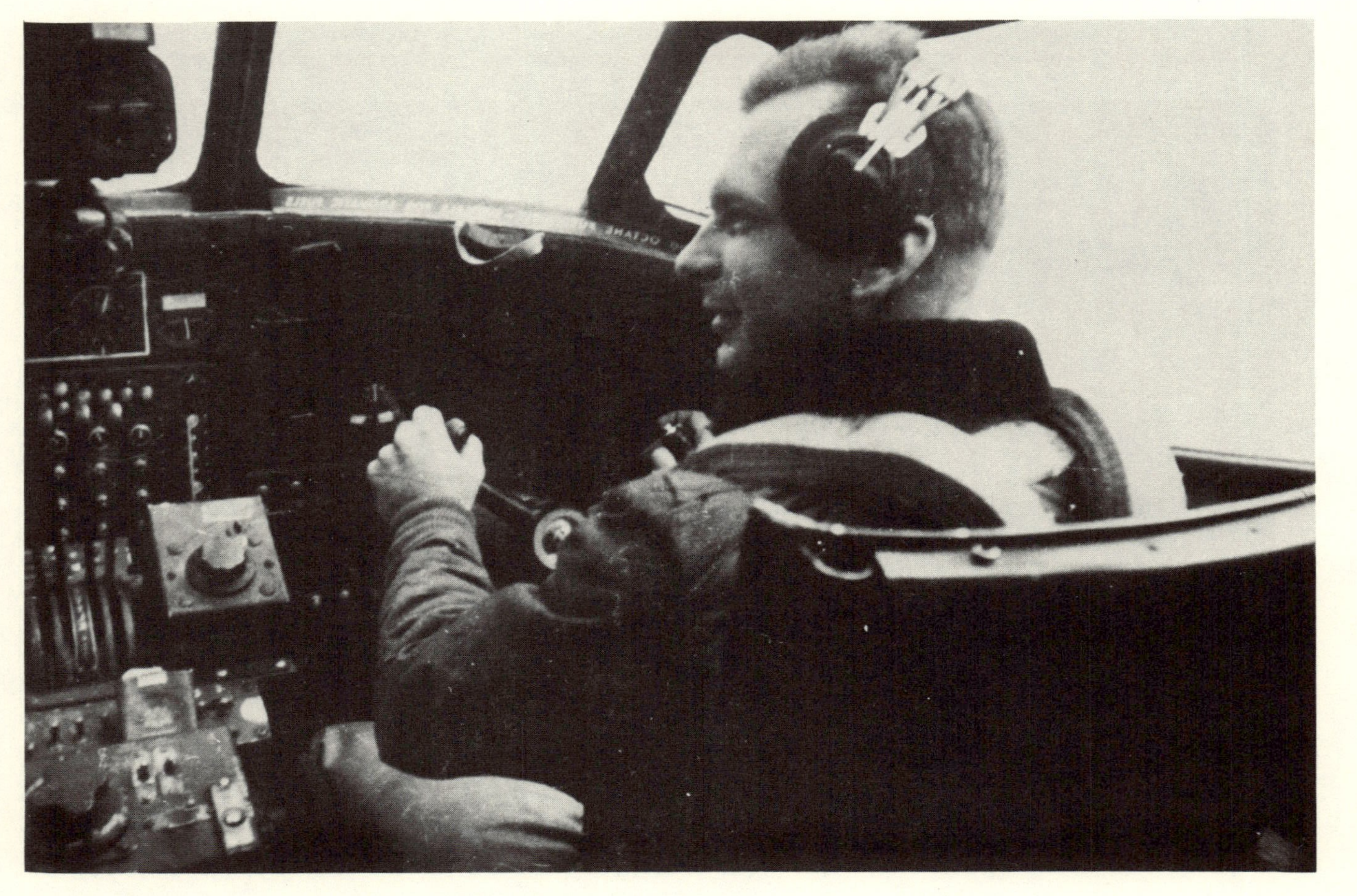

Elmer E. Haynes in the copilot seat of a B-24. *Courtesy Elmer E. Haynes*

An impromptu ''Jing Bow'' party. Left to right: Sergeants Parvola and Singletary of the 3rd Mapping Squadron, Haynes, Miracle, and McClure. *Courtesy Elmer E. Haynes*

Photograph of Major General Claire Lee Chennault, autographed to Captain E. E. Haynes. *Courtesy Elmer E. Haynes*

Street scene in Kunming, China. *Courtesy Elmer E. Haynes*.

Hostel and barracks area at Liuchow airfield. Note the pinnacle rock formations called "ice cream cones." *Courtesy Elmer E. Haynes*

Liuchow airfield as seen from control tower facing west. *Courtesy National Archives #111-SC-227358*

Liuchow airfield. Note the B-24 in center foreground and another to the far left. *Courtesy National Archives #111-SC-227354*

General Claire Chennault at his slit trench command post during a Japanese air attack on Kunming, China. *Courtesy Anna C. Chennault*

Chinese workers busy constructing a Fourteenth Air Force bomber field in western China. *Courtesy Anna C. Chennault*

Bombs and gasoline being unloaded from river boats at Chungking, China, for distribution to Fourteenth Air Force bases.
Courtesy Anna C. Chennault

Flying Tiger pilots dash to their P-40s during an air raid alert. Photo probably taken at Chengkung. *Courtesy National Archives #208-N-6687*

Flying Tiger P-40s over central China near Liuchow. *Courtesy National Archives #208-(M-7T)N-6658P*

Mitchell B-25 bombers from Liuchow, China, attack Japanese shipping in Hong Kong Harbor. *Courtesy Anna C. Chennault*

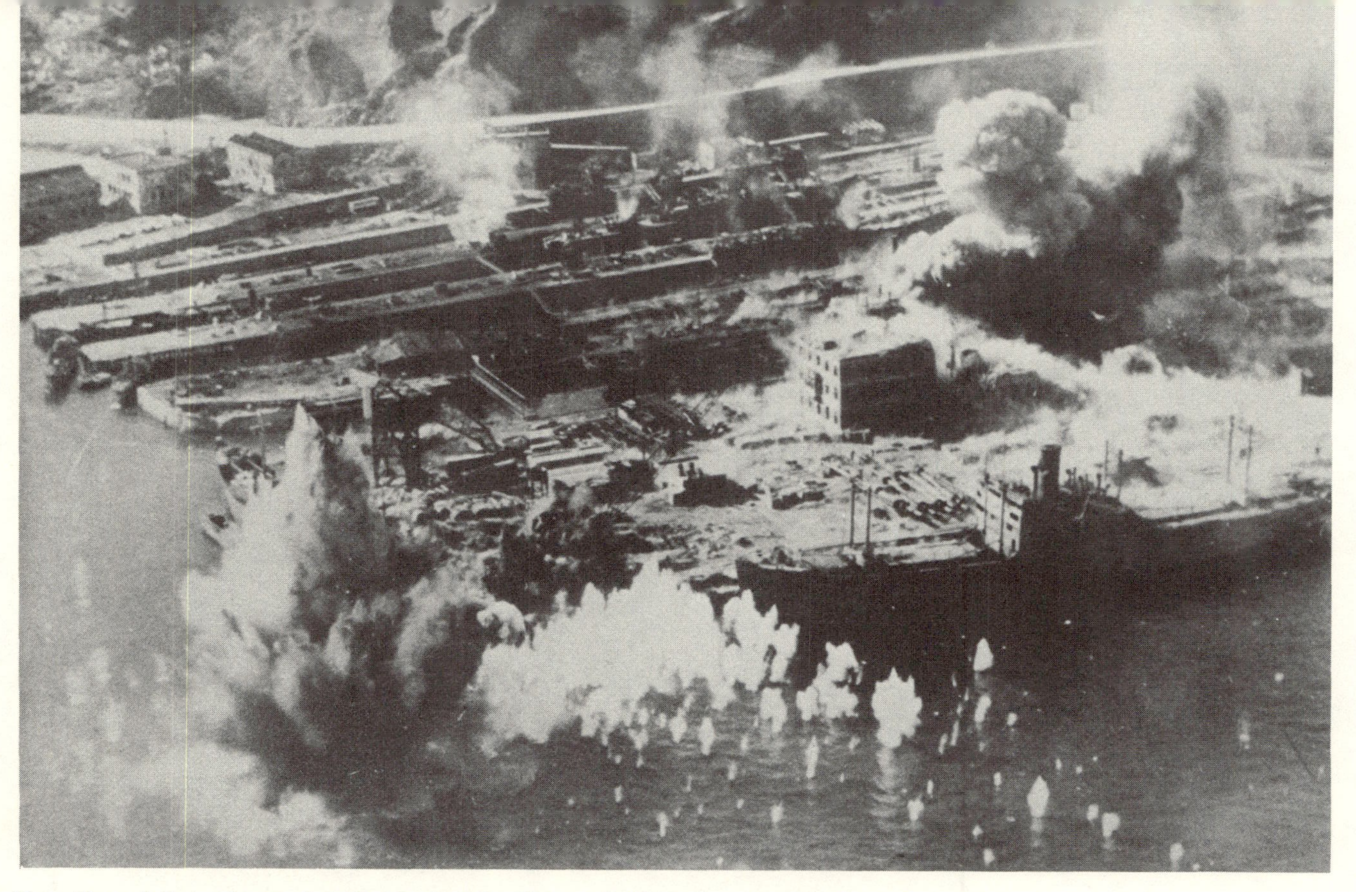

Hong Kong docks under attack by bombers of the Fourteenth Air Force. *Courtesy Elmer E. Haynes*

Hong Kong Harbor under attack by bombers of the Fourteenth Air Force. *Courtesy Elmer E. Haynes.*

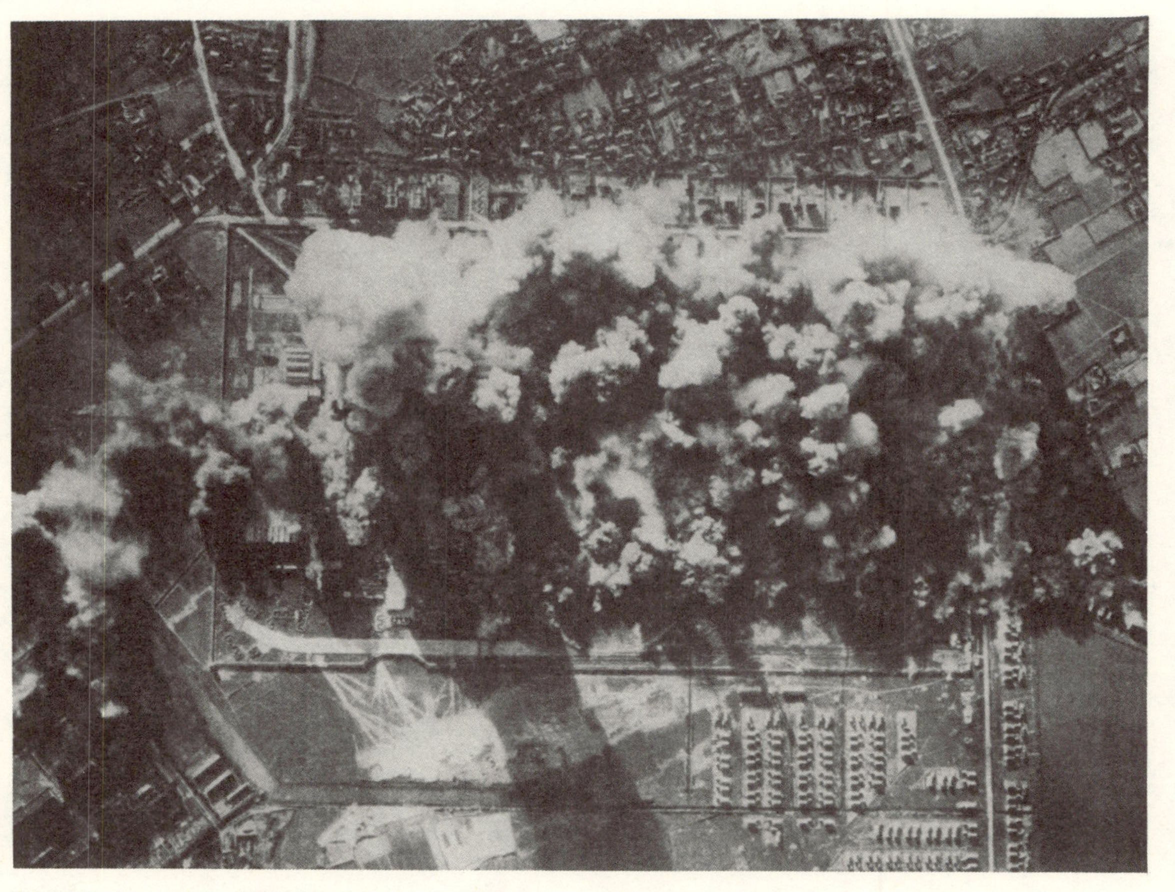

B-24 Liberators of the 308th Bomb Group destroy Japanese railroad repair shops at Vinh, Indochina. *Courtesy Anna C. Chennault*

Japanese installations on Hainan Island under bombing attack by U.S. planes. *Courtesy National Archives #80-G-355273*

308th Bomb Group mission against the railroad marshalling yards at Changsha, China. *Courtesy Elmer E. Haynes*

308th Bomb Group mission, August 1944. *Courtesy Elmer E. Haynes*

308th Bomb Group mission against Fort Bayard. *Courtesy Elmer E. Haynes*

A head-on view of Haynes's and Wind's B-24 that crash landed at Chengkung after a mission on the night of October 26, 1944. *Courtesy Elmer E. Haynes*

Standing under the tail section of their B-24 that crash landed at Chengkung after its return from a mission on the night of October 26, 1944. Left to right: Haynes, Wind, McClure, and Miracle. The aircraft was struck by more than a hundred bullets. *Courtesy Elmer E. Haynes.*

Japanese ship sinking in the South China Sea after being attacked by U.S. bombers. *Courtesy National Archives #80-G-301070*

Aerial view of the first convoy crossing the Hump on the Burma Road. *Courtesy National Archives #111-SC-316923*

A convoy ascending the famous "twenty-one curves" on the Burma Road en route to Kunming, China. *Courtesy National Archives #111-SC-208807*

Aerial view of a truck convoy on the Burma Road. Note the mountainous terrain. *Courtesy National Archives #111-SC-228183*

General Joseph Stilwell. *Courtesy National Archives #111-SC-181569*

General Albert Wedemeyer. *Courtesy National Archives #208-NS-3210*

Generalissimo Chiang Kai-shek. *Courtesy National Archives #80-G-186434*

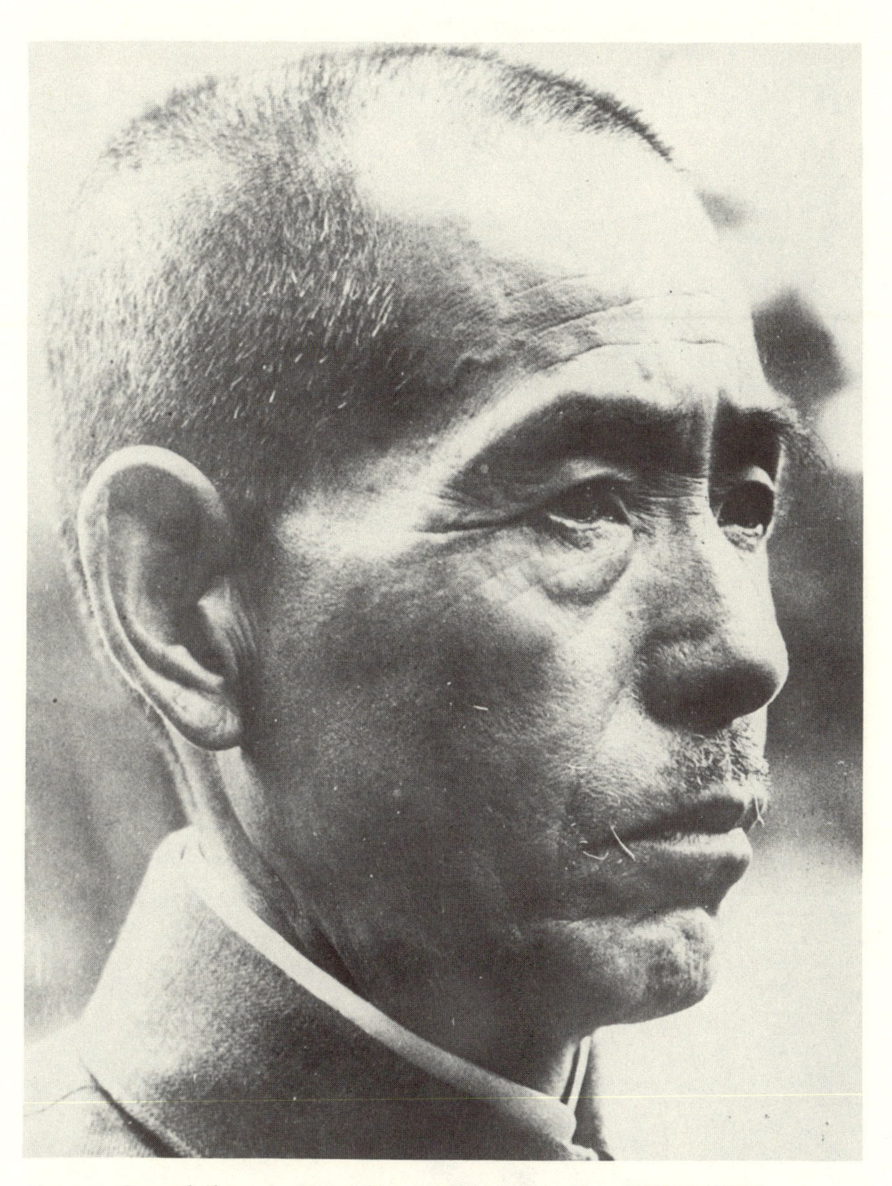

Japanese General Shunroku Hata. *Courtesy National Archives #208-N-43364*

Japanese General Takahashi. *Courtesy National Archives #80-JO-63364*

Major Horace S. Carswell, Jr., 308th Bomb Group. *Courtesy National Archives #111-SC-313635*

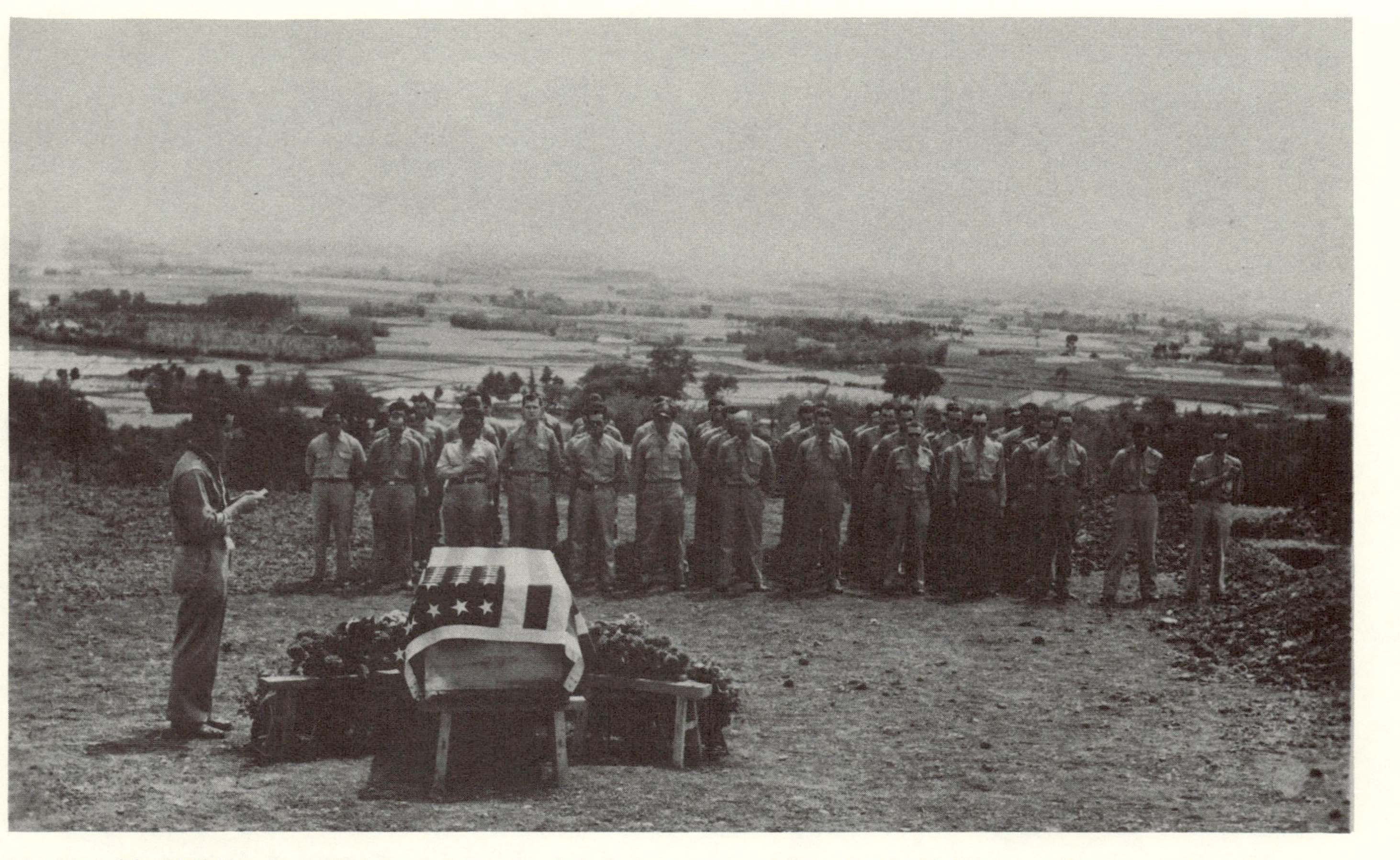

Members of the 375th Squadron, 308th Bomb Group, pay their final respects to a fallen comrade. Photo taken at Chengkung. Note open grave to far right. *Courtesy Elmer E. Haynes.*

Captain George C. Link (left) and Lieutenant Commander Sam Savage (right) celebrating VE-day at Kunming. Link tried on Savage's hat to see if it fit. *Courtesy Elmer E. Haynes.*

Coolie power, not ''horsepower,'' pulling a stone roller to build a runway. *Courtesy Colonel William D. Hopson, U.S. Air Force (Ret.)*

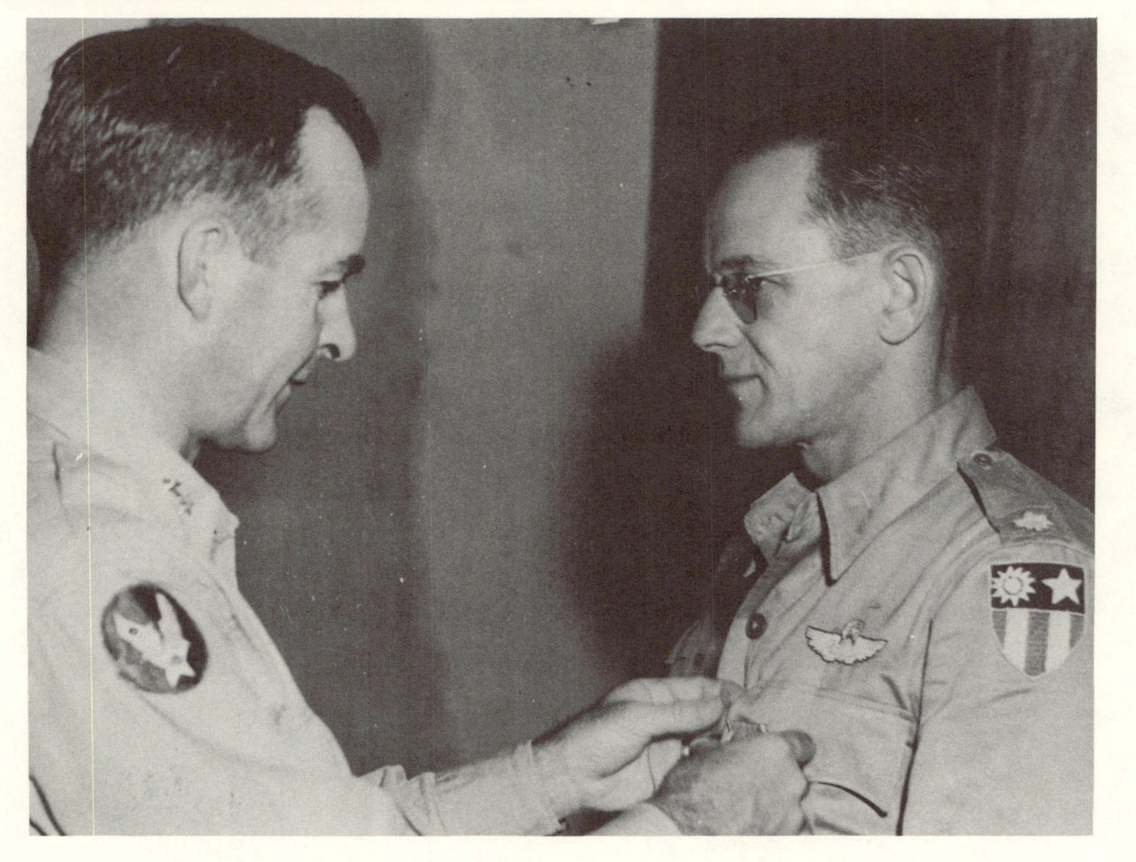

Lieutenant Colonel William D. Hopson receives the Legion of Merit medal from Major General Charles Stone on August 6, 1945. Hopson was promoted to full colonel on August 14, 1945. *Courtesy Colonel William D. Hopson, U.S. Air Force (Ret.)*

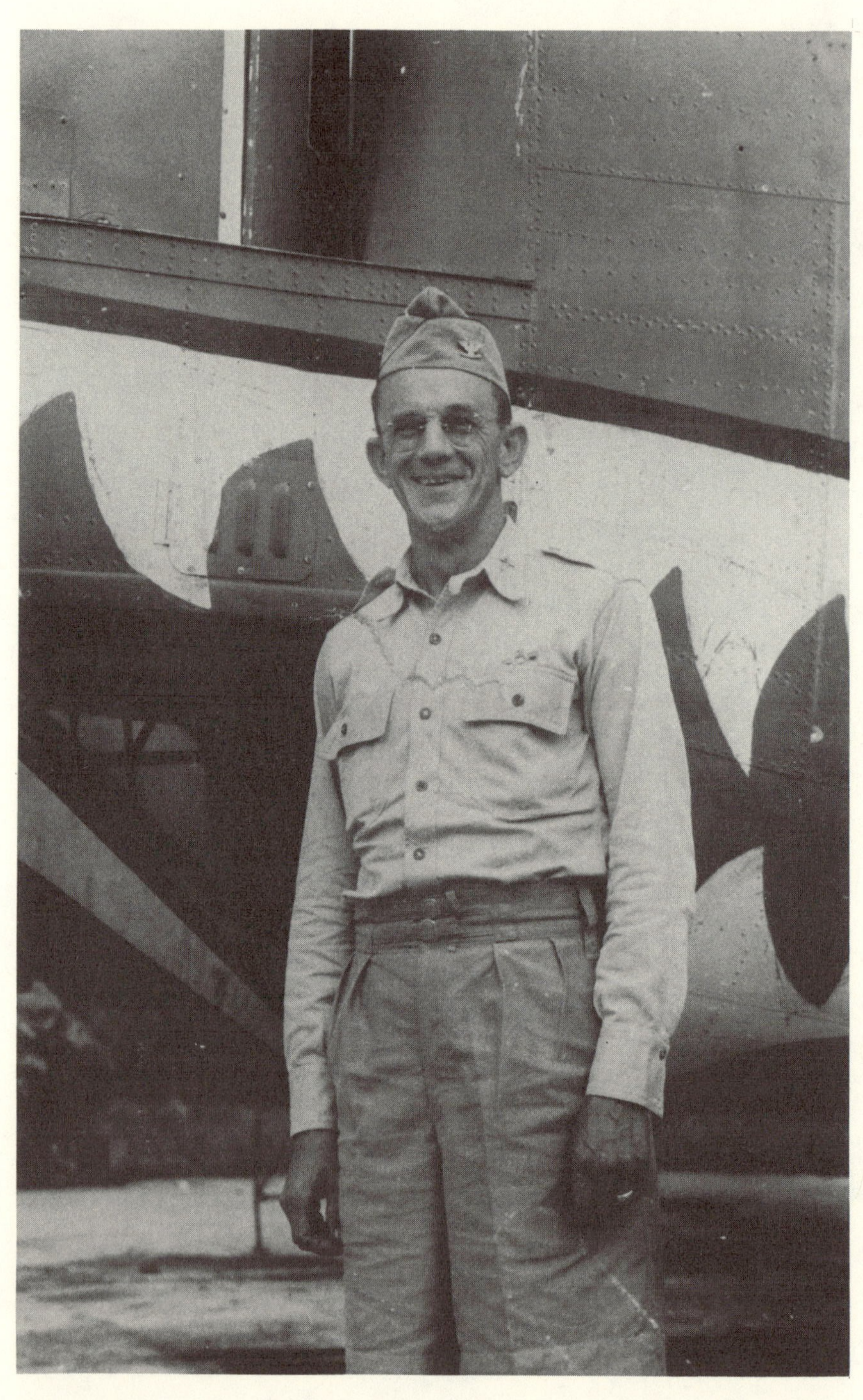

Colonel Hopson standing alongside one of the 308th Bomb Group's B-24s. *Courtesy Colonel William D. Hopson, U.S. Air Force (Ret.)*

Colonel William D. Hopson plants a kiss on the B-24 that he piloted back to the States from Rupsi, India, to Morrison Field, West Palm Beach, Florida. October 1945. *Courtesy Colonel William D. Hopson, U.S. Air Force (Ret.)*

CHAPTER 7

The Legend of "Hainan Harry"

December 22, 1944

At 1400 we took off for Chengkung. The sky was overcast and a wind shift blew us off course. But this did not pose a problem since we could home in on the radar beacon near Kunming. On the negative side, we only had an hour's supply of fuel in our tanks.

Atkins easily picked up the beacon signal and we soon spotted the field. However, when I contacted the tower for landing instructions, I learned that there was an air raid alert and the runway lights were about to be turned off. I immediately told the tower that we were out of gas and were coming in on a straight approach and to leave the damn lights on.

We were cleared to land, but the runway was darkened by the time we rolled to a stop. In order to taxi, I was forced to turn on our landing lights. As members of the ground crew directed us to the parking area, our lights picked up the figure of a Chinese soldier running head-on toward the plane. Our engines had not yet been shut down, and the props were still turning. Miraculously, the fellow dashed between two of the spinning propellers without being sliced to pieces. It was hard to believe that he slipped through alive. The clearance between the tips of the three-bladed props was less than 36 inches.

We related the incident at debriefing and also talked about it with fellow members of our squadron. At first, we could find no reason for the soldier's action. But the little Chinese lad who took care of our rooms supplied the answer to the mystery. According to his story, certain Chinese were superstitious and believed that evil spirits followed them around giving them bad luck. In order to rid themselves of these demons, they would run in front of a moving object—such as a truck, train, or aircraft—hoping the evil presence would not follow. In this soldier's case, it must have worked. I doubt if any evil spirit would have been crazy enough to follow this guy.

A few minutes later, the all clear sounded. The Japs must have had another target in mind. When I returned to my quarters, the room was packed with an accumulation of mail and packages. Mac had heard that our crew returned from Suichwan and burst in to welcome me back to civilization. After I stowed my gear, we headed for the squadron bar to celebrate my safe arrival and exchange news. Compared to Suichwan, this place seemed like heaven. The only thing I could have wished for more was to be going home to the States. But there was a dark side to our festivities—the absence of our missing friends.

December 23, 1944

I spent the morning reading my mail and drooling over the packages that awaited opening on Christmas Day. About noon, I decided to make the rounds of the squadron to find out what had been going on while I had been stuck out in the boonies for three weeks.

One of the big news items was a combined strike, on December 18, by the 308th Bomb Group and B-29s of General Curtis LeMay's Twentieth Air Force. Their targets were Japanese airfields and railroad yards in the Wuhan-Hankow area. The mission was a fantastic success. The B-29s and our B-24s really blew the place apart.

I also learned that four new replacement crews had arrived from Chabua. I met a few of their officers and then strolled over to operations where I was informed that a crew was being put together for me. My group would be composed of men who, because of various factors, still had not flown the required combat hours to complete their tour.

At this stage of the game, the idea of leaving Milt Wind and the other guys I had been flying with, did not bother me that much. McClure was now squadron navigator, George had left for home, and Miracle would finish his time in about a month.

During the evening, Mac and I walked over to the dayroom to relax with several of the squadron boys. We had no sooner sat down than there was an air raid alert. We dashed back to our room for warm clothing before racing to the trenches. After an hour or so with no sign of enemy planes, the all clear sounded. The Japs had bypassed us again, but they hit the 373rd Squadron's base at Luliang.

December 25, 1944

McClure and I awoke early and tore into our gifts like a couple of kids. Minutes later, we were surrounded by the spoils—cigarettes, cigars, candy, dates, razor blades, and much, much more, including, of course, the inevitable fruitcake. We could hardly find room to store our treasures. I turned on the radio for some Christmas music, and Mac and I congratulated each other for still being alive.

In the early afternoon, we had a fine holiday dinner. Even though the meal came out of cans, it tasted like home cooking to us. After stuffing our stomachs, we headed to the squadron bar and exchanged greetings with our fellow airmen. The liquor flowed freely, and the entire gang got into a song fest, with everybody whooping it up and having a grand old time.

The evening meal was leftovers, but the food helped to sober us up. McClure and I had just returned to our room when there was another air raid alert. We spent the next three hours huddling in the bitter cold at the bottom of a slit trench. By the time the all clear sounded, we were frozen. And thus went Christmas Day in China!

December 26, 1944

I was up early again this morning and had just settled down to write a few letters when a messenger showed up with orders for me to report immediately to operations. I met Milt Wind on the way and we entered the office together. Major Edney was waiting for us. He informed Wind and me that we would be flying as check-pilots with the new replacement crews on their first two combat missions. Milt and I had not anticipated this sudden turn of events.

Both of us now had the responsibility of checking out green crews on their initial baptism under fire. It would be our task to assess the pilot's ability to handle the aircraft, the capabilities of the navigator and bombardier, and the proficiency of the rest of the crew members. We were also instructed to pass on to these new men whatever knowledge we had gained from our own combat experiences. I remarked to Wind that if any of these replacements came close to obtaining the expertise of our own original crew, I would turn them loose without any qualms whatsoever. Milt agreed.

Wind and I had been saddled with one of the toughest jobs in combat flying. Checking out new crews was a good way to get yourself killed. There was absolutely no way to know how men would react under the pressures of aerial warfare. We left the meeting discussing our new assignments and wished each other good luck. I knew we both would need as much of that as we could get. I still had 130 combat hours to go before I reached the magic number—400—and I had a gut feeling that they were going to be the toughest hours of all.

When I returned to quarters, McClure was in the room. I told him what had transpired. He was surprised to hear that Wind and I were getting check-pilot jobs at the same time. Mac asked who was mad at us. I had my suspicions but said nothing.

I finished writing letters and then borrowed a jeep to visit my buddies at the 3rd Mapping Squadron across the field. We exchanged Christmas greetings, had a few drinks, and caught up on the latest news. I told the guys about my assignment as check-pilot and my dubious future. They agreed it sounded tough, but thought that it was an honor to be chosen for this type of job. I asked if any of them wanted to trade places, but there were no takers. I am going to seriously rethink this friendship business.

December 27, 1944

I went to briefing at 1030 and learned that I would be flying a recon mission to check out a new crew. We would be carrying a full load of gasoline but no bombs. The first pilot was Lieutenant Bobek. Our plane would be one of three aircraft—each flying a designated search pattern in order to make a complete sweep of the South China Sea, Hainan Island, and the Indochina coast.

During preflight inspection, I discovered that our command radio set was not working. While the ground personnel were busy making repairs, I assembled the crew and gave them a lecture on what to expect on this kind of mission.

About two hours later, the radio was finally repaired, and we took off without further incident. I sat in the first pilot's seat and Bobek flew as my copilot. We climbed quickly to search altitude. I had just leveled off and trimmed for cruising, when the No. 1 engine quit. Bobek became rattled. He had trouble feathering the engine. In the meantime, I was busy wrestling with the controls—trying to overcome the terrific drag caused by the dead motor. I shouted instructions for setting the power on the other three engines so that our plane could maintain altitude. We had already dropped more than 1,000 feet due to the heavy fuel load.

My quick response to the emergency shocked Bobek into action. He wasted no time in feathering the motor, and we were able to get the plane back on an even keel again. I told the flight engineer to check for the cause of the trouble—making sure to inspect the fuel valves. Sure enough, the valve to the dead motor was almost closed. The problem was remedied quickly, and I directed Bobek to defeather the prop and start the engine. It kicked in immediately. We were dangerously close to the mountains below. I pushed up the power and climbed for altitude.

A sudden predicament of this kind is an excellent example of what can happen to inexperienced airmen under stress. With a veteran crew, the loss of an engine would not have posed a critical problem.

After explaining to Bobek the correct procedure in handling an emergency of this kind, I told him to take over the controls while I headed aft to check on the rest of the men. I could tell by the expressions on their faces that they were pretty well shook up. I calmed the boys down, and assured them there was nothing to worry about, and that troubles of this nature were routine.

We soon reached the South China Sea and began our sweep down the Indochina shoreline. The search netted nothing until I decided to check the south coast of Hainan Island. We had barely started our sweep, when the radar operator called excitedly over the intercom that he had picked up four blips at about 20 miles distant. I alerted the crew and advised them that we were dropping down to try and make a visual identification. I warned the men to keep a sharp lookout. We were near the Japanese naval base and could be intercepted by enemy fighters. I descended to 800 feet—close enough for everyone to notice that the blips were sampans. Although the vessels were probably manned by Japs, they did not shoot at us.

We ended our sweep and returned to Chengkung. After making my report, I pointed out to Bobek and his crew that they had completed their first combat flight without being fired upon by the enemy. I sensed that the men were still a little uneasy but told them that everyone is a bundle of nerves on the initial mission.

I realized that my job as check-pilot was going to be a tough assignment. I was far from satisfied with Bobek's performance. He would have to do much better before being permitted to take out a crew by himself. But this was exactly the reason for check rides, and not every man was going to pass the test.

Captain George Link headed the intelligence section of our squadron. He and his men were responsible for scrutinizing the debriefing reports, as well as acquiring information regarding Japanese radar sites, antiaircraft emplacements, and other important data. Link and I became good friends, and he was frequently at my debriefing sessions.

It was Captain Link who pinned the nickname "Hainan Harry" on me. Hainan Island was included in the majority of our search patterns. The sweep usually began down the shoreline of northern Indochina, covering the Gulf of Tonkin. We would then turn east, around the southern tip of Hainan, and up the coast to the north end of the island. The final leg of the mission would be to scout the waters near Hong Kong. Another search pattern included the Hainan Strait, between the island and China's Liuchow Peninsula.

Hainan Island covers an area of 13,000 square miles, with 600 miles of shoreline. Three hours were required to fly completely around the island's coast.

FOURTEENTH AIR FORCE SEA-SEARCH BASES AND SEARCH AREA

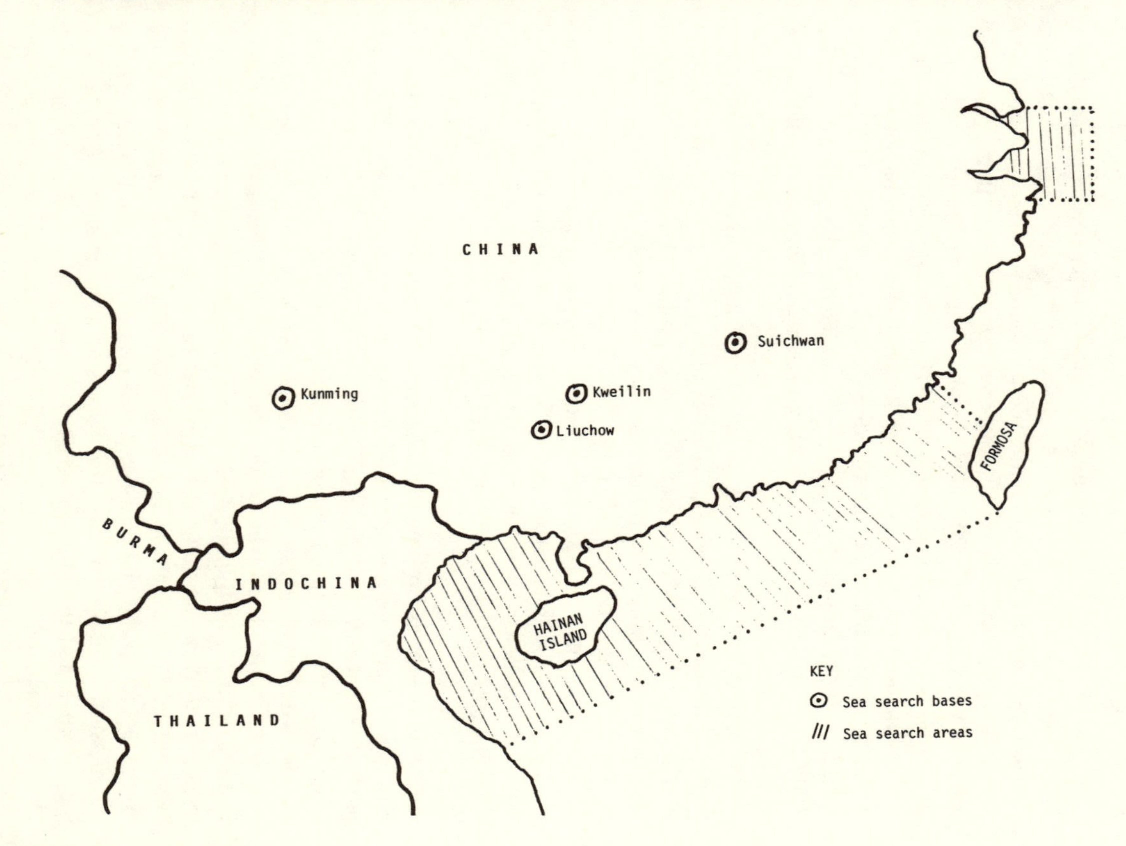

The seas in the Tonkin Gulf-Hainan region were the main shipping lanes for Japanese vessels coming up from southern Indochina. The enemy ships would move inshore as they traveled north.

Samah Bay, located at the south end of Hainan Island, had an excellent anchorage and was home to a Jap naval base and the Yu-Lin airfield. Several radar stations were also situated nearby. Frequently we hit Samah Bay as a secondary target—just to let the enemy navy boys know that they had not been forgotten.

At the northern tip of the island, across the strait from the Liuchow Peninsula, was the harbor of Haikou. This large bay was also favored by Japanese shipping.

On daylight recons, with good weather and perfect visibility, the air search around Hainan was a very scenic flight. I made a careful study of the area, and at one time knew the location of practically every major rock and small island along the coast.

As a rule, the waters surrounding Hainan Island proved to be good hunting. However, the Japs knew that our radar aircraft could easily detect their vessels on the open sea. Therefore, in order to counter our night searches, the enemy ships began hugging the coast of any large landmass. Only an expert radar operator, who was familiar with the shoreline, could detect any changes in its contour.

Gradually, over a period of several months, our charts were amended to show the many little islands and large rock formations along the coast of Hainan. We were then able to spot anything of a suspicious nature. Until the corrections were made, tons of bombs were wasted on targets that refused to sink.

In this respect, the mapping capabilities of radar were invaluable. By the end of 1944, LAB planes had plotted the entire coastline of China—from the Formosa Strait down to the Indochina coast below Hainan Island. We also charted Hong Kong Bay and up the river to Canton. Mapping procedures were handled by the radar operator who took pictures of the scope, while the navigator identified the photos and noted the locations.

Our recons and night strikers kept the Hainan area under a continual watch, and the surrounding waters never failed to provide some kind of target. There was, of course, a great amount of sampan and junk traffic, which made visual identification imperative in order to prevent a waste of bombs.

I spent a great deal of my time lecturing and orienting new crews about the facts concerning Hainan Island. Captain Link got a big kick out of my obsession with the region and continually joked to the men that I had circled around the island so many times that I knew the shoreline by heart. And if they had any questions, they should check with "Hainan Harry." So, I guess the moniker was justly earned.

Usually crews flying LAB radar B-24s did not take part in group daylight

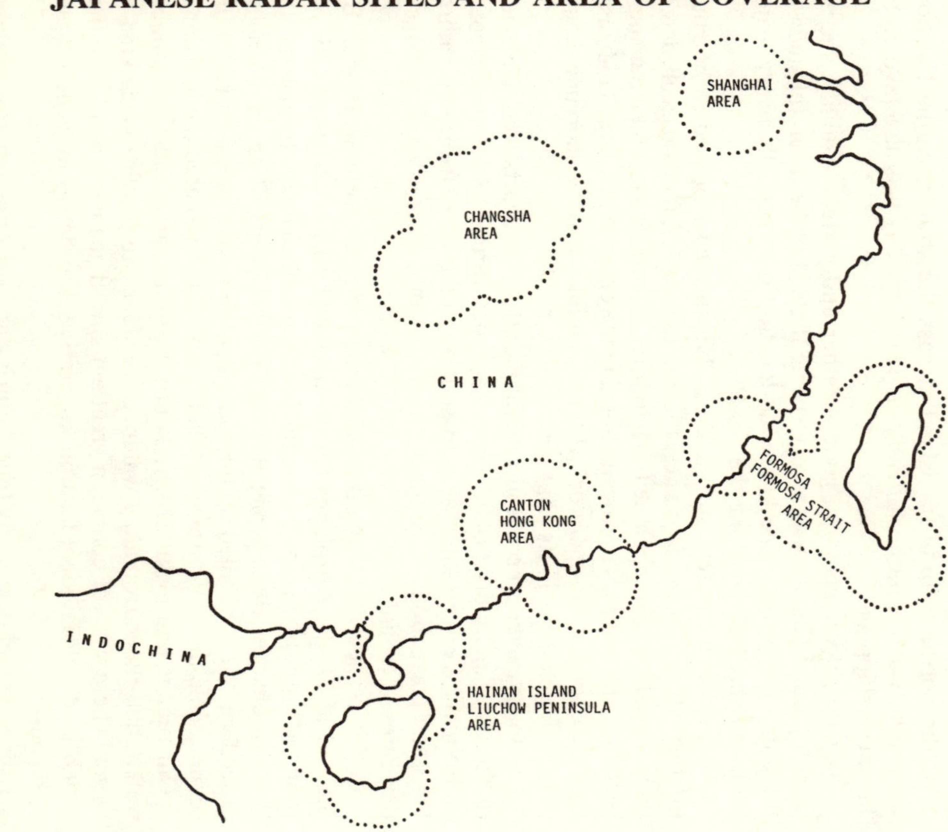
JAPANESE RADAR SITES AND AREA OF COVERAGE
SHANGHAI AREA
CHANGSHA AREA
CHINA
FORMOSA
FORMOSA STRAIT AREA
CANTON HONG KONG AREA
INDOCHINA
HAINAN ISLAND LIUCHOW PENINSULA AREA

raids against land targets. The straight, nonradar aircraft handled this chore. The LAB crews only flew day missions when every available plane was needed for an all-out attack against a particular target.

About half of the new arriving replacements were straight bomber crews. This meant that check-pilots were required to indoctrinate the men who flew day missions as well as the night radar boys.

Since I was not attached to any particular crew, I began to work in the intelligence and operations section—something I had never had the opportunity to do before. The intricate job of running a combat airfield was a new revelation to me. Among the myriad of reports that had to be written was an evaluation sheet on each LAB B-24. This critique was an in-depth study of the function of the plane's radar and included the extreme range at which shipping targets could be detected. Search ranges were known to deviate 50 to 150 miles from one B-24 to another.

Another important factor was the maximum distance from the aircraft to a mapping site that would show up clear enough on the scope for a photograph to be taken. Radar distances, which revealed a number of well-defined blips, often varied 50 miles.

However, the most critical test of the equipment was its ability to pick up our homing beacon at Chengkung. If an aircraft's radar system was operating efficiently, it should be able to latch onto the beacon's signal anywhere from 50 to 20 miles from the field. Usually upon our return after a mission, we would be flying at about 12,000 feet—depending on weather conditions—and the beacon was a great help. But, like everything else mechanical, it had a habit of breaking down and could not be used as a sole navigational aid.

Another function carried out by radar crews was the so-called "ferret mission." These sorties were flown by B-24s equipped with special electronic gear. This specific type of aircraft had the unique capability to intercept enemy radar signals. The purpose of these planes was to locate and plot Japanese ground radar installations that were beginning to appear in ever increasing numbers. This information was relayed to the Fourteenth Air Force Headquarters and to the U.S. Navy. The intelligence gathered by the "ferrets" proved invaluable in planning missions against enemy land targets.

A large number of ground personnel were required to maintain the air base and keep the planes flying. Besides the mechanics and engineers, there were the armament crews. It was their job to handle the different types of bombs, fuse them properly, and secure them in the aircraft. The ordnance men also took care of the .50-caliber machine guns and loaded the ammo belts with the proper assortment of shells—one solid bullet cartridge, one incendiary, one high explosive, and one tracer, for every four rounds in the belt.

However, the unheralded heroes of the air war in China were the men who operated the radio directional finders. The crews of these stations lived in the wilderness of the remote countryside. They worked from a large truck with a van body. This vehicle contained their charts and directional finding equipment. A gasoline generator supplied power to run the station. The boys manning these outposts continually monitored our various radio frequencies and would give a location fix to any aircraft lost or in trouble. Lord knows how many planes and men they guided to safety.

I was now at the point in my combat tour when the strain was beginning to show. I was becoming more aware each day that the odds against my survival were stacking up. When we first arrived in China, the old-timers told us that after 200 hours, a crew starts "sweating out" the missions. I realize now exactly what they were talking about. I am really beginning to "sweat!"

December 29, 1944

The U.S. Navy believed that the Japanese would soon be pulling their troops out of Indochina. The 308th Bomb Group received orders to begin an around-the-clock surveillance of the South China Sea and to be in a position to spot all enemy ship movements.

Bobek and I were briefed this morning. Our plane would be one of four recon flights (a B-24 from each squadron) for the initial 24-hour period. I told Bobek to fly in the pilot's seat, while I handled the copilot's job. We took off at 1100 with a full load of gasoline but no bombs.

At 1900, near the end of our search pattern, the radar operator picked up two blips on his scope. It was a bright moonlit night and visibility was excellent. I called the crew on the intercom and told them we were dropping down to make visual contact. I also informed the boys that from the general position of the blips, the vessels were probably freighters—and the firepower from merchant ships usually was not heavy or accurate at long range. I impressed upon the men to remain calm and instructed the radar operator to keep me posted on distance as we neared the target area.

We descended to 1,000 feet. About two miles from the blips, I instructed Bobek to commence circling. Moments later, we spotted two large Japanese freighters silhouetted in the moonlight. As we raced in for a better look, the ships opened up with machine gun fire. Bobek and his crew became excited at their first taste of combat. I settled the men down and reminded the boys that this was a recon mission. Our job was to locate Japanese vessels and identify them. We circled the freighters a couple of times and then headed for home.

When we reached cruising altitude, I told our radioman to contact Kunming and report the number of ships sighted, their types and location.

I was very satisfied with the results of the recon and the manner in which the crew had conducted themselves on their second mission. We landed at Chengkung about 0130—after 14 hours in the air. While being debriefed, I gave Bobek and his men the "green light." They were now on their own.

December 31, 1944

New Year's Eve in China. The squadron bar opened for business at 1400. I bumped into Paul Brosious, and we decided to start the celebration early. After downing a couple of glasses of the local home brew, Paul suddenly became lonesome for his buddies of the 425th Squadron stationed at Kunming. He insisted that we pay them a visit. It was a lousy, cold day, but I thought we probably had enough antifreeze coursing through our veins to make the trip.

The idea seemed great, except for the fact that no transportation was available. However, I solved the problem in a hurry. I called Lieutenant Stanton at the 3rd Mapping Squadron. I knew that Stanton had his own vehicle and asked him if he would be interested in taking a "scenic" drive to Kunming. I laid the crap on pretty thick about the advantages of such a journey—big parties, and probably Stateside food and booze. Stanton had already guzzled a few drinks and unhesitatingly agreed to go with us. In fact, he insisted that we use his jeep, and a few minutes later we were on our way over the bumpy road to Kunming. It was a good thing that traffic was light, because as loaded as we were, it was a wild ride.

The 425th was located at the south end of the airfield and at 1800, we slid sideways to a stop directly in front of their squadron bar. We had just mixed a round of drinks to melt our frozen arteries when Captain Harry Marshall slapped me on the back. He had been transferred from Suichwan to Kunming and was appointed commanding officer of the 425th. Marshall and I had a few drinks in his room. I told him about Wind and me being split up and assigned check-pilot jobs. The captain was impressed. He tried to convince me that it was the same thing as a promotion. According to Marshall, I was making headway in the service. I agreed that I was making progress, but as far as I was concerned, it was in the wrong direction.

When Marshall's supply of booze ran out, he sent me to the bar for another bottle. I immediately ran into Colonel Hightower Smith. He insisted that I return with him to his room and meet several of the men from the 308th Bomb Group Headquarters. A full-blown party was in progress. Smith's quarters were packed with top brass—majors, colonels, and brigadiers.

I had left my jacket, with attached rank insignia, in Marshall's room, and Colonel Smith decided to have some fun at my expense. He proceeded to introduce me as one of his old pals from Langley Field—*Lieutenant Colonel* Haynes. Of course, without insignia to prove otherwise, nobody questioned my sudden promotion. But I was feeling very uncomfortable and embarrassed by the joke and finally managed to escape the clutches of Hightower Smith.

I hurried back to the bar. Brosious and Stanton had been waiting for me. They wanted to drive into the city for dinner. The thought of food sounded good to me. I dropped off Marshall's bottle, retrieved my jacket, and we headed to town.

We finished our meal and had just returned to the squadron barracks, when an air raid was signaled. Stanton said the hell with the alert, he wanted to get back to Chengkung. We drove the twenty-odd miles without lights. However, we had plenty of moonlight to guide us. Miraculously we completed the trip without running over anyone or anything. When the new year arrived, we were sitting in the guardhouse waiting for the all clear to sound so that we could enter the base.

Stanton and I ended up the evening at his quarters having drinks with the mapping squadron's enlisted men. I finally hit the sack at 0230 and immediately passed out. What a New Year's Eve!

January 2, 1945

Since our arrival in China last summer, General Chennault had been steadily increasing the number of LAB planes and crews to make up for heavy losses. As we entered the new year, 308th Headquarters and the 425th Squadron were based at Kunming. The 373rd Squadron remained at Luliang, while the 374th and 375th Squadrons were stationed at Chengkung.

The U.S. Navy continued its request for constant surveillance of the seas south of China. Each of our squadrons sent out a recon every 24 hours—each flight separated by a six-hour interval.

I was briefed early this morning for a regular reconnaissance patrol. I would captain the aircraft on this trip. It would not be a check flight. Lieutenant Victor Del Masso was my copilot, and the rest of the crew was made up of personnel who needed additional hours to complete their combat tours.

We took off at 1240 and commenced our radar sweep from an altitude of 6,500 feet. About two hours into a search pattern down the Indochina coast, the radar operator called excitedly over the intercom that he had picked up many blips on his scope, He said that the contact appeared to be a large convoy approximately 60 miles southwest of Hainan Island. I told Del Masso that this must be one of the convoys the Navy was expecting.

Observation weather was perfect—unlimited visibility with scattered clouds at 8,000 feet. I notified the crew to put on their flak suits and helmets. Any large Japanese convoy was certain to be escorted by a few naval vessels—maybe even an aircraft carrier. In any event, we could expect a great deal of flak and possibly enemy fighters. I pushed up the power and headed into the cloud cover—it would give us some protection in case we were intercepted.

I instructed the radar operator to keep me posted at regular intervals, and to let me know as soon as he had a clear picture of the exact number of ships. The navigator was advised to make sure that he had the correct coordinates of the convoy's position. And the radioman was told to be prepared to transmit the information, in code, to the Fourteenth Air Force Headquarters.

I also directed the men to break out their binoculars. We would be dropping down through the clouds to make a visual sighting. I impressed upon the crew the necessity of a fast, but accurate, ship identification. I did not want to hang around long enough for the Japs to get our range.

When we were about 25 miles from the contact area, the radarman reported eleven clear blips on the scope. I told him to advise me when we were within five miles. I then alerted the crew and told Del Masso to be ready to push up full power. I did not intend to be a sitting duck for the Jap gunners.

We started our descent and broke out of the clouds at 7,800 feet. The enemy convoy was three miles dead ahead. And what a thrilling sight—one aircraft carrier, one heavy cruiser, three destroyers, two large troop transports, and four cargo vessels. The convoy was heading northeast on a 40°-course.

Our plane was spotted the moment it popped through the clouds, and the enemy ships began to take immediate action. The cruiser and destroyers swung toward us—firing every gun in our direction. I noticed aircraft lined up on the carrier's flight deck, and shouted to my crew to watch that floating airstrip like a hawk in case any fighters took off.

The sea below was a brilliant blue, and wakes of the fast maneuvering vessels plowed snow-white rows of foam through the water. It was a beautiful scene—if one could overlook the streams of tracers and black bursts of exploding shells.

After their initial attack, the cruiser and supply ships moved in near the carrier to protect the vulnerable man-of-war, while, at the same time, the destroyers began circling the convoy and continued shooting at us. Antiaircraft fire was coming uncomfortably close. I got on the intercom and asked the crew if they had identified the ships. Their answer was affirmative. I threw the B-24 into a shallow dive and banked away from the Jap flotilla. I leveled off at 1,000 feet and eased back on the power. Moments later, we were out of the enemy's range of fire, but we had been dangerously close to the convoy for about three minutes. We climbed to 6,500 feet, and flew a wide circle while the radio operator transmitted the report of our sighting.

After returning to Chengkung, I asked Captain Link if he had any idea why the Japs did not scramble their fighters. Link said that perhaps they thought their planes might lose us in the clouds—or else they figured we were a decoy of some sort.

January 3, 1945

Milt Wind woke me at 0900 with news that he was promoted to operations officer and that Major Benjamin McCary had replaced Major Edney as squadron commander.

Wind asked if I would mind flying a mission today—just another "easy" 14-hour recon like the one I had just finished. I would be piloting Lieutenant Nathan Traylor's crew. Traylor was sick and unable to make the flight. I was still half asleep, and before I had a chance to wipe the cobwebs from my mind. I agreed to do the mission. Milt gave me a heap of thanks and then told me that I had one hour to get over to briefing. I managed to clear my head, showered, shaved, grabbed a bite to eat, and made it to operations exactly on time.

We took off at 1145—a flying bomb, with 3,400 gallons of gasoline stashed in the wing tanks and bomb bay. I headed for the coast to begin our sweep, and turned on the IFF. Every LAB aircraft was equipped with this device, which sent a continuous coded signal that was changed at regular intervals. This secret communication was received by friendly aircraft and naval vessels who were also transmitting. The exchange of signals enabled our ships and planes to identify each other.

The search pattern took us within sight of Samah Bay. Although there was always the risk that the Japs would send up fighter planes, it was necessary to approach near enough for our radar to pick up any targets anchored in the bay. Nothing important was sighted in the area, and we turned east to continue the search.

We were 600 miles out to sea when the No. 3 engine sputtered and quit. Fortunately Traylor's crew were all experienced men. It was a ho-hum affair to these boys. We feathered the motor and began to hunt for the trouble. As usual, the fuel system was at fault. After setting the valves properly, the engine restarted without any difficulty.

However, while going through the checking procedure, the fuel gauges showed that we had barely enough gas to make it home. I began to sweat. I did not see how we could have used up so much gasoline unless we had a bad leak somewhere. But there was no evidence to indicate a break in the lines. My only choice was to abort the mission. I notified the navigator to plot a straight-shot course to Chengkung.

The more I studied the gas gauges, the less sure I was that we would be able to reach our base. I leaned all four engines back as much as possible, and with a lot of sweat and prayers, we landed safely. The needles were on empty when we touched down at 0300.

At debriefing, I reported the flight problems. The ground crew checked the aircraft and informed me that there was still 700 gallons of gasoline in the tanks. The fuel gauges were giving a faulty reading. By this time, I was hot under the collar. I told the guys at operations that this was not the first time I had trouble with those damn gauges, and they had better test that gasoline in the tanks, because half of it was probably our sweat.

When my bosses figured I was through spouting off, I learned that I had been scheduled for another mission the following day, but the plane's radar was not working, and no other LAB aircraft was available. I thanked them for the information and remarked sarcastically that I was very disappointed. I had been looking forward to another 14-hour recon.

I was so tired when I hit the sack that I could have slept for a week. I had logged 55 hours in my last four flights. Mentally and physically I was shot.

CHAPTER 8

R&R: Rest and Recreation in China

January 6, 1945

No flying today, and I was really enjoying the time off. McClure rushed into our room about noon. He had just come from operations and showed me his orders promoting him and James Otis to captain. Harry Marshall was also raised in rank to major.

Because Mac was now our squadron navigator, a good deal of his time was spent at 308th Headquarters for briefing on forthcoming missions and working out navigational problems. He told me that some of the top brass were aware of my accomplishments as a check-pilot and flying make-up crews. Hightower Smith told McClure to pass the word down to me that I was making a name for myself. The news made me feel good, but after my last experience with the colonel, I wondered whether this was just another one of his practical jokes.

Mac had no sooner left than a messenger came by and said I was wanted at squadron headquarters immediately. I sauntered down to the office, thinking that another recon was planned for my benefit. I had been spending more time in the air during the past few days than a migrating bird. Imagine my surprise when I learned that the members of our original crew had been authorized for one week of R&R at an air force rest camp. Wind and McClure would not be going along because they were attached to squadron headquarters.

I hunted up Jim Miracle and gave him the good news. Both of us ran over to the enlisted men's quarters and told our boys to get their gear ready for an early morning departure. They were as excited as we were.

I should have realized, however, that fate would deal us a blow to dampen the happiness. Sure enough, late in the afternoon, Mac returned from Kunming with upsetting news. Hightower Smith, Harry Marshall, Seymour Richmond, and six other men were missing on a flight over the Hump to pick up supplies at Chabua. They had taken off from Kunming at 0700 and had not been heard from since. A few ATC pilots reported that icing conditions were prevalent over the mountains.

McClure and I knew what the words "missing over the Hump" meant. There was very little, if any, chance that the men were still alive. I remember looking at Mac in dead silence. The first thoughts that crossed my mind were of Pierpont, Tomenedale, and their crew still listed as missing after the raid on Takao, and not one word as to their fate. My stomach twisted into a tight knot, and long with the feeling came the inevitable question, "Which one of us will be next?"

I had been looking forward to rest camp, and the welcome break in the monotonous routine. But somehow, after this shock to my senses, it did not seem to matter whether I went or not. I was down in the dumps for the rest of the day—too wrapped up in my thoughts to do much talking. Mac felt the same way. We kept ourselves busy, privately contemplating about life in China and the price we were paying in friends to win this war.

January 7, 1945

Jim Miracle and I managed to get our gear together and left for the rest camp at 0900. We arrived about noon. The camp was located alongside a lake, 50 miles south of Chengkung. The lake itself was ten miles long and three miles wide. A long dock extended from the recreational facility out into the water. The surrounding terrain was rugged and mountainous.

The camp, however, was a pleasant surprise. It had been constructed almost like a resort in the States, with tennis and basketball courts. I noticed many sailboats and rowboats tied up at the dock and was told that the fishing was very good.

Miracle and I unloaded our baggage and headed for the mess hall. The food was better than we had expected. After lunch, we scouted around the camp to learn what kind of recreational activities were available. Considering the site was in an isolated area of China, it had everything necessary for a relaxing vacation. The camp was well stocked with fishing tackle, tennis and baseball equipment, and ping-pong tables. For the duck hunters among us, there were shotguns and a plentiful supply of ammunition.

Jim and I had no sooner returned to our quarters than an alert sounded. We hurried outside to see what was happening. Everyone was running toward the dock. We joined the group and noticed that a small sailboat had capsized about 200 yards offshore. The sergeant in charge of the boats had taken one of the craft out in the lake to check its sails. A sudden gust of wind tipped the boat over. The sergeant was wearing a Mae West life preserver, but the water was extremely cold. He had been apparently knocked out, because when his body was finally located, he had never inflated the Mae West. We were all shaken by the tragic accident. What a way to start a vacation! It seemed as though death is always present everywhere in China.

January 8, 1945

This afternoon, Miracle, Cuva, Thomas, and I armed ourselves with shotguns and headed south along the lakeshore in hopes of shooting some game. We hiked for more than five miles up and down hills and through ravines. It was tough going, and we did not even see a rabbit. After a few hours of acting like big game hunters on safari, we held a conference. The decision was unanimous—get our tails back to camp before they froze off.

By the time we returned to barracks, the four of us were bushed. But everyone enjoyed the so-called sport. It was certainly a change in the routine. In fact, Jim Miracle was so enthusiastic that he thought we should give duck hunting a try in the morning. However, the rest of our crew chickened out. They would rather remain indoors and play ping-pong.

January 9, 1945

At 0500, my alarm clock went off with such a racket that I thought it would wake the entire camp, but the noise did not faze Miracle in the least. After much shaking, punching, and yelling, I finally managed to get him out of the sack. Jim moaned and groaned, and complained bitterly about being awakened "in the middle of the night." I reminded my roommate that it was his idea to get up early and hunt ducks. Miracle argued that he must have been out of his mind to agree to anything this stupid.

As soon as we dressed, and I poked my nose outside, I realized that maybe Jim was right. The ground was completely covered with heavy frost, and the air was bone-chilling cold. Miracle vouched that even ducks would not be crazy enough to paddle around in ice water waiting for us to shoot at them. But, after discussing the situation, we decided that maybe we were dumber than ducks. So, we bundled up in warm clothing and set out along the shore.

The first traces of daylight found us straining our eyes through a thick mist rising from the water. After standing shivering, and half frozen, for several minutes, we heard quacking, and spotted a few ducks far out in the lake. Although the birds were out of range, we fired at them, in hopes they might fly in our direction. They took off as expected but then landed again farther out in the water. By this time, they were so far away that it would have taken a .50-caliber machine gun to hit them. I told Miracle that this was an asinine way to spend a vacation—and besides, "Who likes ducks anyway!" We aborted the mission and trudged back to camp for breakfast.

But, idiots never learn. After wolfing down the morning vittles, we plotted another attack on the water fowl—only this time from a different direction. We hiked north, using all available cover, and crept toward the shoreline. Within a few minutes, quacking was heard. I peeked through the protective brush and saw ducks—lots of ducks—paddling among the reeds, but still out of shotgun range. Jim and I scratched our heads and cussed birds in general. We held a quick conference and came up with the brilliant scheme of using a boat to go after our prey.

We rushed two miles back to camp and commandeered a rowboat, trying to be as quiet as possible with the oars. But, although we sighted plenty of ducks, plenty of ducks spotted us too. Every time we came within range, the birds would take off, fly about a hundred yards, alight on the water, and wait for our boat to catch up. We were stupid enough to chase those damn ducks halfway around the lake. I fired a few desperation shots, but that was it.

The air was numbing cold, and both of us were soon out of energy and patience. I told Miracle that our little feathered friends had more sense than we gave them credit for, and besides, I was tired of being a human outboard motor. We agreed that playing ping-pong might not be such a bad idea after all, and rowed our blistered hands and frozen bodies back to the camp dock.

January 10, 1945

Early this morning, I rounded up our crew, and we hiked to a small Chinese community at the north end of the lake. It was a typical village for this part of the country—the usual smells, disease, worn-out coolies, and hungry-looking children. Apparently the people had not seen many Caucasians—especially Americans. They seemed more curious about us than we were about them. However, the villagers were very friendly and smiled as we greeted each other with "Ding How." The entire populace, both young and old, were extremely interested in our Fourteenth Air Force patches with the "flying tiger" embroidered on them. It turned out to be a very interesting day—and I am sure that the "strange visitors from another world" will be a main topic of conversation in the village for many years to come.

Upon our return, we were introduced to the camp chaplain, Reverend Bryan. He was very informative and told us that he had been stationed here for the past year. During our talk, I mentioned to the chaplain my frustrated attempts to bag a few ducks. The reverend was very sympathetic. He also stated that he knew the best hunting areas and would be happy to accompany us as our guide the next time we wanted to go duck shooting.

January 12, 1945

Miracle and I decided to take the chaplain up on his offer, and all arrangements were made. We met Reverend Bryan at his quarters at 0500, and the three of us started out on a long trek. We hiked seven miles, practically all uphill, to one of a few small lakes south of camp. The weather was freezing, and my teeth were chattering so loud that I was sure the ducks could hear them.

Just before dawn, we were in position at the chaplain's favorite location. As soon as the sky was light enough to see the birds, we began blazing away. I had always considered myself pretty good with a shotgun, but all I accomplished was to scatter a few feathers on the water. Jim Miracle and the chaplain also came up with a big zero for their efforts.

Hoping to change our luck, we walked to the next nearby lake and tried to sneak up on a flock of geese. But these birds were as cunning as the ducks, and once again we were unable to hit anything. After this latest fiasco, Miracle, Reverend Bryan, and I decided that we were poor excuses for hunters, and began the cold trek back to camp. The chaplain tried to console us by remarking what a nice sunny day it had turned out to be, and besides, we needed the exercise. We reached the mess hall in time for lunch, and spent the rest of the day catching up on lost sleep.

Our vacation was quickly coming to an end. It was the first time that I had a chance to forget about the war since I arrived in China. The rest camp had served its purpose to get my nerves back in shape for the final tough missions of my tour.

I feel like a man who is running a close race and approaching the finish line with death at his elbow. Combat teaches a grim lesson—the thread by which we hold on to life can be severed in a second. When an airman in my situation makes it this far, it is not the thought of dying that is frightening. But rather the tension of wondering when and how the grim reaper will pluck him from the sky.

January 14, 1945

This was our last day at camp. We packed our belongings and at 1400, climbed on a truck for the long, bumpy ride to Chengkung.

When I reached my quarters back at the base, I found a week's accumulation of mail waiting for me. I had just opened one of the letters when Jim Miracle rushed in to show me his orders to go home. Sergeant Milt Atkins would be leaving with him. I could not help feeling a certain amount of envy. I told Miracle how happy I was for him and that I wished I was going along. Jim promised to phone my wife when he returned to the States.

A few minutes later, Wind showed up with some good news. He had just heard that Harry Marshall, Hightower Smith, and all the people on their plane had parachuted into the jungle. They had been rescued and were now back at Kunming. It was hard for me to believe that they had survived. I told Wind that I wanted to see Marshall at the first opportunity. I imagined that he would have quite a story to tell.

CHAPTER 9

Ordeal in the Jungle: Harry Marshall's Story

January 16, 1945

I had been scheduled for a group mission, but it was postponed for a day because of bad weather. The delay gave me a chance to drive to Kunming and see Harry Marshall. I was anxious to hear the account of his rescue.

It was the middle of the afternoon when I walked into Marshall's office. He was glad to see me again. We headed for the squadron bar to pick up a bottle and then went to his quarters. Harry poured us a couple of stiff drinks, made himself comfortable, and proceeded to tell his hair-raising story.

It seems that Marshall and Hightower Smith needed to pick up some flying time for the month. The 425th Squadron needed supplies, and this looked like a good opportunity to get in their flight time by making a routine trip over the Hump to Chabua.

At 0950, on January 6, the supply plane took off from Kunming. Colonel Smith was at the controls as first pilot, and Harry Marshall was copilot. Seymour Richmond flew as navigator. Sergeant A. W. Rhoades was the radioman, and Sergeant Edward Wilson was the flight engineer. Four passengers also made the journey, Captain P. J. Tea (Chinese Liaison Officer), Captain Joseph Morrone, and Lieutenants Ewing Baker and Curtis Mitchell.

According to meteorological reports, weather conditions over the Hump were unpredictable—as usual for this time of year. Hightower Smith and Marshall were about three hours en route—flying at 14,000 feet through thick overcast—when they encountered icing conditions. Smith tried to climb above the sleet, but the freezing rain accumulated so fast and heavy that they were forced to descend. During their drop through the clouds, the continued buildup of ice snapped off the radio antenna.

Without radio contact, there was no way that the plane's crew could positionally orient themselves. Marshall said they tried everything in the book to keep the aircraft flying. But, because of the loss of airspeed and lift, the B-24 began to stall. In a matter of moments it would crash into a mountainside. Smith gave the order to bail out. At least, if they hit the silk, there was a slim chance of survival. But, everyone realized that there was not much hope either way.

The passengers jumped first, and then the crew. Marshall was the last person to leave the plane. Harry said that it seemed as if he was falling for several minutes, instead of seconds, before his chute opened. He recalled the tense moments of his first parachute jump: "As I dropped like a cannon ball through the clouds, pictures of my past life flashed at top speed across my mind. Suddenly, I felt the impact of tree branches snapping under me, and I came to a jarring halt—my chute had tangled in the tree, and I dangled from the harness like a puppet on strings."

Marshall checked his arms and legs—nothing was broken, but he could only see a few feet through the fog and mist. Momentarily the jungle was silent as it sized up the strange intruder. Then quickly, like a sudden gust of wind, the air was filled with ominous sounds. At first, Harry worried that his parachute would rip loose—and the thought of tigers lurking below also did little to settle his nerves.

After about an hour, the mist began to clear, and Marshall saw that he was hanging nearly 20 feet above the jungle floor. When he looked upward, he could see the path his body made as it smashed through the foliage. Harry shook the cobwebs loose from his head and carefully surveyed the surrounding area. It appeared safe. He hit the chute harness release button and dropped into the heavy underbrush.

Although it was still early afternoon, the jungle was so dense that very little light seeped through the trees. An unnatural darkness crept slowly over the region, and strange night noises began to fill the air. For the time being, however, Harry felt secure enough. He was wearing his winter flying gear, boots, and jacket, and carried a .45 and a survival pack.

Marshall noticed that he had parachuted into a small valley surrounded by high bluffs. He decided to climb a nearby hill, in hopes of reaching a clearing where he might be able to get his bearings.

Harry trudged through the tenacious undergrowth for almost two hours before coming to a narrow trail that snaked up the hillside. The path was steeper than it had looked, and by the time he was approaching the summit, Harry was out of breath and very tired. As he rounded a bend, he came face-to-face with a native woman who was busy filling an earthen jug from a spring. The moment she saw the strange looking airman, the girl screamed, dropped the pitcher, and ran up the trail. Marshall remarked that he did not know which of them was more scared. The sudden sight of the bare-breasted woman, wearing only a loincloth, and with long matted hair and weird dangling earrings, was not his idea of a sex symbol.

Harry drank his fill of water from the spring, and rested to catch his breath. Obviously there was a village in the neighborhood, but, by now, the girl must have alerted the inhabitants of his presence. Marshall hoped the people were friendly. However, just to be sure, he checked his .45 to see if it had a full clip of ammunition and then continued up the path.

After climbing a few more minutes, Harry rounded a curve at the crest of the hill and came upon a small clearing where several bamboo huts had been built along both sides of the trail. He was about 20 yards from the nearest dwelling. The air was dead silent, and there was no movement anywhere. Marshall yelled out a greeting, but there was no answer. He waited a short time, then raised his right hand as a gesture of peace and approached closer to the native settlement. As he moved cautiously forward, Harry observed about a dozen huts. They were without windows. Each dwelling had a small, closed wooden door that faced the trail. The roofs were thatched with vines and bark.

Marshall began to break out in a cold sweat as he neared the closest hut. He decided that if nobody appeared, he would proceed through the village. Maybe the people would realize that he was nonbelligerent. With his blond hair and blue eyes, Harry knew that he could not be mistaken for a Japanese.

Marshall walked past the first hut. There was still no noise or movement. He felt uneasy. The whole atmosphere of the place seemed to exude hostility. He was well aware that many cannibal and headhunter tribes inhabited the region.

Harry was halfway along the path through the village when he heard the sound of doors opening. He turned around swiftly. Several men, carrying spears and long knives, were behind him. The natives gave a frightening appearance. Their faces were painted, and they had bones sticking through their long, tangled hair.

The nearest man, about 40 feet away, shouted and threw his spear. Marshall ducked just in time. More spears began to zip through the air. Harry yanked his .45 from its holster, fired a couple of times, and ran for his life. A couple of spears came uncomfortably close as he sprinted, zigzag fashion, down the trail.

Harry related what happened next: "I took a quick look back. The natives were still racing after me, waving their weapons and yelling. At a bend in the path, I spotted some thick underbrush to my right. I dove headfirst into the thicket and plunged down the steep slope. After I had stopped sliding, I could hear the sounds of the savages running along the trail above me. I remained quiet and listened. My heart was pounding so loud that I was sure they could hear it. I waited until dusk, and then sneaked quietly down the hill. I stopped every few minutes to listen for signs of pursuit, but evidently the natives had given up the chase.

"It was dark by the time I reached level ground. I was hungry, thirsty, and so tired that I could barely walk. I decided to climb a tree to spend the night, but it was a restless sleep. By morning, I was so cramped up that every bone in my body ached.

"As soon as I felt safe, I dropped to the earth and headed in another direction across the valley. I intended to put as much distance as possible between myself and the hostile village. The jungle was full of all kinds of birds, but I was afraid to shoot one for fear of giving away my location.

"I had walked for about an hour, when I came upon a wide trail that looked like it had been well traveled. I followed the winding path and soon saw and smelled smoke. I knew I was nearing another village. I checked my gun—there were still five rounds remaining in the clip and chamber. I put two extra ammunition clips in a pocket close at hand, said a prayer, and headed toward the smoke.

"I followed the trail up a small hill and when I reached the crest and looked down, I saw many huts indicating a fairly large settlement. Most of the dwellings were surrounded by vegetable gardens.

"It was about noon, and I was very thirsty and weak from hunger. I decided to take my chances and trust to luck. I stumbled down the slope and walked toward the village. As I approached the huts, I noticed natives working their gardens, and other people looking in my direction. Several children were among the villagers, which gave me some sense of comfort. I figured that they would be inside if any hostile action was planned.

"When I came within shouting distance, I raised my right hand and called out, 'American! American!' A couple of men started up the path. They welcomed me with smiles and a thumbs-up gesture of greeting.

"I was led into the village and met by a large group of inhabitants. An elderly man, wearing a hat, stepped out from the crowd and said, 'Hello.' I was startled to hear English spoken in the middle of the jungle—especially in the rugged Hump region.

"The old man motioned me into his hut, where I was given water and some kind of cake. He told me that he was the village chief and had served as a guide for the British in an attempt to subdue tribes of headhunters in this part of the Naga Hills. The chief showed me an old Enfield rifle and bayonet and his army uniform jacket. He also brought forth his collection of human heads that he had confiscated from the savages. The chief said that he knew I was in the vicinity from drums reporting that airmen had parachuted nearby."

Harry stopped for a moment to pour us another drink, and then continued his story: "I was told that the tribesmen who chased me were definitely headhunters, and my blond head would have been a rare trophy. The only reason those painted savages stopped hunting for me was the fact that I had escaped in the direction of the chief's village. The practice of headhunting had been outlawed by the English Government, and the offending natives avoided contact with tribes that were friendly to the British.

"I learned that the savages did not have any firearms except a few ancient rifles that would probably explode if they were ever fired. Therefore, the headhunters had a healthy respect for my .45—especially after I shot at them a couple of times."

Marshall spent the night as a guest of the chief. And the following morning, with two native guides, set out on a three-day journey to another village. When Harry arrived at the settlement, he was greeted by Colonel Smith, Lieutenants Baker and Mitchell, and Sergeant Wilson. It was a joyous reunion.

After a short rest, the survivors headed toward a British mining operation in the mountains. On January 11, they were sighted by a C-47 rescue plane that dropped food and supplies. The next day, the men reached a military outpost where they were met by an aircraft and flown to Chabua. The other members of Hightower Smith's crew had been picked up the day before, and were waiting at the 308th Headquarters when Marshall and his group landed. A real celebration took place that night.

I listened to Harry's story with intense interest and amazement. It was a miracle that all nine men survived with only minor injuries. There were not many people who made it back to civilization after bailing out over the Hump.

We had several drinks during the conversation and discussed other subjects. Marshall asked me if I would consider staying on in China for a while after I finished my tour. He said I would be able to make captain before going home. I explained to Harry that I did not believe I had much of a chance for promotion in the 375th Squadron. There were not any openings now that Wind had filled the vacancy in operations. I congratulated Harry again on his fortunate rescue and hopped in my jeep for the drive back to Chengkung. It had been a very interesting and unusual day.

CHAPTER 10

Panic in the Skies

In early January 1945, the first supply convoy of 113 vehicles departed Ledo, India, for the long journey over the newly opened Burma Road to Kunming, China. The trip would cover more than 1,000 miles of narrow, treacherous highway. The trucks were delayed repeatedly. Besides mechanical breakdowns, the roadbed and bridges were in constant need of repair. In one instance, the convoy had to stop and wait while Chinese soldiers cleaned out a pocket of Japanese troops.

Finally, on February 4, 1945, the convoy rolled into Kunming. The entire population of the city turned out for the celebration complete with ribbon cutting, fireworks, and music.

The opening of the Burma Road meant that a continuous river of supplies could now flow into China without having to be airlifted across the Hump. By the time the war ended, 5,000 trucks had hauled 30 tons of supplies over the road that many people said could never be built.

Although the Burma Road was a remarkable engineering feat, there was one major drawback—it was one way. Every vehicle that traversed the highway from India was unable to return and had to remain in China. The area around Kunming became a large parking lot for trucks, vans, jeeps, and anything else that crossed the Hump on wheels.

January 17, 1945

I was up early and checked with operations on the status of a group mission scheduled for tomorrow. I learned that I would be flying as check-pilot with Lieutenant Edwin Baxter and his crew. They had just flown a new plane over from the States, and this would be their first combat strike.

I gathered Baxter and his men together for a question-and-answer session. Their aircraft was a straight B-24, not equipped with radar. I explained to the navigator the importance of accurate plotting and told the crew that they should know their jobs, keep cool, and above all, not panic.

Baxter and I sat down together, and I laid out the specifics of the operation. It would be a daylight group mission, flown in formation, with all four squadrons participating. Our target was the Hong Kong docks, and bombing runs would be made from an altitude of 16,000 feet.

I also let Ed Baxter know the grim news. We could expect heavy flak, and possibly enemy aircraft. However, we were promised fighter cover, which would virtually eliminate a threat from the air. All things considered, I thought it would be a good flight for a first combat mission.

However, during our conversation, Baxter dropped a bombshell in my lap. His plane was a gas hog. On the trip over here from Stateside, each engine burned more than 60 gallons per hour, and the cruising airspeed only averaged about 155 MPH. I did not have to be a mathematician to figure out what these statistics meant. I knew we would be carrying eight 500-pound bombs and 2,750 gallons of gas. If Ed's Liberator burned as much fuel as he claimed, we would be cutting the round trip too close for comfort.

Baxter and I went to the flight line to check on his aircraft. I told him to have the ship inspected thoroughly, while I went over to operations to have a talk with Wind. I let Milt know that I was very concerned about Ed's aircraft and the gas consumption problem. The flight to Hong Kong was 770 miles each way, and there was a question as to whether I could make it back to Chengkung. Wind agreed that it was a bad situation to be in, especially with a green crew.

I hit the sack early but had a hard time falling asleep. I had no doubts that tomorrow would be the most dangerous day of my life.

January 18, 1945

We were briefed for the mission at 0615. A total of 29 planes would take part in the strike. An hour later, seven Liberators from each of our two squadrons (the 374th and 375th) took off from Chengkung. We rendezvoused over Luliang with eight B-24s from the 373rd Squadron and seven from the 425th. We formed a shallow diamond formation and headed to pick up our fighter escort at a point 125 miles north of Hong Kong. However, our formation was late in arriving at the rendezvous spot. After making a few circles, we gave up hope of contacting the fighters, and turned south toward the assigned target.

Baxter's plane gave me trouble during the entire flight. It handled poorly, was sluggish in response to controls—and it drank a lot of gas. As if I did not have enough problems, the group formation was very ragged—with aircraft scattered all over the sky. I thought to myself that this whole damn mission must be made up of new crews.

When we reached Hong Kong, the entire area was obscured by heavy overcast. We circled the region for an hour, hoping for a break in the clouds—but no luck. We then turned north to our secondary target, the White Cloud airdrome at Canton. I instructed every member of the crew to keep a sharp lookout for Japanese planes. We would be flying over one of the enemy's largest airfields, and without fighter escort, we were sitting ducks.

Luckily, when we sighted White Cloud, the clouds began to disperse. We made our bomb runs. But, because of the group's sloppy formation order, the strike was far from satisfactory. Several planes dropped their bombs prematurely, not anywhere near the target area. Intermittent cloud cover prevented us from seeing how much damage we actually caused. Accurate flak was a problem. But, for some unknown reason, no Japanese aircraft came up to a challenge us.

As soon as we were clear of danger, I held a conference with Ed Baxter and the flight engineer. From all indications, we were burning gasoline at an alarming rate. We had been using a much higher power setting than normal in order to keep up with the other B-24s, and this was causing our plane to eat up more fuel than necessary.

I realized that if we ever expected to make it home, we would have to quit the formation. I called the group leader, told him of our gas situation, and that we were dropping back and would fly on our own.

After we broke formation, I instructed Baxter to lean out the fuel mixture as much as possible. I also had the navigator come up to the cockpit. His performance so far had been substandard, and I told him that he had better get on the ball. I impressed on the fellow that we would be flying over clouds most of the way, and I was relying on his "dead reckoning" navigation to get us to Chengkung.

I was very concerned about our predicament but tried not to show it. The crew was green, and the navigator did not seem to have much confidence in himself. The sky above us was also beginning to cloud up, which meant we would be unable to get a celestial fix on our position. And, without radar, we could not home in on the radar beacon. Our only choice was to rely on radio navigation. However, with the existing weather conditions, static would be breaking up our transmission and reception. But, my main problem was the plane itself. It handled like a truck with a flat tire, and guzzled gasoline like a sot. As I watched the fuel gauge readings, I knew it was going to be a nip and tuck battle to make it back to Chengkung. There was no margin for error!

I got on the intercom and told the navigator to keep a sharp eye on the cloud cover below and to use his drift meter if he sighted ground through a hole in the overcast. If I had some idea of the wind direction, I would be able to adjust our present heading to allow for drift. I also ordered the navigator to give me an ETA [estimated time of arrival] as soon as he had one calculated.

The time was now 1630, and the sky was starting to get dark. I instructed the radioman to get busy on his set and begin calling for a radio directional fix so we could determine our present location and to let me know immediately when he made a contact.

I trimmed the aircraft to a fine point, and we began flying on the step. The mixture controls were leaned farther back. I kept my fingers crossed that the engines would not detonate [backfire]. At our present rate of gasoline consumption, I estimated that we had about three hours of fuel remaining.

I kept in constant touch with the crew, giving them words of encouragement and telling them to keep calm. I assured the boys that we would return to base safely. Convincing myself was another matter!

My imagination began to run wild. By this time, we should have been in range of somebody. I got on the intercom and told the radio operator to start calling the Chengkung and Kunming stations at 15-minute intervals and to continue attempting to raise a radio directional finding station. I was positive that our powerful command set would be able to reach 50 miles—even through all the static. There was no question in my mind that if we did not contact anyone within the next hour, we were definitely off course. I had a gut feeling we had drifted—otherwise, we would have received some kind of answer to our signal.

The sky soon became very dark. The clouds were beginning to break up, and I could see the terrain below but the countryside looked unfamiliar. I was positive that we had been blown northeast. I told the navigator to try and get a drift reading. In the meantime, I turned west. There was one consolation, however, we had to be over friendly territory.

Baxter and I noticed that the No. 3 engine was using the most fuel. I instructed the engineer to level off the remaining gasoline into the four main wing cells—then cut off the cross feed, letting each engine run on its own tank. At least when the No. 3 motor quit, we would still have plenty of time to bail out before everything went dead.

I remarked to Ed that this was a hell of a way to begin a combat tour—lost on his first mission, running out of gas, and the prospect of abandoning his aircraft. I also told him that although this mission was a great experience for the crew, I had already had my share of experiences, and would do my damndest to keep this crate in the air. I was not about to make my first parachute jump this late in the game. I reassured Baxter that we were not finished yet. We were still flying—and in the right general direction.

During all this time, Harry Marshall's story of bailing out over the Hump kept running like a continuous film before my eyes. And now I was preparing to do the same thing. Fortunately, however, my plane had no ice buildup, and I was not over headhunter country.

After flying an hour on the new heading, we had still not made radio contact. I called the crew on the intercom and told the men of our situation. I reminded them to keep calm, not to panic, and explained the bail-out procedure. I told the boys to check their chest chutes, tighten and adjust the harnesses, and be ready to abandon ship on command.

I informed everyone that the bomb bay doors would be opened the moment the No. 3 engine sputtered. I would immediately ring the alarm bell, and they were to jump in an orderly manner—staying as close together as possible. Hopefully they should land near enough to each other to join up. If a man was injured in the bail out, he was to fire three shots as a signal that he required assistance. I told Baxter that I would be the last person to leave the ship and not to get in my way when I headed down the bomb bay aisle.

I had barely finished giving the crew their jumping instructions when the engineer tapped me on the shoulder—our radio had picked up some type of contact. I jammed my headset down over both ears—switched to the incoming channel, and, sure enough, I heard a voice. It was too faint to make out the message, but my heart began to beat faster. Maybe we still had a chance!

I shouted to the radioman to keep calling on the same frequency, while we tried to get a bearing on the sending station. I knew that if the voice started to come in clearer, and volume increased, then we were flying in the direction of the transmitter. I made a slight correction in our heading, and the signal came in stronger. I was back on the intercom in less than a second. I told our radio operator to keep up the chatter, and to tell the person doing the sending that we were trying to home in on his signal. And, if he was transmitting from an airfield, to turn on plenty of lights, as we were about out of gas.

The clouds below us had broken up considerably, and I noticed that we were flying over very rugged terrain and high hills. But, overhead, there was still a high, hazy overcast, and no stars were visible.

The crew was instructed to keep a sharp lookout for any kind of light. But, of course, even if something was sighted, there was still the question of whether we would have enough fuel to reach its location.

I began to sweat as the minutes continued to tick off the clock, and the gas gauge needles kept dipping toward zero. Suddenly, our engineer yelled that he spotted a flickering light in the distance. If appeared to be a rotating beacon. I shouted at Baxter to get on the radio and call for landing instructions. And to tell the tower that we were practically out of gas and needed to come straight in. He was unable to get an answer. But, by this time, I could see the lighted runway of an airfield straight ahead of us.

I told the engineer to put all tanks on cross-feed. I could not risk losing the No. 3 engine on our landing approach. The fuel gauges indicated we had less than 200 gallons of gas—if they were accurate.

We were within five miles of the field. I could see it plainly, but the strip was strange to me. I knew that I had never landed here before. I made a tight circle to inspect the length of the runway and check for obstacles. Everything looked clear and I set up the plane for landing. I made two tight left turns and began my final approach. I told Baxter to turn on our landing lights and give me full flaps—then I chopped the throttles. However, I had leveled off a little high, and the ship dropped about 15 feet to the ground. We bounced hard. I struggled with the controls to keep from stalling out. Our wheels finally grabbed the runway and we rolled to a stop. The plane was safely on the ground at last—even if it was a lousy landing.

I turned the aircraft around and taxied up the runway. A truck came out of the darkness and directed me to the parking area. After unloading, I discovered that we had landed at Luliang, about 70 miles north of Chengkung.

At our debriefing, I learned that we were damn lucky to get back at all. There had been a strong windshift that, along with the heavy overcast, had scattered the squadrons all over southwest China. Several planes had still not reported and were probably lost.

I went with Lieutenant Baxter and his crew to the mess hall, and then arranged for officer and crew quarters for the night. By the time I fell into my bunk, I was physically and mentally exhausted. We had been in the air under the most stressful conditions imaginable for almost 12 hours.

January 19, 1945

I was up early, had breakfast, and walked over to operations to check on the status of our aircraft. I was informed that the plane's fuel cells were nearly bone dry—less than 200 gallons remained in the tanks. And the way this clunker ate gas, once more around the block and we would have cashed in our chips. Just to be on the safe side, I convinced the ground crew that we needed a thousand gallons to get home.

Ed Baxter rounded up his crew, and we climbed aboard for the trip back to base. I was ready to go but, for some reason, the stubborn plane refused to cooperate—two of the engines would not start. A team of mechanics worked on the motors for a couple of hours. Finally, about noon, all four engines cranked up and we were ready to take off. I called the tower, gave them my thanks, and said that we were heading to Chengkung—that is, if a thousand gallons of fuel would be enough to fly this crate 70 miles.

About an hour later, we touched down on our home trip. Boy, did it feel good to get back. I reported in at operations. They had been nervously sweating us out. Milt Wind was happy to see I returned safely. He had not been notified we landed at Luliang. There was no direct communication between the two bases and the terrain was so rugged that radio signals were unable to get through.

I gave Wind my opinion on the performance of Baxter's crew. All passed with flying colors, with the exception of the navigator. I told Milt that the fellow could stand some coaching from an old hand to give him more confidence.

McClure was waiting for me when I got to our room. He had just flown back from a trip to Calcutta. Mac could hardly wait to tell me his tale of woe—how rough life was down there, with all the booze, good food, and English girls running around all over the place. He gave me a bunch of crap about how much he missed China, and how he could barely wait to get back to Chengkung. I felt like pinning his hide to the wall.

January 22, 1945

I was briefed for a night recon mission. Lieutenant Jessie O'Neal was my copilot. We were airborne at 1730 with a full load of gasoline. I climbed to 12,000 feet and leveled off. But, just as I began transferring fuel from the bomb bay tanks to the wing cells, our No. 4 engine quit. We finally located the trouble—a valve was in the wrong position. The problem was corrected quickly, and the engine restarted with a roar.

Once over the coast, we commenced our sea search at 6,000 feet. I flew my usual pattern around Hainan Island, but without any sightings of importance. On one occasion, we dropped down to investigate a few blips, but they turned out to be sampans.

Although I hit turbulence on our return to Chengkung, we landed without mishap at 0630. It had been another long night, but with no serious problems for a change.

January 23, 1945

I finally pried my eyes open about noon and, after a shower and shave, headed for the mess hall. While having lunch, I learned that our squadron had lost a B-24 on a flight to Chabua. The crew was forced to bail out when the plane's controls jammed. The last man to jump barely got out of the ship before it went into a steep dive. Sergeant Henry Thomas, one of my original crew members, was aboard the flight, but bailed out safely. The other men sustained various injuries.

The airfield at Chengkung was constructed in a level valley, but the surrounding terrain was rugged and mountainous. The doomed aircraft had just started to climb over the first high mountain range when the accident occurred. Consequently, the crew had almost no chance of bailing out without breaking bones or sustaining internal injuries. Fortunately, the incident happened in broad daylight, so at least they could attempt to guide their chutes. I can easily imagine what their chances would have been on a night jump into this wilderness. We play for keeps here. Even a routine flight is fraught with danger.

During the evening, I had just settled down to write a few letters when Sergeant Thomas stopped by my room. He described the bailout, and said he was lucky to escape unhurt. Thomas also remarked that if he had been flying with me, nothing like this would have happened—because I lead a charmed life. I told the sergeant that I doubted if his assumption was correct—but, if he was right, I sure hoped it would continue.

January 25, 1945

I was briefed in the morning for a noon recon. However, the aircraft had a radar problem, and take off was postponed for a few hours. The trouble was fixed by 1430. My crew was aboard and I was ready to taxi out to the runway when Milt Wind drove up in his jeep. He shouted to me that a couple of new B-24s assigned to our squadron had just arrived in India, and he wanted me to take a crew over the Hump and bring one of the planes back to Chengkung. He said that I would be leaving early the next morning, "so try and get some sleep during the recon." There were a few choice words that I felt like shouting back at him, but I held my tongue.

Our route was the usual sea-search pattern around Hainan Island. But there were no sightings, and we returned to base at 0430.

January 26, 1945

I stumbled awake at 0800 and packed my gear for the flight to India. I do not know who made the arrangements for this trip, but they must have had rocks in their head. We were to hop a truck to Kunming, then wait for a plane to arrive from Luliang to ferry us over the Hump.

The ride to Kunming is not a pleasure trip in any sense of the word. And, after being bounced about for 20 miles, my back felt as if a couple of vertebrae had been knocked loose.

We drove up to the Fourteenth Air Force Headquarters at 1030, checked in, and waited for our transportation to show up. My crew and I waited—

and waited—and waited. Finally, after six hours of twiddling our thumbs, I was notified that the plane from Luliang had developed engine trouble, and the flight was called off until the following morning.

To say I was irritated would be putting it mildly. And I was not called "hot-under-the-collar-Haynes" for nothing. I was boiling mad. A whole day had been wasted, I lost a lot of sleep, and besides, I almost ruptured myself on that "obstacle course" riding to Kunming.

I stormed into Harry Marshall's office and flat out told him that this was the dumbest way to fly to India I ever heard of—and that my crew and I were not intending to spend the night. I borrowed a truck to take us to Chengkung, and we were back at our quarters by 1900—all of us in a nasty frame of mind. As far as I was concerned, it was just another screwed-up day in the military.

January 27, 1945

At 0900, we were on the road again to Kunming. But this time, we only had to wait an hour for our "taxi" to arrive. The plane was piloted by James Otis. Four crews, one from each squadron, climbed aboard to pick up new aircraft.

We took off at 1330. Our destination was Ondal, India—about 950 miles southwest of Kunming. We had good weather over the Hump for a change, but when I looked down at the murderous terrain where Harry Marshall had bailed out, a cold chill ran down my spine. I tried to imagine what it must have been like—parachuting through the dense clouds and into the jungle.

We touched down at Ondal about 2100, but during our landing roll, the No. 4 engine suddenly caught on fire. Otis slammed on the brakes as we skidded along the runway. Two men jumped out the waist window—one sprained his leg and the other suffered a broken wrist. The rest of us exited the ship through the bomb bay doors—the *proper* method of evacuating a B-24. Crash trucks were on the scene immediately and had the fire under control before it did too much damage.

I reported in at operations, arranged quarters for my crew, and then joined the other officers on our flight at the air base Officer's Club. Everything at Ondal was first class—including the club. It was real Stateside—not like our little shack at Chengkung. I was instructed where to bunk for the night, and then headed to the bar.

Ever since I have been in the service, I often marveled at how many times I have had the occasion to exclaim, "It's a small world!" And tonight was no exception. I had no sooner ordered a drink than I ran into my old sergeant from basic training days at Camp Roberts, California—Robert Bartolec. He had made lieutenant and was now stationed at Ondal.

Bartolec was easy to recognize, with a face that was hard to forget. He was big, tough, and mean looking—with a voice like a foghorn. He was not the kind of person to have as an enemy. We got along fine in basic training, but others, much to their regret, ran afoul of Robert Bartolec's "gentle nature." Bob and I closed up the bar, and I finally hit the sack about 0130. Surprisingly, I had one day ending on a positive note for a change.

January 28, 1945

I met with Otis at 0900, and we walked over to operations to check on the status of the planes that were to be ferried to China. We learned they were still being serviced and would not be ready until the next morning.

Bob Bartolec had mentioned to me that if we were still around today, he would be glad to take our group on a tour of the area. I managed to locate Bob, and six of us jumped in his truck for an eye-opening trip. Bartolec drove to another air base a few miles away. The buildings and general layout of the field gave all the appearances of a plush country club in the United States. The first place we checked out was the Officer's Club. It was magnificent. This was top brass territory all the way.

Our next stop was the PX. It was also first rate—with everything imaginable on the shelves. I made a few sarcastic comments about how rough it was to be stationed in India. But I felt more than a little irritated when I thought about all the goodies they have over here compared to what we have in China.

I taunted Bartolec and asked him if he would like to climb aboard my plane tomorrow. I would show him the Hump and take him on a guided tour of Chengkung. But Bob bowed out of the deal. He said that he already knew about life in China—and would just as soon "sweat out" the war in India.

It was late afternoon by the time we arrived back at Ondal. The tour had been a very interesting experience for me. I came to the conclusion that we were fighting two different kinds of war over here—the "lounge war" and the "bust-your-butt" war.

We had a terrific dinner upon our return—topped off with ice cream. It was the first time I had tasted that treat since I arrived in Asia. I was very tired by the time I hit the sack, but I had really enjoyed the day.

January 29, 1945

My plane was ready about noon, and Bartolec drove out to the runway in a jeep to see me off. The return trip over the hump was a smooth ride. The ship flew beautifully and handled like a dream. It was, without a doubt, the finest B-24 I had ever flown. The earlier models required a lot of physical effort, but not this baby. Even the autopilot worked perfectly.

I landed at Chengkung about 1800—just in time for supper. It felt great to be back. Although we did not have the luxurious setup like the boys stationed at Ondal, this was still my home away from home.

January 30, 1945

I checked in at operations to learn if anything important had happened while I was away. Milt Wind gave me the sad news that one of our planes was missing from a routine flight. Lieutenant Bobek and his crew were one of four recons that took off on the evening of January 27. Two of the search planes reported radar contact with unidentified aircraft in the vicinity of Hong Kong. According to headquarters, Bobek's plane may have been intercepted and shot down. They were one of the new replacement crews, and it hurt me to hear that Bobek and his men were probably gone forever.

But that was not the only shock Milt had in store for me. Effective February 1, I was to be leader of "C" Flight—and both Wind and I had been recommended for promotion to captain. However, there was one requirement. Once I was promoted, I would have to remain in China until May—and maybe longer. I was between a rock and a hard place. If I finished my tour, and went back to the States as a first lieutenant, there was a good possibility that I could be sent back to China for another tour of duty. But, if I put in the necessary time as captain, I would be able to return home for good. In any event, there was nothing I could do about the situation, except sweat it out and hope for the best.

February 4, 1945

The first truck convoy to cross the Burma Road arrived in Kunming today and rumors are spreading like wildfire everywhere.

Wind called me into the operations office. He told me to sit down while he gave me some bad news. I still lacked about 20 combat hours to finish my tour. On top of that, Milt said he heard that my captaincy had been turned down—not enough flying time. I was positive that Major McCary squashed my promotion. We never did get along. It was a personality clash I suppose.

I was very disgusted when I returned to my quarters after the conversation with Wind. In fact, I was getting madder by the minute. After doing some hard thinking about my predicament, I decided to find out exactly what the policy was regarding the required combat hours for first pilots—and also what the rumors were all about.

I borrowed a jeep and drove to Kunming. I hunted up Hightower Smith and Harry Marshall and told them what had happened. Smith said that there was nothing I could do about the combat time since 400 hours was a rigid requirement for first pilots. However, they both agreed that there was something fishy about my promotion being turned down.

I did get the answer to all the rumors flying about. The straight B-24s of the 374th, 375th, and 425th Squadrons would be moving very soon to Chengtu. The 373rd Squadron and all LAB radar planes would be stationed at Luliang. A lot of changes were definitely in the works.

February 5, 1945

Another one of our planes is missing. George Turpyn and his crew took off on a recon a couple of days ago and have not been heard from since. His is the second plane lost from our squadron in the last few days.

I hurried over to operations and told Milt Wind that something must be happening around Hainan Island. It was too much of a coincidence that two aircraft, flying the same search route, turn up missing in such a short time. I also mentioned to Milt that I had often worried about being intercepted while searching the southern tip of Hainan near the Jap naval base. I knew from intelligence reports that the Japanese had radar stations operating in the area, and they might be effective enough to spot our recons. Wind remarked that I could be right and suggested I tell my theory to Captain Link.

During our talk, Milt informed me that I would not be flying any more missions—just casual hops here and there and testing planes. He had also heard that orders would be coming through about February 20, sending me back to the States whether or not I had 400 combat hours.

February 6, 1945

The days are really beginning to drag now. It seems hard to realize that this nightmare I am living in might finally be coming to a close. Before I started this combat tour, I had always taken life for granted—but not anymore. I learned the hard way that men do not live forever—especially fighting this war in China.

CHAPTER 11

Formation of the 308th Radar Control Detachment No. 1

With a continuous ribbon of supplies now moving over the Burma Road into China, Generals Wedemeyer and Chennault implemented a new strategy to halt the Japanese land offensive. Straight B-24s of the 308th Bomb Group were moved to the Chengtu area, where they would be more readily available for attacks against enemy land targets and to support Chiang Kai-shek's crack army units.

The LAB radar planes were sent to Luliang and placed under one command, instead of being scattered among the four squadrons of the 308th. The radar-equipped aircraft concentrated on cutting Japanese shipping lanes. And their recon patrols would notify the U.S. Submarine Force of enemy flotillas. The South China Sea soon became known as "Convoy College" by the submariners.

February 12, 1945

Ever since I first arrived in China, I had been accumulating a lot of junk and now began giving it away or throwing it out. Rumors were still flooding Chengkung about where our squadrons would be heading. Although I knew the answer, I could not tell anyone what I had learned. I had high hopes of getting out of here before the changes took place. But something bothered me. It was too easy.

February 14, 1945

This was one Valentine's Day I shall never forget. Late in the afternoon, a messenger stopped by my room with a message that Major McCary wanted to see me immediately. The first thought that entered my mind was that my orders to go home had come through. I hurried down to the CO's office. After we exchanged formalities, McCary looked me straight in the eye and said, "Lieutenant Haynes, your orders to return to the States have been canceled. You will remain here as our operations officer during the forthcoming move and reshuffling of the squadron. I expect you will be promoted to captain shortly and will be required to stay in China until at least June."

McCary added that my name had been chosen for a special assignment by some "higher-ups" at group headquarters. I looked at the major in disbelief. Here I was, practically on a plane going home, and all of a sudden I could be stuck here for a few more months.

McCary remarked that the news came as a surprise to him also. But, he said, at least I had finished my combat tour and would not have that worry hanging over my head. From now on, I would only have to fly four hours a month to receive flight pay.

What a blow! And there was not a damn thing I could do about it. But this was not Major McCary's decision. Somebody had gone over his head—and I did not think he was very happy about it. However, that was small consolation to me. I trudged back to quarters thoroughly disgusted. I wrote my wife a letter telling her what happened. She was really going to love this piece of news.

February 15, 1945

All enlisted members of my original crew received their orders to go home today. The whole gang stopped by my room to say goodbye and wished I was going with them. They were certainly a happy bunch of guys. Our farewell became quite a choked-up affair by the time they left.

A short time later, I was called to McCary's office. He was rather curt and told me to get my gear together as soon as possible and report to Major Marshall at Kunming.

February 16, 1945

McClure helped me with my baggage and rounded up a jeep and driver for me. We had been roommates for a long time and had a lot of good times together. There was a big lump in my throat when I waved goodbye to him.

I walked into Harry Marshall's office at 1330 and asked him what the hell was going on. He just laughed and said I was stuck here—after all, we had a war to fight, and I had to do my bit. We went to his quarters, and he filled me in on what my "bit" was to be.

Marshall did not waste any words and got right down to the business at hand. He told me that the war with Japan was now entering a very crucial stage. Events occurring in the Pacific had put the enemy on the defensive. The Japs had been losing one island after another and were desperately trying to get their troops out of Indochina. Intelligence reports revealed that the enemy was carrying out mass evacuations by means of any seagoing transportation available. It was imperative that we cut the Japanese shipping lanes and destroy their vessels. The success of a venture of this type depended entirely upon a concentrated effort by our LAB B-24s and U.S. Navy submarines.

The 308th Bomb Group would be working directly with a naval detachment to be stationed at Kunming. In order to effect the liaison, a new organization was set up called the 308th Radar Control Center. I had been chosen as chief controller. And, along with two assistants, I would handle the around-the-clock operation of the station.

Lieutenant Colonel William D. Hopson would be commanding officer of the radar center. The organization was classified as top secret and would consist of about 20 officers and enlisted personnel.

Marshall said that this idea had been in the works for some time. But, now that the Burma Road was open, we would have the wherewithal to put the plan into effect. Since nothing of this kind had ever been attempted before, it was up to me to see that it worked as efficiently as possible.

I sat like a man in a trance listening to Harry talk. I felt detached from reality. This must be some kind of dream. It surely could not be happening to me. I must have looked like I was in shock, because Marshall suddenly stopped and asked if I was awake. I quickly came back to earth, and said that I heard what he was saying—but why was I picked for the job? Of all people, why me?

Harry patted me on the shoulder to calm my fears and said that Colonel Hopson was looking for men who had taken their early radar training at Langley. He knew that they were older, more experienced, and more likely to have the qualifications for a task of this kind. The pilots would also have completed their required combat time and flown LAB aircraft on night striker missions in the South China Sea.

Major Marshall and Colonel Hightower Smith had submitted my name, along with their recommendation that I had the capabilities of handling the chief controller job—because of my background with the Sea-Search Attack Group at Langley and my combat record in China.

I told Harry that I appreciated the big buildup for an assignment that nobody knew anything about. And, although I was grateful for his confidence in my ability, I was inclined to think that maybe he had bitten off more than he could chew—me included. Besides, my wife would probably shoot both of us if we ever made it back to the States.

Marshall only laughed and said that he and Colonel Smith had the utmost faith in me. "Thanks a lot!" I answered, as I headed out the door to find the colonel.

I located Hightower Smith in his quarters, and the first thing he asked me was what I thought of my new job. I told him that I was still in a state of shock. And, as far as the work was concerned, I did not have the faintest idea what it was all about.

Smith told me a few facts while we walked over to the building that housed the radar control center and the Navy detachment. I would be working directly under Colonel Hopson, and Hightower would be going to Luliang as commanding officer of the 373rd Squadron. Lieutenant Colonel Allan Crockett would be the new group operations officer.

Smith and I entered the control center. It was protected by armed guards. We walked down a long, narrow hall and entered a large war room. Lieutenant Colonel Hopson was waiting for us. He was a tall man, wore glasses, and spoke with a quiet measurable drawl. He had been an Arkansas lawyer in civilian life.

I liked Hopson from our very first meeting. He had a direct approach to any problem and did not waste time coming to the point. He was very sharp, and his entire manner commanded respect.

The three of us sat down at a table, and Hopson related the framework of what we hoped to accomplish. Our radar control organization would be working with a Navy intelligence unit that was under the command of Lieutenant Commander Sam Savage.

The offices of the naval section were located directly across the hall, and the Navy boys would provide us with information and other data pertinent to our LAB striker missions.

The Radar Control Center would be the central information repository for all known Japanese shipping in the South China Sea and along the Indochina coast. Our job would be to plot the location of all vessels in our control area. We would have the responsibility of directing the LAB strike force against enemy shipping anywhere in our zone and within range of the aircraft.

We were also instructed to prepare a daily report of our activities and the results of the LAB missions. These reports were to be hand-delivered to the Fourteenth Air Force staff meetings every morning—and given personally to General Claire Chennault. In addition, we were told to be prepared to answer questions from members of the staff regarding the contents of the reports.

Colonel Hopson said that, as a rule, he would attend the staff meetings. But, in his absence, I would take his place. Hightower Smith smiled at that statement. He knew that it hit me like a brick between the eyes. I looked at Hopson in amazement. I could not believe what I was hearing. After catching my breath, I blurted out, "You mean that I, a lowly first lieutenant, will have to go into that room full of generals and other top brass—personally hand the reports to General Chennault—and then stand there answering questions?"

It was Colonel Hopson's turn to smile this time as he tried to calm my fears. "It won't be all that bad," he said. "The men at those staff meetings are just like the three of us sitting in this room. They just have more rank."

Hopson then elaborated on the extent of my duties. As chief operations officer, I would have complete authority over the radar center and would be answerable only to the colonel himself. In Hopson's absence, it would be up to me to make the decisions regarding how many LAB planes to send out against Japanese shipping targets in our control area. I would receive the data on the results of our strikes before anyone else—with the exception of the naval unit, whose radio messages would come in from their submarines, and other intelligence sources.

I would always have first-hand information on the daily progress of the operation and would keep Hopson up-to-date on the situation. A minimum of two controllers would be working for me—with one on duty (or instantly available) in the war room at all times.

Hopson glanced at his watch. He said there was much more for me to know, but at least I now knew the basics. We would be getting together tomorrow with the radar control personnel to go over our jobs and various other functions of the organization. The colonel then hurried out the door, leaving Hightower Smith and me sitting alone in the war room. I was silent and busy trying to sort out everything I had heard. I was so wrapped up in my thoughts that I did not realize Hightower was talking to me. "Haynes! Haynes!" he shouted to get my attention, "You sure got yourself a job here!"

"Colonel," I answered, "You sure got yourself some kind of a sense of humor. I think you and that Harry Marshall just love to see me suffer!"

Smith walked with me from the Radar Control Center over to my new living quarters. The barracks for the radar personnel was only about 40 yards from where we would be working. While I was signing in, Hightower introduced me to my two assistant controllers—First Lieutenants Forest O. McClure, Jr., and Luverne M. Freeman. The three of us were LAB pilots who had finished flying our combat tours. Colonel Smith left us to get acquainted while he went back to his office.

I talked with McClure and Freeman for quite some time. They did not have the faintest idea what was going on. I brought them up-to-date, explaining what I had learned so far—and that we would probably get all the facts the next morning.

After we parted company, I went to my room. As I unpacked, the shock of the day's events began to wear off. I looked over the notes I had scribbled during Colonel Hopson's talk, and tried to make some sense out of the information. This was going to be a real challenge. I did not get much sleep that night. Too many thoughts were racing through my head—and too many questions without answers.

February 17, 1945

By 0800, seven officers and fifteen enlisted men had assembled in the war room. One familiar face was Captain George Link. He had been assigned as our intelligence officer.

Colonel Hopson introduced each member of the organization and explained their duties. He told the men that the actual operation would be under my supervision and that of my assistants, Freeman and McClure. The rest of the personnel were to render any help required to get the design phase of the project completed. And anyone with a workable idea should bring it to my attention.

After he finished his speech, Hopson departed, leaving my two aides and me looking at each other, and wondering where to begin. Captain Link came over to me and said that he was glad to be part of the outfit, and would assist us in every possible way. Link already knew a few of the naval intelligence people from his dealings with them in the past. He remarked that he would introduce me to the Navy fellows at a combined group meeting scheduled for the next day.

Orders also came through designating our unit as the 308th Radar Control Detachment No. 1.

February 18, 1945

At 0900, Captain Link and I entered the war room where I was introduced to the Navy section and Lieutenant Commander Sam Savage. We discussed how to go about setting up our operation with the resources we had available.

Savage contributed a great deal of information concerning the Navy's techniques of gathering intelligence. In addition to a powerful radio—which picked up messages from their surface ships and submarine patrols—Savage also received surveillance data from a secret network of coast watchers. These observers were stationed at strategic locations along the China and Indochina coasts, Hong Kong, and the Strait of Formosa. Using portable, high-powered radio transmitters, these scouts reported any movement of Japanese shipping, the kinds of vessels, and their course. The information was then immediately relayed to Fourteenth Air Force Headquarters at Kunming.

At the present time, most of the naval action in the China seas was being carried out by U.S. Navy submarines. The data received by Savage and his intelligence unit was evaluated and radioed to the submarine fleet.

The subs also picked up information from our LAB recons patrolling the South China Sea.

We discussed operational details until noon, and then quit for the day. After lunch, when I returned to my quarters, I suddenly realized that this was my first wedding anniversary. And, here I was, in China—12,000 miles from home—holding a hot potato for a job and not knowing when I would get back to the States. What a hell of a way to spend an anniversary.

Later in the afternoon, I went back to the war room to continue working out the particulars for forming our control center. As I studied all the problems and possible solutions, I discovered that one function led to another. I became so engrossed in the project that I worked until 0300 the next morning. However, I accomplished a great deal. The operation was really beginning to shape up.

February 19, 1945

At 0900, I met with Colonels Hopson and Smith. I told them about my meeting with the Navy people and my ideas on how to proceed with setting up the control center. I explained that, due to the increased traffic of Japanese shipping in the China seas—and the enemy's desperate attempt to move their forces out of Indochina—it was imperative that we maintain a 24-hour-a-day surveillance of the areas within the 1,000-mile range of our LAB B-24 reconnaissance aircraft. The recons were able to haul additional gasoline in a tank placed in the bomb bay. The extra fuel supply gave them the advantage of covering greater distances than the strikers—which were saddled down with the added weight of eight to twelve 500-pound bombs. Therefore, I mapped out two separate sea-search patterns—one for reconnaissance planes, and a "blind bombing line" for the strikers.

The bomb line would extend from Vinh, on the Indochina shore, to Dongfang on the west coast to Hainan Island. It would then continue from the northeast tip of Hainan to Takao, Formosa. After the hours of darkness, any vessels within the area encompassed by the "blind bombing line" would be subject to attack by our LAB strikers.

Navy submarines operating in this zone would be required to remain submerged at night—or better yet, stay away from the region entirely. Even though our LAB planes were equipped with IFF, there was always the possibility that a set would fail, or someone would use the incorrect code for a given date. With the cooperation of the Navy, our strikers could safely assume that any target picked up on their radar would be the enemy.

All sightings of Japanese targets by our recons would be sent by coded radio transmission to the Radar Control Center. The targets would then

FOURTEENTH AIR FORCE RECONNAISSANCE ROUTE AND BLIND BOMBING LINE

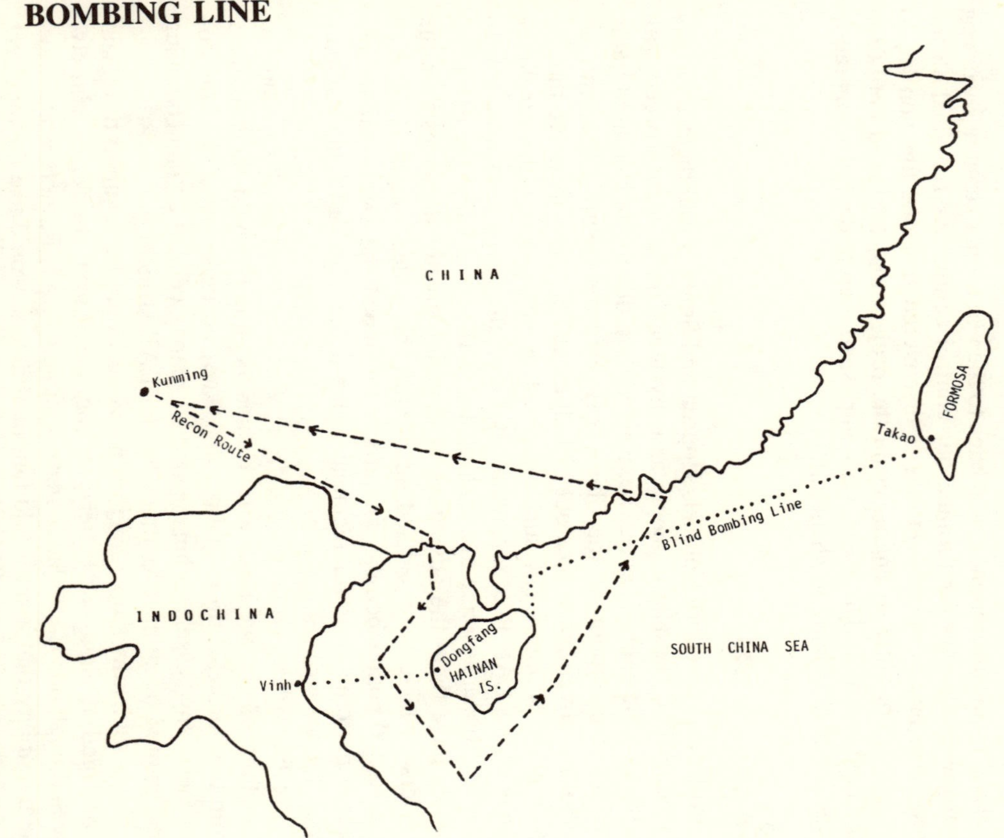

be plotted according to location, course, and types of vessels. The Navy would also be consulted regarding the top speed of the various ships. After correlating every piece of information available, additional plotting would be made on the map, and I would decide on a course of action for the striker aircraft.

If the targets were within the bomb line, I would have the option of sending out as many planes as necessary to destroy the enemy ships. Any vessels out of striker range would continue to be shadowed by our recons. Theoretically, nothing could move for any length of time in the control area without our knowledge.

In fact, it was not even necessary for us to know a target's course. The ships moved relatively slowly—and by extending their range in a circle of a predetermined number of miles, the radar-equipped B-24s would have little difficulty in locating a specific objective.

Our attack aircraft would be instructed to keep the control center apprised of the results of their bombing missions. A ship was to be reported as sunk, probably sunk, or damaged. In the case of a crippled vessel, if one of our submarines was within intercept distance, it would be instructed to close in for the kill.

In order to accomplish these goals, an adequate striking force of LAB B-24s would be required to be on constant alert and standby every night. The aircraft and crews would have to be ready to take off, with the necessary gas and bomb loads, within an hour's notice. This effort would also demand additional ground personnel and an abundant supply of parts in order to keep the whole operation functioning efficiently.

I presented all of my recommendations at the meeting and outlined the general framework of our planned operations. Both Hopson and Smith were pleased with the progress to date, and I was given their joint approval on practically everything we discussed.

February 21, 1945

For the past couple of days, I was kept continually busy putting the radar center in shape. I had Freeman and McClure round up all available aeronautical charts of our control zone and paste them together on the wall of the war room. By the time they finished, we had fabricated an eight- by ten-foot plotting map.

It was a lot of map, but it had to cover an area from Kunming to Luliang, then down the coast of Indochina to the 15th parallel, across to the Philippine Islands, north to the 24th parallel, and extending over to Formosa. It was a large territory—450,000 square miles.

After the chart was completed, we worked out a location grid of the entire sea-search area for reporting purposes. The grid was then drawn on the plotting map. The next item on the agenda was to set up an accurate scale and to figure distances from the LAB base at Luliang.

We covered the map with acetate film and attached a scaled cord and compass card to a pin that was located at Luliang. By stretching the cord out to any spot on the chart, we could immediately figure the distance and compass heading from the LAB airfield to a target.

After taking into consideration distances and weather factors, the scaled cord enabled us to determine the amount of fuel required to reach an objective and return safely.

The system sounded simple. However, our charts were not exactly accurate. We had to make compensations and relocate several islands and cities to achieve the necessary accuracy.

I devised a method of using colored pins to indicate the different kinds of ships, their locations, and what action had been taken against them. We could also use various colored grease pencils on the acetate to record data directly on the map itself.

In the meantime, Captain Link had been working out the details of the morning report that Colonel Hopson would be delivering to the Fourteenth Air Force staff meeting.

Besides a specific accounting of the LAB missions, the report would also include information concerning the activities of our three squadrons that were based at Chengtu. When all the incoming data had been categorized, General Chennault would be receiving a complete daily operational record of the 308th Bomb Group.

The project seemed to be running smoothly, except for one stubborn problem—an irritating disruption of communications between the Radar Control Center and Luliang. For some unknown reason, our teletype machines were continually breaking down. And, without them, we were forced to rely upon radio transmissions. However, this method proved unsatisfactory—especially during bad weather.

Something had to be done, and fast, if the control center was ever going to get off the ground. Every member of our group, including the Navy unit, immediately got busy trying to find a solution to the difficulty.

Sam Savage was the one who finally came up with a workable answer to the dilemma. The Navy would station submarines along the north-south "blind bombing lines," where they would wait for shipping traffic entering or leaving the area. The subs, acting as a relay station between our control center and Luliang, solved the problem. We now had the Japs covered—both coming and going.

February 23, 1945

My controllers and I had been putting in 18-hour days, but the war room was operating efficiently, and we were beginning to get good results.

Colonel Hopson asked me when our organization would be ready to be inspected by the Fourteenth Air Force Headquarters staff. I told him that we should have all the maps up and be ready for visitors in a couple of days.

February 24, 1945

Hopson delivered our morning report to the staff meeting, and returned to the war room about 1030. He was jubilant and said that the people at headquarters were very impressed with what we were trying to accomplish, and for us to be ready the following morning for an informal inspection to be held directly after the regular daily meeting.

The colonel also told me to be prepared to answer a lot of questions about the Radar Control Center and how it worked. I called a conference of all my personnel, including the Navy unit, and alerted them about the upcoming visit. I instructed everyone to make sure that their respective sections were cleaned up and in good shape.

February 25, 1945

I was up early, put on my best uniform, had a quick breakfast, and hurried to the control center. The war room looked very impressive. Our last display panel had just been put into place. It was the status board that showed the number of LAB planes that were operational and the crew strength to man them. For security reasons, I had a draw curtain installed. When it was closed, the drape covered the wall where our plotting map and various boards had been placed.

At 1100, Colonel Hopson and the Fourteenth Air Force staff officers arrived. Among the party was Colonel John G. Armstrong, commanding officer of the 308th. The visitors were conducted through the different sections of the control center and then were seated in the war room where I had set up folding chairs for the occasion.

Hopson introduced me and my assistant controllers and briefly explained the operation of the radar center. Then he turned the meeting over to me. Needless to say, I felt extremely nervous at first—standing alone in front of a large group of generals, colonels, majors, and a few high-ranking naval officers. But, as I began my speech, the anxiety disappeared. I commenced with a hypothetical case, and then proceeded with the steps taken in our systematic process of dealing with a sighting—from the discovery of an enemy target by a reconnaissance plane until the final action by a striker in sinking or damaging the vessel.

When I finished my talk, I was asked numerous questions concerning our tactics, most of which I answered without difficulty. Other inquiries, dealing with the workings of the center, I turned over to Colonel Hopson. All things considered, the session moved along very smoothly.

In less than half an hour, the visitors had acquired a working understanding of the radar center and its possibilities. As the airforce staff left the room, they complimented my men and me. They were impressed with what they had just seen and heard—especially with the results we had already achieved in only a few days of actual operation.

February 26, 1945

Colonel Hopson flew to Chengtu today to attend a group meeting—so it was up to me to deliver the morning report to General Claire Lee Chennault. I parked my jeep in front of Fourteenth Air Force Headquarters and entered the conference room. The place was jam-packed. I took a quick look around and realized that I was the only lieutenant in a room filled with top brass. The chief staff members seated themselves in a row of chairs directly in front of General Chennault's desk, and I was able to get a good look at the man I had read and heard so much about.

The commanding general fully lived up to his description. He had the face of a fighter pilot. It was the color of antique leather and deeply lined from exposure to the wind and sun of an open cockpit. This was the man of legend—"*The* Flying Tiger," and he looked every bit the part. The general's bearing was that of a leader. And, when he called the meeting to order, his voice rang with authority.

The sessions began with the discussion of a few routine matters, and then General Chennault called for the 308th Bomb Group report. After a few anxious moments, I worked up my courage and raised my hand to indicate that I had the data. I had been standing with my back to the wall several yards from where Chennault was seated. He riveted his eyes in my direction and told me to step to the front of the room where I could be seen, and he could hear me better.

To say I was nervous would be an understatement. But, as I picked my way through the crowd of officers, I recognized several faces from the control center inspection. The men gave me reassuring smiles, and one of them whispered to me, "Speak up loud son, the general's hard of hearing!"

When I reached General Chennault's desk, he asked me to introduce myself and state my duties. I gave my name and rank and said I was chief controller of the 308th Bomb Group, Radar Control Detachment. While I stood at attention, reciting the information, the general's eyes seemed to be boring holes right through me.

Chennault said that he had heard a lot about our radar section and the excellent results we were getting from its operation. Since I had put most of the material together myself, I was able to give him many of the details from memory—only referring to the document for data of our squadrons based at Chengtu. As I started to narrate the information concerning our recon and strike missions, the general asked me to speak louder. He had his hand cupped behind his left ear and smiled when I raised the volume of my voice.

General Chennault asked me several questions concerning the particulars of the report. I answered promptly and without hesitation, and the general appeared to be quite pleased with what he had heard.

I was finally dismissed—and very much relieved when I worked my way back to my spot against the wall. It seemed as if I had been standing in front of the general, and the entire Fourteenth Air Force staff, for quite a long time. But, in reality, it had been less than 15 minutes. I did feel a little proud of myself though. In my opinion, I had done a good job in representing the 308th Bomb Group.

[Haynes recently remarked, "Meeting General Claire Lee Chennault for the first time was truly one of the greatest experiences of my life. And, even after many years, the memory of that occasion is still very clear and vivid in my mind."]

CHAPTER 12

The South China Sea: Cauldron of Death

After his return to the United States, Joseph Stilwell continued to criticize General Chennault and the fact that the Fourteenth Air Force was unable to stop the Japanese advance across China. However, Stilwell neglected to mention his failure in providing Chennault with the necessary supplies, gasoline, and bombs needed to halt the enemy juggernaut.

The differences between the two generals were well known in Kunming and at Fourteenth Air Force Headquarters. But the presence of General Wedemeyer proved to be a positive factor on the side of Chennault.

With the help of Chiang Kai-shek and his generals, Wedemeyer was able to put together a viable fighting force and mounted a successful counteroffensive against Japanese troops in the Liuchow and Kweilin area. This action, along with the constant pounding of enemy supply lines by units of the Fourteenth Air Force, finally stopped the Japanese drive about 300 miles from Kunming.

March 11, 1945

Colonel Hopson was deputy group commander of the 308th Bomb Group, which necessitated his frequent trips to group headquarters at Chengtu. This left me with the responsibility of representing the Radar Control Center whenever Hopson was called away.

At 0800, I was once again at the Fourteenth Air Force staff meeting. But this time I was prepared for what lay ahead of me, and I was able to make my report to General Chennault without swallowing my Adam's apple. I answered questions from the general and other officers in a very professional manner. I had the information that they wanted, and everyone seemed pleased with the results of our LAB strikes.

The work of our radar section has been picking up every day. The Japs are trying desperately to evacuate their troops out of Indochina and Thailand, and the tempo of their shipping has increased dramatically. The enemy is using any kind of vessel that will float—even sampans and junks. However, to our disadvantage, the small wooden boats do not show up very clear on radar. They are also shallow craft, and can hug the shoreline in their attempt to escape detection.

Because of the sudden heavy traffic in the South China Sea, Colonel Hopson decided to start sending out armed recons. This tactic would serve a dual purpose. Not only would the LAB planes be flying search patterns but also, upon locating a target, they could make a couple of bombing runs without having to call for assistance. The new strategy eliminated the need for unarmed reconnaissance aircraft, which, although they had the ability to scout a larger area, did not have the attack capability.

If an armed recon sighted a convoy of several vessels, it could call for aid, and we would dispatch the necessary strikers to the target area. Even though each LAB B-24 was capable of handling twelve 500-pound bombs, it proved more expedient to send out aircraft carrying nine bombs. By employing this safety factor, a plane could make three passes over a target, and still return the extra air miles to Luliang.

We were obtaining fantastic results with this new plan of action—but we were also losing a large number of planes and crews. Our losses were small compared to the enemy's. Nevertheless, we were suffering a dangerous attrition of men and aircraft.

I knew many of the squadron members personally—and each time I ordered out a mission, I wondered if any of them would ever make it back. I did not relish the responsibility, and often stayed up until the wee hours of the morning, sweating out their return.

I may have been an "old hand" at trying to survive out there—making bomb runs in the blackness of night and wondering if the next run might be my last. But that was little comfort when the casualty reports started coming in, and I saw the names of friends on the lists.

Our frustrating losses were a deep concern to all of us in the war room. I had discussed this with Colonel Hopson and told him that the responsibility of sending men to their death was beginning to weigh heavily on my conscience. Hopson said that he also felt the burden, but somebody had to do the job if we were ever to bring this war to an end. He also made a point of reminding me that everyone in our section (including himself) had already put in their combat hours. We had all lost friends—

but now it was up to us to make sure that we achieved the maximum results from the available planes and men.

Although I knew the colonel was right in what he said, it was still a difficult decision for me to make. I justified the job by trying to convince myself of the fact that, during my combat tour, someone had been sending me out—and now I had the same unpleasant task. It was a bad business either way.

March 5, 1945

I attended another Fourteenth Air Force staff meeting this morning, and it proceeded smoothly and according to plan. I am accustomed to the routine now and have become quite friendly not only with General Chennault but also with General Alfred Hegenberger (Chennault's deputy commander), General Albert Wedemeyer, and several other staff members.

Sitting in on these sessions was an unheard-of opportunity for a first lieutenant like me. It was a once-in-a-lifetime experience conversing with this group of famous military leaders—no one under the rank of major.

March 7, 1945

Colonel Hopson arrived back at Kunming from Luliang. I stopped in at his office to talk to him about my getting in some flight time. I had not flown a plane since I left Chengkung.

Hopson sent me over to the 308th Group Detachment Center. The operations officer assigned me a pilot, and I was checked out in an L-5 (liaison plane). It was the first single engine aircraft I had flown since my flight training days at Columbus, Mississippi. It certainly felt strange, flitting around the sky like a moth in that two-seater wind-knocker. It was like flying a kite. I really had a lot of fun.

After we landed, the check-pilot asked me what it was like flying an airplane instead of a boxcar. I told him that I would be more than happy to return his courtesy by giving him instructions in piloting a B-24. He declined the invitation.

After I returned to the control center and told Hopson that I had passed my "flying test," he asked me to take one of the naval officers to Luliang for a briefing on a mine-laying mission. I would be using the L-5.

When I landed at Luliang, I parked on the flight line alongside a B-24. Everyone in the vicinity got a big laugh from seeing my plane standing next to that big flying boxcar. I was jokingly asked how it felt to be a puddle-jumper pilot flitting around the "wild blue yonder."

I was back at Kunming at 1600, and headed directly to the control center. When I arrived at the war room, I was greeted with good news.

The orders promoting me to captain had finally come through. Forest McClure also received his captaincy on the same dispatch. Both of us were congratulated by the men in our section, but we did not have a chance to do much celebrating. A recon had just reported some sightings, and everyone went to work. It was 0200 the next morning when I finally hit the sack. I was completely exhausted.

March 8, 1945

Since I was now doing very little flying, the feeling of being cooped up was beginning to bother me. Despite the critical work we were doing, and the significant results achieved, it was the same routine day in and day out. I was the only man from my old gang working here. I did not see any of my buddies anymore. They were scattered throughout the squadrons in the Chengtu area. Most of my friends had already finished their combat tours and would be going home soon—unless they were stuck with further assignments like myself.

I received a message from Milt Wind this afternoon. He had heard about my promotion and sent his congratulations. He also said that Mac McClure had been transferred to the 308th Headquarters at Chengtu. Mac was now group navigator and would stop by and see me the next time a group meeting was held at Kunming.

Jim Miracle was the only officer of our original crew who had not yet made captain, or was picked for a higher position in the 308th organization. Jim was certainly good enough to at least be squadron bombardier. However, by the time he finished his combat tour, there were no openings available. Otherwise, I am sure he would have been promoted.

March 11, 1945

Luverne Freeman will be going home shortly. Captain William R. Fulk is his replacement, and I began breaking him in immediately. It was a good day to show him our operation. We were very busy. Lots of sightings and plenty of action. It gave Fulk a good idea of what was going on and the proper procedures to take under all kinds of circumstances.

March 13, 1945

Late this evening, our control center was visited by three lieutenant colonels from air force headquarters. They arrived at an opportune time. Several sightings had been reported, as well as information being fed into the war room by the naval section. The building was a hubbub of activity. The visitors stayed around for nearly three hours watching us work. They finally left at 2300—very impressed with what they had seen.

About 0300, we had an earth-shaking thunderstorm. I was busy in the control center at the time, and the crashes of thunder sounded exactly like exploding bombs. From force of habit, I made a dash for the exit to hunt for a slit trench to dive into. I asked the guard at the door if we were having an air raid and how come we had not been alerted. He gave me a strange look and calmed me down by saying it was only a storm. I told him that I guess I was getting nervous in the service, but from where I was sitting, it sure as hell sounded like bombs going off.

All of our electrical energy was supplied by gasoline generators. During the thunderstorm, the high winds knocked down an electrical pole, and the power lines fell into a large mud puddle near the entrance to the enlisted personnel quarters. One of the men accidentally stepped on the submerged line and was electrocuted. By the time I reached the scene, the generator had been turned off—but it was too late. It never ceases to amaze me how a person can be killed anywhere in a theater of war without ever coming close to the combat zone. This was a freakish way to die—and very depressing for all of us. I could not help remembering the sergeant who drowned at the rest camp a short time ago.

March 16, 1945

Because of bad weather along the coastal areas and in the South China Sea, there has been very little action. I had the day off, so I went with a couple of other officers into Kunming for dinner. We had just started back to the base when we heard the scream of sirens going off and noticed a large fire at the north end of the field. We raced to the site and learned that a C-47 had crashed into a small village near the end of the runway—killing 32 villagers and everyone aboard the plane. It was a tragic accident, but I had come to the conclusion long ago that there is no way to escape the specter of death in China. It hovers over our heads like a hungry vulture.

March 19, 1945

I had a long talk with Colonel Hopson this morning. He remarked that our efforts and results to date had far exceeded his expectations. He was very pleased with the progress and how the operation of the control center was being managed. I could not help feeling elated. Hopson was not one to hand out compliments on a wholesale basis.

After going off duty early in the evening, one of the boys suggested driving into Kunming for dinner. So we borrowed a jeep belonging to the center and drove into town.

I parked in front of the restaurant and told the doorman to keep an eye on our vehicle. But, when we were ready to head back to the base, the jeep was missing. I was frantic, and asked the doorman what happened. He pointed to a couple of MPs farther down the street. We ran and caught up with them, and asked what was going on. The police told me that a new order had been put into effect a few days ago. The directive prohibited the parking of military vehicles on public streets after dark. My jeep had been impounded, and I would have to go to the provost marshall's office to get it released.

I phoned the Radar Control Center and told them what had happened. Within a short time, a man from our unit pulled up in a jeep, and we took off to rescue my vehicle. Upon reaching the provo's office, I learned that the marshall would not be available until the next morning—and the jeep could not be released without his authorization. After a great deal of arguing—which accomplished nothing except raising my blood pressure—we returned to the control center. I took a short nap and then went back to the war room about midnight.

I now had the unpleasant job of telling Colonel Hopson my story of the missing vehicle. He was not exactly pleased with the news. But that was not the worst part—Hopson was required to report "in person" to the provost marshall in order to get the damn jeep released.

As a result of my screwup, the colonel informed me that it might do me good to walk for a while—unless I needed transportation for official business. I was grounded! Never a dull moment in this man's war!

March 20, 1945

I had a big surprise this morning. Major Harry Marshall showed up at the Radar Control Center, and I gave him a thorough tour of the building. We spent considerable time in the war room. I showed Marshall our routine, and how we handled the sightings—a few of which were coming in while we talked.

I also told Harry that I had been representing the 308th Bomb Group at Fourteenth Air Force staff meetings and giving my reports directly to General Chennault. Marshall was impressed and gave me the same old blarney that I was going places in the service.

The major stayed overnight, and we caught up with all the latest news from home. We both had some good laughs and toasted ourselves several times on our good fortune to still be in the land of the living.

March 23, 1945

Mac McClure flew in this afternoon from Chengtu. He will be going home next month. That will leave Milt Wind and me as the only members of our original crew still cooling our heels in China. I could not help wondering how much longer it would be before we received our orders to return to the States.

However, I knew that the work being done at the control center—cutting the enemy's supply line to Japan—was critical to the war effort. The Japanese were losing a staggering number of ships, and it was bound to have an effect sooner or later.

CHAPTER 13

Japan's Last Hurrah in China

The Japanese attempted to consolidate their positions in central and southern China—around major cities and along the railroad to Hanoi. Small craft and every sampan the enemy could find were used in a desperate endeavor to move men and equipment from Indochina to ports along the South China coast. The troops were to be transported by rail to the fighting fronts.

General Chennault's Fourteenth Air Force concentrated its efforts on Japanese targets along the rail lines. At both high and low altitudes, Chennault's fighters and bombers attacked like a swarm of locusts—inflicting heavy losses on enemy troops and disrupting communications. Japan's decimated war machine slowly began grinding to a halt.

By the end of April 1945, the 308th Bomb Group's armed strikers were returning to base without sighting any large merchant vessels. The enemy's supply line—carrying oil and other vital war materials to Japan—had been cut. The LAB missions were now mainly devoted to reconnaissance flights and to aiding the U.S. Navy in locating Japanese warships.

April 2, 1945

I received my first pay today as a captain. I am now drawing $478 per month. Out of this amount, I have to put out approximately $50 for meals, GI Insurance, and other incidentals. Most of the rest will go home to my wife. There is no place to spend money over here—except gambling and a few restaurants in town.

April 6, 1945

I had a talk with Colonel Hopson this morning. Among other things, we discussed my prospects of going home. To my surprise, Hopson agreed to put my name in for orders. Unless the unexpected happens, I should be back in the States sometime in June.

April 16, 1945

The map in our war room is now completely marked up by grease pencil, indicating sinkings, probable sinkings, and damaged vessels. Multicolored pins—showing the location of these ships—are scattered along the Indochina coast, around Hainan Island, and the Strait of Formosa. Information from naval intelligence concerning vessels sunk by U.S. Navy submarines is also marked on the chart.

The map reveals a very impressive picture of the cooperative efforts of the Fourteenth Air Force and the Navy during the few weeks we have been in operation. Japanese shipping had slowed to a crawl. The enemy had lost so much of their maritime and naval fleet, that they had practically nothing left that could float.

I have been slaving over a report describing the workings of the Radar Control Center and its achievements. The information was requested by General Chennault for the U.S. Army Air Force Headquarters in Washington, D.C. And since this data would probably wind up on General "Hap" Arnold's desk, both Colonel Hopson and I are very critical of its contents. I hope to have the final draft ready for the colonel's approval sometime today.

April 18, 1945

I was notified that my going home orders should be coming through next month. The news came as a big relief to me. I heard from Milt Wind, and he should be leaving about the same time. It would be great if we could go together. However, along with these happy thoughts came the somber realization that many of the boys from our Langley Field gang would not be going home—ever!

Of the approximately 45 LAB B-24s that made up the original Hopson Project, most had either been lost in action or so badly damaged that they were used for spare parts.

Naval intelligence had learned from various sources that the Japanese considered themselves as good as dead if they entered the Strait of Formosa or the South China Sea. Few of them ever returned from these voyages.

We were also paying a price, but nowhere near what the Japs were suffering. There was no doubt that we were winning the war with Japan. Anyone looking at the map on the wall in our war room could see that.

The daily report I prepared for the Fourteenth Air Force staff meeting not only detailed the results of our LAB strikers but also gave accounts of the 308th Bomb Group missions flown from Chengtu. The vivid description and photographs clearly showed the tremendous destruction and havoc our planes were creating on railroads and other important land targets. We were annihilating the Japanese forces on both land and sea.

April 19, 1945

I did not have a chance to do any flying so far this month, and was beginning to sweat out the required four hours to receive my flight pay.

The problem was solved, however, when Milt Wind flew in from Chengtu. His Stateside orders had come through early, and he asked if I could fly with him to Calcutta and bring the plane back to China. In this way, he could get to Calcutta, and I would get in my flight time.

Colonel Hopson gave me permission to make the trip. Milt and I took off from Kunming about noon and headed over the Hump to Chabua. The weather was great for a change. And, flying at 18,000 feet, with unlimited visibility, I could see forever. I looked down at the winding ribbon of the Burma Road and wondered how many lives had been lost in its construction. I never could forget that remarkable highway or the courageous men who built it.

We landed at Chabua at 1400, and made arrangements to stay overnight. Several of the Langley Field boys were there, including James Otis. We threw a party to celebrate Wind's "release." It was a great bull session, and with plenty of beer. It reminded me of the old days back at Langley.

April 20, 1945

We were airborne at 0800, and landed at Calcutta two hours later. Milt and I spent most of the day running around trying to find lodging. The city was jam-packed with servicemen trying to get home. We were finally billeted about five miles from town at the estate of the Maharajah of Burdan. We had a fabulous meal and plenty of mixed drinks. I even tasted ice cream for the second time in two months.

April 22, 1945

I was up at 0600, showered, shaved, and bid Milt farewell. I wished him a safe trip home. He promised to call my wife when he got back to the States, and let her know that I would be seeing her shortly. I left for the airfield—leaving Wind standing forlornly alone in the room.

It was a sad parting. We had been through a lot together, and it was not easy to hide our feelings from each other. But, I was alone now too—the last member of our crew still stationed in China.

I took off from Calcutta at 0900, and since I had to pick up a planeload of supplies at Chabua, I decided to stay there the rest of the day and spend the night.

I had no sooner landed and reported in, than I ran into James Otis again. We made the rounds of the various Officer's Clubs surrounding the field, and before the evening was over, I had to pour him into his bunk. I always could drink Otis under the table.

April 23, 1945

I was off the ground early but ran into very rough weather crossing the Hump. I climbed to 22,000 feet before getting above the high winds and turbulence. After not having flown a B-24 in quite some time, I had forgotten how difficult it was to wrestle with one of these babies in rough weather. By the time I landed the ship at Kunming, I was worn to a frazzle. The soft life I had been leading finally caught up with me.

However, on the positive side of the ledger, I had picked up 13 hours of flight time. I now had a shade over 395 hours and had completed 41 missions.

April 25, 1945

It has taken me a couple of days to get caught up on my work at the control center. Colonel Hopson was off again to Chengtu, and I worked from midnight until eight this morning to get our daily report ready to submit to the Fourteenth Air Force staff meeting.

General Chennault asked me how much action we had been having during the past few days. I told him very little. The general smiled and said that maybe the Japs were running out of ships for us to sink. That comment brought laughter from everyone assembled in the room—including me.

April 28, 1945

I had become quite friendly with one of the staff officers at headquarters, and he visited me quite often at the control center. Today he showed up with a photograph of General Chennault that had been personally autographed to me. I was very much surprised—and certainly did not expect it.

[Elmer Haynes stated: "I prize this picture as a true treasure. General Chennault was a great leader of men, and I have always considered it a privilege to have served under him. It was an honor for me to meet the general face-to-face on numerous occasions, and for him to have listened to my reports with avid interest—even though, the first couple of times, I was shaking in my boots."]

April 29, 1945

I stopped by the censor's office to find out about the procedure I had to follow in order to send my photographs and diary home. I was told that I could send the pictures, but my diary would be impounded and returned to me after the war was over.

The censor shoved the photos into a large manila envelope, sealed it with official tape, and told me that he would mail the packet within a few weeks. I explained to the fellow how much work I had put in the diary and how I would hate to lose the material. The censor was sympathetic and said he understood my feelings. He calmed my fears by insisting that my journal would be treated the same as all classified documents, and assured me that it would be safe.

After my diary was confiscated, I began a new one—only this time I stuck to irrelevant topics. The classified information, I would have to keep in my head.

Colonel Hightower Smith was waiting for me when I returned from the censor's office. He was leaving for the States in a few hours and had come down to say goodbye. We went over to my quarters and had a can of beer to celebrate the occasion. The conversation drifted to our old gang, and we both damned the war for the friends it had cost. I told Smith that I was still receiving letters from Pierpont's sister and Tommy's wife, and I was at a loss as to how to answer them. We both had sad looks on our faces, and asked the same question, "What do you say to them?" They were praying for any ray of hope—and we had none to offer.

I drove Smith to the airfield. We shook hands as he jumped from the jeep. Then he slapped me on the back and told me I had done one hell of a job—just as he and Harry Marshall knew I would. We were both choked up when he climbed up through the bomb bay of the B-24 and squeezed into the pilot's seat. Hightower waved to me as he taxied to the runway. I waited until he was airborne before turning my jeep around and heading back to the radar center. I do not know whether the windshield of my vehicle was dirty or not—but I seemed to have a hard time seeing through it for a few moments. Colonel Hightower Smith had always been a good friend and buddy to me. That was the last time I ever saw him.

Harry Marshall and I were now the only members of the old gang left. I was beginning to feel more and more alone. It seemed as if all I had been doing for the past couple of months was saying goodbye to friends. It was taking a lot of the spirit out of me.

May 8, 1945

Some amazing news came through today. Lieutenant George Turpyn and his crew had been rescued after bailing out over southwest China on the morning of February 4.

Turpyn's interrogation report revealed a fascinating account of the different factions and warlords that Chiang Kai-shek had to deal with during China's war with Japan.

George Turpyn was returning from a routine reconnaissance mission over Gulf of Tonkin when, about 0200, he began to pick up ice. George tried to establish radio contact with Chengkung, but without success.

His No. 1 and No. 3 engines ran away and had to be feathered—and No. 4 was only putting out half power. There was no choice but to bail out and abandon the plane.

However, without realizing it, Turpyn had been blown off course. He was about 55 miles west of Chaotung—halfway between Chungking and Kunming. Five of the first seven crew members to jump landed near the headquarters of a friendly guerrilla leader, Lu Kai Fan, on the east bank of the Yangtze River. The other two men dropped on the west bank, and were captured by a rival chieftain and held for ransom. Lu Kai Fan negotiated a release for the prisoners in exchange for two German type pistols.

Because of a severe snowstorm, the airmen stayed at the guerrilla camp. Finally, on February 14, accompanied by a detachment of Lu Kai Fan's soldiers, the seven flyers set out for Chaotung, where they were rescued a week later.

Lieutenant Turpyn and the remaining four members of his crew were the last people to jump from the aircraft. However, they parachuted deep into Lolo country, west of the Yangtze. This area was unfriendly territory, and the aviators were captured by tribesmen armed with spears and ancient rifles.

Under the pretext of examining their prisoners' .45s, the natives confiscated the weapons and then proceeded to take any other valuables that they could find on the crew—watches, rings, money, and survival packs.

Other members of the tribe soon arrived and also wanted "souvenirs." The airmen were quickly stripped down to their underwear and shoes. The weather was very cold and the aviators shivered as they were led to the native village. A sympathetic tribal chief had some of the clothing returned to the captives so that they would not freeze to death before ransom negotiations had been completed.

Lieutenant Turpyn and his men were held by the natives for a week before being released to a friendly guerrilla leader.

May 9, 1945

VE-day in Europe. The entire base went crazy. Everyone was jumping around, shouting, and slapping one another on the back.

We opened our hostel's bar in the afternoon and broke out the booze that had been saved for a special occasion. Some of the boys from the Fourteenth Air Force Headquarters joined our personnel in the celebration. Sam Savage and some of his officers showed up as well. It was a great party and a welcome break from the monotony.

May 11, 1945

The big day finally arrived—my going home orders came through. The directive also included Forest McClure. We would be leaving together.

I had plenty of warning concerning the probable date of my departure, and was all packed and ready to go. McClure was caught by surprise, but he had everything bundled up in short order.

The only thing I had to do now was say goodbye to the control center personnel and the Navy boys. It was the moment I had been waiting for—but, now that it arrived, I began to dread this goodbye more than all the others.

I stopped in at Colonel Hopson's office first. I was very humble as I thanked him for the opportunity he had given me and the trust he had placed in my ability. Hopson walked over to his desk, picked up a large envelope, and handed it to me. He said that the contents would reveal how he felt about my work, and our relationship. It was a personal commendation to put in my 201 (service record) file for any future references that I might need.

I was completely surprised by this gesture on his part, and it showed as I told the colonel how much I enjoyed our association. Hopson was not a man known for outward shows of emotion, but I could tell that he was just as flustered as I was. However, he composed himself quickly, and wished me a safe and speedy journey home. I had a big lump in my throat when I left the colonel's office—and I believe that he did too.

I continued my tour through the control center, saying my last goodbyes to our group's personnel, and then across the hall to the naval section where I said my farewells to Savage and his men.

My last stop was the war room to take one more look at the plotting map, with all its colored pins and notations. I said a silent prayer for the gallant men who gave their lives to destroy the ships that the pins represented. I had tears in my eyes when I finally turned my back and walked out the door for the last time.

When I returned to my quarters, I opened the envelope from Colonel Hopson. The commendation said it all. It stated exactly what the 308th Bomb Group had been able to accomplish and depicted a true picture of the unit's contribution to our war effort against the Japanese in the CBI theater.

[Haynes also said: "I have always considered my work in helping to set up and operate the Radar Control Center to be one of the greatest achievements of my life. The 308th sunk more Japanese shipping than any other air outfit during World War II. This successful effort weakened Japan's military position and contributed to the early end of the war. It was truly an honor and a learning experience to have had the benefit of Colonel Hopson's keen tactical talent and knowledge of radar-equipped B-24 aircraft. I still consider Colonel Hopson and General Claire Chennault as the two finest officers I ever had the pleasure to serve under. And to be able to call them by that noblest of titles—friends!"]

CHAPTER 14

Homeward Bound and the Death of Harry Marshall

May 12, 1945

Forest McClure and I drove out to the Kunming airfield and hopped on a B-24 for our last trip over the Hump. It seemed strange to be riding as a passenger. It was a beautiful day in more ways than one, and I was able to really enjoy the scenery for a change.

We landed at Chabua late in the afternoon and arranged for quarters to spend the night. Naturally, I had to say goodbye to my old buddies, and we partied it up until late night. For some reason, I felt that my trip back to the States was too good to be true. I was afraid that I would awake in the morning and discover it was all a dream. But, God! It was great to be alive and heading home. However, much to my sorrow, many of my friends would never be making the trip.

May 14, 1945

About noon, McClure and I climbed aboard another Liberator and arrived at Calcutta in record time. The city was a madhouse. Now that the war was over in Europe, thousands of men were trying to find passage home. After standing in line at the billeting office, for what seemed hours, we were finally assigned quarters at a maharajah's estate on the south side of Calcutta. The accommodations were first class. Forest and I had an entire bungalow to ourselves. It was modern, with all the newest conveniences—even a tiled bathroom. Now, all we had to do was wait for transportation to the States—and I mean *wait*.

May 20, 1945

Enjoying the sights of Calcutta was interesting, but the novelty began to wear off fast. Everyone was desperately hunting for some way to get out of here. I happened to run into a Fourteenth Air Force colonel whom I recognized from General Chennault's daily staff meetings. He commanded the night-fighters and had been here a week before I arrived. The colonel had heard of a method that some airmen were using to fly home, and we decided to check it out. We took a taxi to a nearby airfield where hundreds of war-weary aircraft had been parked. We were given permission to take any plane we wanted—if we were willing to chance a trip of thousands of miles in one of these wrecks.

But, after inspecting a couple of hundred crates, I finally shook my head in disgust. I told the colonel, "After looking at all these 'used cars,' I think I can wait a little longer to get home. I've risked my neck too often to die in one of these death wagons." The colonel agreed.

The day after we toured the "junkyard," I learned that one of these planes had crashed in North Africa, killing the five men aboard who were trying to get back to the States.

May 25, 1945

The Officer's Club at Calcutta was very plush, and I spent quite a bit of time hanging around the place. The war seemed very far away in the opulent surroundings. But, this evening, while hanging around the bar, the terror was brought home to me with a vengeance.

I recognized one of the Langley boys of the 425th Squadron. He had just landed in Calcutta and was glad to run into me. He thought possibly that we might go home together. In the course of our conversation, he happened to mention that Major Harry Marshall had been killed soon after I left Kunming. He immediately saw, from the expression on my face, that I had not heard the news and apologized for breaking it to me that way. I almost choked on my drink but finally caught my breath and asked what the hell had happened.

According to the story, Marshall was piloting a bombing mission against several railway bridges in the Singtai area—the main rail line running south from Peking to Indochina. He was carrying a new type of bomb called the Azon. It was an experimental radio-guided bomb that was designed specifically for use against bridge targets. It could be controlled by the bombardier to strike pilings under the bridge, instead of exploding on the top surface.

Major Marshall's target was approximately 750 miles northeast of Chengtu. He picked up two P-51 escort fighters at Sian. It was about noon when Harry dropped his bombs and then decided to take his B-24 and the P-51s on a low-level strafing attack against nearby railroad yards.

But the Japs were not asleep at the switch. Machine guns on the top of several boxcars put up a stubborn defense, and Marshall's plane was pitted with many bullet holes. This arrogant display of force by the enemy only made Harry more determined than ever to crush any vestige of Japanese resistance.

On his third pass over the yards, Marshall turned around to look through the open bomb bay doors. He remarked to the copilot, "Those damned Japs can't shoot worth a. . . . " Those were the last words out of his mouth. A bullet, shooting up from the open bomb bay, struck Harry under the chin, plowed through his brain, and smashed against the inner lining of his flak helmet. Marshall never knew what hit him.

The copilot flew the plane to the fighter base at Sian, so that the bombardier, who was also wounded on the last pass, could receive medical attention. However, the ironic part of the story was that Harry was due to receive his Stateside orders any day. And, worse yet, he did not have to fly the mission. Harry just wanted to see how the Azon bomb worked. He did make a few direct hits, knocked out some bridges, and accomplished his mission—but what a way to die. Marshall had flown night-bombing sorties in the South China Sea, survived bailing out over the Hump and being chased by headhunters. Now to have his life snuffed out by one lousy Jap bullet—it just was not fair.

The fellow from the 425th said that he did not know how close Harry Marshall and I had been and only wished that somebody else had broken the news to me. I told him that I appreciated the information. Then we shook hands and he left.

I ordered another drink and sat at the bar alone with my thoughts. What a hell of a war! I began to wonder why I was still alive. Harry's death sure took the thrill out of returning to the States. In fact, I even felt guilty that I would soon be going home—while so many others would not.

May 30, 1945

McClure and I had been booked on a Coast Guard troop transport, the *U.S.S. General Greeley*. We were all set to sail from Calcutta when, at the last moment, Forest came down with a sudden attack of malaria and was hospitalized. I visited him just before we shoved off. He was a heart-broken man. I hated to leave him behind but did not have much of a choice.

The voyage got off to a great start. We ran aground on a mudbank in the Hooghly River on our way to the Bay of Bengal. After sitting for 12 hours in the sweltering India heat, the ship finally floated free at high tide.

I was informed that this was the *Greeley*'s shakedown cruise. Breakdowns kept occurring at frequent intervals—and more than once we were sitting ducks for Jap submarines reported in the vicinity. Being an airman, I was not prepared for a slow crawl across the ocean. I remember pacing up and down the transport's deck like a crazy man. I would never have made a sailor. A ship was too confining, too slow, and too monotonous. And the prospect of looking at nothing but water day after day was definitely not for me. I could hardly wait to get my feet on dry land again.

June 22, 1945

After three weeks at sea, we finally docked at Newport News, Virginia. I stepped off the ship only 12 miles from the spot where I had taken off on that fateful day nearly a year ago. It seemed like I had been gone a lifetime—and, in a sense, for many of us it was.

Epilogue

During its three years of operation, General Claire Chennault's Fourteenth Air Force destroyed approximately 2,600 Japanese aircraft, with another 1,500 listed as probables. "Flying Tiger" losses were amazingly low—only about 500 planes.

Beside 2,230,000 tons of enemy merchant ships and naval vessels destroyed, the combined efforts of the Fourteenth Air Force bombers and fighters also sunk or damaged 13,000 sampans, junks, and river boats, and killed approximately 67,000 Japanese troops. More than half of all Japanese opposition in China was generated by the "Flying Tigers."

In his book, *Way of a Fighter*, General Chennault praised the 308th Bomb Group with the following remarks:

> The 308th was unique among heavy bomb groups. It was entirely self-supporting across the Hump, and operated from tactical bases from 500 to 900 miles from its supply bases.
>
> The Liberators did many things their designers never intended. They skip-bombed ships from mast height, strafed at low-level, ferreted out enemy radar stations, mined rivers and harbors, flew transport missions, and on one occasion functioned as fighters.
>
> After the war, when Army Air Force Headquarters in Washington tallied the bombing accuracy of every heavy bomb group in action, I was astonished to find that the 308th led them all.

Elmer E. "Bud" Haynes was discharged from the U.S. Army Air Force on August 8, 1945, at Camp Beale, California, and later the same year, he and his wife moved from the West Coast to St. Louis, Missouri.

Haynes joined the Missouri Air National Guard at Lambert Field, where he served as pilot and Education and Information Officer with the 131st Aircraft Control Squadron. Bud was also a licensed commercial pilot (multi-engine rated) and flew chartered passenger flights throughout the United States.

In the spring of 1952, Elmer Haynes and his family relocated in Roanoke, Virginia. Bud served in the U.S. Air Force Reserve for five years, and then flew for a company based at Hopewell Field, Virginia.

Haynes retired in 1982 and is currently enjoying his "golden years" in Roanoke playing golf. He still has that touch of "luck" too. Bud recently made his first hole-in-one.

Appendix I: Air Bases and Targets, with Approximate Headings and Distances

	Heading	Miles
Chabua (India Base) over Hump to Kunming (China base 14th AF Headquarters)	105°	500
Chabua (India Base) to Myitkynia (Burma Hump Base)	130°	150
Myitkynia (Burma Hump Base) to Yunnanyi (China Hump Base)	80°	185
Yunnanyi (China Hump Base) to Kunming (China Base 14th AF)	100°	165
Kunming (14th AF Base) to ChengKung (375th & 374th Squadrons Base)	175°	20
Kunming (14th AF Base) to Luliang (373rd Squadron Base)	90°	60
Kunming (14th AF Base & 425 Squadron Base) to Myitkynia (Hump)	280°	350
Kunming to Chihkaing (fighter base)	70°	435
Kunming to Liuchow (Forward Base LAB B-24's)	100°	450
Kunming to Kweilin (Forward Base Fighters & B-24's)	88°	470
Kunming to Suichwan (Forward Base LAB B-24's)	85°	740
Kunming to Canton (Target area White Cloud and Tien Ho)	102°	680
Kunming to Philippines (North End)	112°	1250
Kunming to Ft. Bayard (Jap Field & Supply Base target area)	120°	550
Kunming to Samah Bay (Jap naval base & field target area), Hainan	140°	650
Kunming to Hong Kong (Kowloon Docks target area)	105°	770

Kunming to Changsha (Jap railroad yards & supply area target)	73°	725
Kunming to Hankow-Wuhan (Jap railroad yards, ferry supply target)	63°	850
Kunming to Cam Ranh Bay (Harbor shipping supply, Indochina)	160°	1125
Kunming to Ondal (U.S.A.F. Base, India)	260°	950
Kunming to Calcutta (U.S. & British Base, India)	255°	925
Kunming to Chengtu (Hdqrs 308th Bombardment Group & 20th AF B-29's)	10°	410
Kunming to Chengtu (375th, 374th and 425th Squadrons)	10°	410
ChengKung (374th & 375th Sq. Base) to Luliang (373rd Sq. Base)	45°	70
Liuchow (B-24 forward base) to Kweilin (B-24 & Fighter Base)	35°	70
Liuchow (B-24 Base) to Pukow-Nanking (Railroad yards & supply)	48°	850
Liuchow (B-24 Base) to Shanghai (Jap harbor shipping & supply)	58°	925
Liuchow (B-24 Base) to Takao Harbor, Formosa	102°	675
Liuchow (B-24 Base) to South China Sea coastal area	160°	250
Liuchow (B-24 Base) to Suichwan (B-24 Forward Base)	65°	350
Kweilin (B-24 & Fighter Base) to Suichwan (B-24 Forward Base)	75°	275
Liuchow (B-24 Base) to Hong Kong (Jap supply, harbor, docks)	112°	325
Suichwan (B-24 Forward Base) to Hong Kong coastal area	185°	275
Kunming (14th AF Base) to coastal area of Tonking Gulf	130°	415

Appendix II: Missions Logged by Elmer E. Haynes

July 27, 1944	Chabua, India to ChengKung, China (Hump)	525 miles
August 23, 1944	Liuchow from ChengKung	435 miles
August 25, 1944	Liuchow to Hong Kong (Kowloon docks)	325 miles
August 29, 1944	Liuchow to Shanghai (Mining)	925 miles
August 31, 1944	Liuchow to Takao, Formosa (Mining)	675 miles
September 2, 1944	Kweilin to Liuchow (Return)	70 miles
September 3, 1944	Liuchow to PuKow-Nanking (Railroad)	850 miles
September 6, 1944	Liuchow to sea (sea sweep)	850 miles
September 7, 1944	Liuchow to sea (sea sweep)	850 miles
September 10, 1944	Liuchow to sea (sea sweep)	850 miles
September 11, 1944	Liuchow to sea (sea sweep)	850 miles
September 14, 1944	Liuchow to Kunming	450 miles
September 17, 1944	Kunming to Changsha (Day Bombing)	725 miles
September 22, 1944	Kunming to Hankow (Day Bombing)	850 miles
September 25, 1944	ChengKung to Liuchow	435 miles
September 25, 1944	Liuchow to PuKow-Nanking (Railroad)	850 miles
September 26, 1944	Liuchow to ChengKung (Return)	435 miles
September 30, 1944	Kunming to Canton (Tein Ho Airfield)	680 miles
October 15, 1944	Kunming to Canton (White Cloud Airfield)	680 miles
October 17, 1944	ChengKung to Chabua, India (Hump)	525 miles
October 17, 1944	Chabua to ChengKung (Hump)	525 miles
October 20, 1944	ChengKung to Chabua (Hump)	525 miles
October 21, 1944	Chabua to Yunnanyi (Hump Emergency Landing)	330 miles
October 23, 1944	Yunnanyi to ChengKung (Hump)	170 miles
October 24, 1944	ChengKung to Liuchow	435 miles
October 26, 1944	Liuchow to sea (Striker)	435 miles

October 26, 1944	Return to ChengKung (Crash Landing)	435 miles
October 29, 1944	ChengKung to Liuchow and return	435 miles
October 30, 1944	ChengKung to Liuchow	435 miles
October 31, 1944	Liuchow to sea (Recon Mission)	435 miles
November 6, 1944	Liuchow to ChengKung (Evacuation)	435 miles
November 10, 1944	ChengKung to sea (Recon Mission)	435 miles
November 13, 1944	ChengKung to sea (Recon Mission)	Abort
November 17, 1944	ChengKung to sea (Philippines Recon)	435 miles
November 20, 1944	ChengKung to sea (Fort Bayard)	550 miles
November 24, 1944	ChengKung to sea (Striker)	Abort
November 26, 1944	ChengKung to Samah Bay, Hainan Island	650 miles
December 3, 1944	ChengKung to Suichwan	775 miles
December 7, 1944	Suichwan to sea (Striker)	775 miles
December 22, 1944	Suichwan to ChengKung	775 miles
December 27, 1944	ChengKung to sea (Recon Mission)	775 miles
December 29, 1944	ChengKung to sea (Recon Mission)	775 miles
January 2, 1945	ChengKung to sea (Recon Mission)	775 miles
January 3, 1945	ChengKung to sea (Recon Mission)	775 miles
January 18, 1945	ChengKung to Hong Kong (Kowloon Docks)	770 miles
January 19, 1945	Luliang to ChengKung	70 miles
January 22, 1945	ChengKung to sea (Recon Mission)	775 miles
January 24, 1945	ChengKung to Chabua & Return (Hump)	525 miles
January 25, 1945	ChengKung to sea (Recon Mission)	775 miles
January 27, 1945	ChengKung to Ondal, India (Hump)	950 miles
January 29, 1945	Ondal, India to ChengKung (Hump)	950 miles
April 19, 1945	Kunming to Chabua, then to Calcutta	925 miles
April 22, 1945	Calcutta to Chabua, then to Kunming	925 miles

Appendix III: Letters of Commendation

LETTER OF COMMENDATION TO ELMER E. HAYNES FROM LIEUTENANT COLONEL WILLIAM D. HOPSON

308TH BOMBARDMENT GROUP DETACHMENT NO. I
Office of the Commanding Officer
A.P.O. 627, c/o Postmaster
New York City, New York

11 May 1945

SUBJECT: Commendation.

TO : Captain Elmer E. Haynes, 0-803618.

1. The services you performed between 13 February and 13 April 1945 in assisting in the establishment and operation of the 308th Bomb Group Control Center at Kunming and gratifying to me and must be a source of considerable personal satisfaction to yourself.

2. To the system which you helped perfect and untiringly operated can be attributed, in a large measure, the unusual success during this period of our anti-shipping forces which resulted in the sinking and damaging of forty-five (45) Japanese Merchant and Naval ships.

3. To have performed these services in addition to a complete tour of combat duty is highly commendable and I want to express to you my personal appreciation.

/s/ WILLIAM D. HOPSON
Lt. Col., Air Corps,
Commanding

PROCLAMATION FROM COLONEL JOHN G. ARMSTRONG, COMMANDING OFFICER, 308TH BOMB GROUP

PROCLAMATION

Saturday 5th May 1945 marks the second anniversary of the first combat mission of the 308th Bombardment Group. Our versatility as a heavy bombardment group has been proven by day and night attacks, high medium and low altitude bombing, mine laying and radar bombing. These sorties were against a variety of targets, most of which were heavily defended, in all kinds of weather and over poorly charted terrain. Units of this group have operated from behind enemy lines. Our men have become acclimated to enemy air raids and bombings, paucity of supplies and long periods of adverse weather conditions.

In these two years, during which time the group has never exceeded 90% of its authorized strength, we have flown 4039 combat sorties totalling 34,975 hours, flown 6486 ferrying sorties totalling 21,603 hours, shot down 222 enemy planes confirmed, dropped 4090 tons of bombs, layed 433 tons of mines, expended 481,000 rounds of ammunition, hauled 9827 tons of freight and supplies, and actually sank 185 enemy vessels totalling 678,000 tons. We lost 116 A/C and 53 crews. 164 men have been killed, 70 wounded, 312 are missing. A great many more have bailed out, but walked back safely.

This is only part of the story. No attempt is made here to describe the devotion to duty of the officers and men of this group or the heroism of the flyers whose deeds lie behind these statistics. In paying tribute to those men who have given their lives in order that the success we have achieved could be attained, we should resolve, as we enter our third year of tactical operations to devote our energies and resources to one common goal, that of speeding in every way possible the final defeat of the enemy.

JOHN G. ARMSTRONG
Colonel, Air Corps
Commanding

Source: Courtesy Simpson Historical Center, Maxwell Air Force Base, Alabama. This document is declassified in accordance with DOD DIR. 5200.30.

COMMENDATION FROM GENERAL C. L. CHENNAULT TO ALL UNITS OF THE FOURTEENTH AIR FORCE

HEADQUARTERS FOURTEENTH AIR FORCE
A. P. O. 627, c/o Postmaster
New York City, New York

4 November 1944

SUBJECT: Commendation

TO : Commanding Officer, 308th Bombardment Group, APO 627.

1. The success of the sea search missions flown by the 308th Bombardment Group (H) in cooperation with the naval activities in the Philippine area have elicited the following radio message of praise from Admiral Nimitz, commander in chief of naval operations in the Pacific (reparaphrased):

"Admiral Halsey, Commander of the Third Fleet, says: 'Please express my appreciation to Chennault for cooperative efforts of Fourteenth Air Force searchers and the value of their information.' At same time, I wish to extend my sincere thanks for outstanding cooperation by your forces on this as well as other occasions that have played important roles toward Japan's final defeat."

2. This sincere tribute from two great commanders of a brother service speaks for itself.

3. I desire to add my commendation to the officers and men of your organization for their wholehearted efforts and the success they have achieved in this assignment.

/s/ C. L. CHENNAULT
Major General, U.S.A.
Commanding

Source: Courtesy Simpson Historical Center, Maxwell Air Force Base, Alabama. This document is declassified in accordance with DOD DIR. 5200.30.

COMMENDATION FROM GENERAL C. L. CHENNAULT REGARDING MESSAGE FROM ADMIRAL WILLIAM HALSEY TO THE FOURTEENTH AIR FORCE AND THE 308TH BOMB GROUP

HEADQUARTERS FOURTEENTH AIR FORCE
A.P.O. 627, c/o Postmaster
New York City, New York

27 October 1944

SUBJECT: Commendation

TO : Commanding Officers, all units, Fourteenth Air Force.

1. Generalissimo Chiang Kai-shek, president of the Republic of China and Commander-in-Chief of the Chinese armed forces, has commended the officers and enlisted men of the Fourteenth Air Force in the following radio message (reparaphrased):

> "I am most pleased with the effective and close cooperation between the Fourteenth Air Force and the Chinese ground forces in the Liuchow area. So that the enemy will soon be destroyed, I hope you will continue your unrelenting efforts in this direction. I herewith express my highest commendation of you and the men under your leadership."

2. This firm tribute from His Excellency, the Generalissimo, may be taken as a personal compliment by each member of this command. It will serve to spur us on to even greater efforts to aid our gallant Chinese Allies in their hour of greatest need and to hasten the final defeat of the enemy.

/s/ C. L. CHENNAULT
Major General, U.S.A.,
Commanding

Source: Courtesy Simpson Historical Center, Maxwell Air Force Base, Alabama. This document is declassified in accordance with DOD DIR. 5200.30.

Appendix IV: Documents on the Operations of the 308th Bomb Group Radar Control Center

HISTORY AND OPERATIONS OF THE 308TH BOMB GROUP RADAR CONTROL CENTER, FOURTEENTH AIR FORCE HEADQUARTERS, KUNMING, CHINA

I. History

II. Establishment of 308th Control Center
   A. Purpose
   B. Sections
      (1) Communications
      (2) Intelligence
      (3) Naval Shipping
      (4) Control Operations
      (5) Weather
      (6) Mining Naval

III. A. Maps
      (1) Plotting
      (2) Enemy Air Operations (Radar and Fighters)
      (3) Enemy Ground Opposition
         (a) Large Map
      (4) Coordination Friendly Philippine Forces
      (5) Map Showing Attacks on Shipping
      (6) Map of Sightings for Shipping Trends
      (7) Mining Program
      (8) Weather

   B. Boards
      (1) Daily Schedule Board
      (2) Status of Aircraft and Crews
      (3) Daily Operational Results

   C. Records
      (1) Air, Ground Communications Procedures
      (2) Written Log
      (3) Verbal Message Log
      (4) Controller's Handbook

IV. Duties of Controller

V. Evaluation
   A. Navy
   B. 14th Air Force (Tab A)

Source: Courtesy Simpson Historical Center, Maxwell Air Force Base, Alabama. This document is declassified in accordance with DOD DIR. 5200.30.

308TH BOMBARDMENT GROUP DETACHMENT NO. I
Office of the Commanding Officer
A.P.O. 627, c/o Postmaster
New York City, New York

HISTORY AND OPERATIONS OF THE 308TH BOMB GROUP CONTROL CENTER

I. History

A. Anti-shipping units of the 308th Bomb Group had been in operation from advanced bases in Eastern China during 1944 and were successful. However, the loss of these bases forced the Group to conduct operations against shipping from Western bases and divide these operations between the four (4) Squadrons of the Group. Each Squadron dispatched one (1) unarmed Recon daily for a total of four (4) each day at six (6) hour intervals. Strikers were available at the Squadrons to go out after sightings, but this method of operations did not prove satisfactory due to poor communications and lack of centraliized responsibility.

B. When the 308th Group moved to Chengtu, it transferred all its LAB and other radar equipped aircraft to the 373rd Bomb Squadron at Luliang. This change was completed and operations were started 13 February 1945.

II. Establishment of 308th Operational Control Center

A. The 308th Bomb Group Detachment was organized for the main purpose of directing radar operations of the aircraft at Luliang. Elements of the 308th Bomb Group Detachment and the U.S. Navy Unit, Headquarters 14th Air Force, were incorporated into a combined organization, known as the 308th Operational Control Center. These two (2) units moved into the same building to simplify communications and liaison problems. This center was located in Kunming because all intelligence reports and Leyte intercepts were being received originally by some agency in Kunming and the only radio station powerful enough to operate our aircraft at the extreme limit of their range was located at Kunming.

B. The Control Center was established by the Detachment for the following purposes:

(1) To provide one center for the receipt, evaluation and semination of shipping intelligence.

(2) To plan, schedule and direct the air effort against shipping.

C. The Control Center was organized in the following sections:

(1) Communications Section: Communications facilities were:

(a) A teletype direct to Luliang with a device for security.

(b) A point to point radio for liaison with Luliang.

(c) Arrangements were made to utilize WLIF, a 500 watt radio station operated by the 14th Airforce, to communicate with aircraft in the air and to monitor Philippine stations and aircraft.

Cont'd

(d) A direct telephone line to WLIF from the control room.
(e) A telephone to Luliang.
(f) The Control Center also had the use of the following Navy communications: Teletype to Chungking, teletype to 14th Air Force Teletype Center, Weather teletype.

(2) Intelligence Section.
(a) An Army Intelligence Section was formed. This section handled all intelligence work on shipping, the flash reports on sorties flown, intelligence files, maps and charts, records and results. This section worked in direct contact with the Navy Shipping Section.

(3) Navy Shipping Section.
(a) This section kept all types of enemy shipping intelligence and had personnel trained especially for this type of work. This section aided in recognition, estimation of courses and speeds of enemy shipping, and proved to be of great help in determining lengths and weights of enemy vessels sunk, probably sunk, or damaged.

(4) Control Section.
The Control Section was formed to direct air power against enemy shipping. This section was run by Army personnel and operated twenty-four (24) hours a day. It was equipped with the necessary maps, charts, boards, and communication facilities to implement this operation. By use of maps, the controller kept a constant visual check on the existing tactical situation. The track of striker aircraft and enemy shipping was plotted hourly. The location of enemy radar search areas and land based fighter installations were maintained on charts. The controller had rapid and reliable communications with aircraft in the air, and immediate access to Navy Intelligence and communications facilities. At his disposal was the aid of the Navy Shipping Section Personnel, in estimating courses and speeds of enemy shipping. The Control Section personnel were pilots that had the necessary experience in LAB tactics and procedure to evaluate the situation and properly direct the air effort.

(5) Weather Section.
A Naval Weather Section was established in the same building. From this section, the Controller could get weather and forecasts whenever needed. The weather of the entire operational area was plotted by the Naval Weather Section at least once every twenty-four (24) hours on a large chart in the Control Room.

(6) Naval Mining Section.
This section was established in the same building and kept up the records and results of the joint Army-Navy Mining Program. This section advised Army as to types, tactics, schedules, and results of the Program.

Cont'd

III. Records And Maps Used In The Control Room

A. Maps.
(1) Plotting Map. This was a large wall map covering the entire operational area. The controller plotted all sightings, attacks, plane positions and tracks on this one map, and used these plots to analyze the situation.
(2) Enemy Air Opposition Map. This map covered the same area. Enemy airfields, enemy air strength at each field and areas covered by enemy search radar were shown. This map was kept up by the Army Intelligence Section.
(3) Enemy Ground Opposition Map. This was a large scale wall map of China, French Indochina and the Philippines. Enemy occupied territory, directions of drives and all other pertinent information were indicated. This map was kept up by both Army and Navy Intelligence Sections.
(4) Coordination with Friendly Philippine Forces. This was a small scale map showing the Philippine Fields and overwater search areas.
(5) Attacks on Shipping. This was a large scale map showing the attacks on enemy shipping by 308th planes. These attacks were plotted as sunk, probably sunk, damaged and missed. The Army Intelligence Section kept this map up to date.
(6) Map of Sightings. Kept by the Navy Shipping Section and served to determine shipping trends.
(7) Chart Showing Mine Fields. This chart showed the mine fields used in the joint Army-Navy Mining Program. On this chart was kept the number of mines dropped in each field, and the date the mines were dropped. This map was kept up to date by the Controller.
(8) Weather Map. A small scale map of the entire operational area was kept up by the Navy Weather Section. The weather was plotted at least once every twenty-four (24) hours, or as often as necessary for the Controller's use.

B. Boards in the Control Room.
(1) Daily Schedule Board. This was a board listing the planes flying for the period, type of mission, call signs, take off times and ETA's.
(2) Status of Aircraft and Crews. This listed the planes and crews in the 373rd Bomb Squadron.
(3) Daily Operational Results. This was a board kept up daily and having on it the following information: Number of sorties, results of attacks, number of ships sighted, number of secondary targets hit, number of bombardment sorties, number of turnbacks.

C. Records in the Control Room.
(1) Air-Ground Communications Procedures. To eliminate errors in air-ground communications, the Control Section

Cont'd

devised standard reporting procedures as follows:
(a) Position Report - This form was used by the radio operator in the plane to transmit the position of the plane every hour on the hour to Operational Control. The Controller then plotted this position on the plotting map. The plane was tracked along its entire course. Its position and ground speed could be computed within a very few miles, and thus the Controller knew where the plane was at any given time during its flight.
(b) Sighting Report - This form was used to report all sightings of shipping to the Control Center. It consisted of time, position of sighting , composition of sighting, course, speed, whether the sighting is visual or radar, the cloud ceiling and percent cover and authentication. It was always transmitted prior to attack.
(c) Attack Report - This report was transmitted immediately after attack, and gave the time of attack, position, type of ship, results, and whether the run was made by radar or aided by visual reference.
(d) Emergency Landing Report - This report was used in any case where the plane had to land at any other than its home base. It included the following: Time over the field, pilot's name, name of field, nature of trouble.
(e) Distress Position Report - This was a coded report transmitted when ditching appeared imminent. This position was relayed to rescue submarines thru Chungking. The procedure had but three (3) factors:
(1) First a given coordinate that had a code name.
(2) Position was given <u>from</u> code name as a bearing in degrees.
(3) Miles were given <u>from</u> code name.

D. <u>Message Logs</u>.
Handling of messages was very important due to the classification of any information concerning shipping. Permanent records were kept showing who handled the messages, either written or verbal, what time the message was received, nature of message, and the action taken.
(1) Written Message Log - This log was kept in the Control Room, and all messages of written nature were entered on this log. The operating period of the control was started 0600 hours every morning and ran until 0600 hours the following morning, and all records were kept on this basis. Written messages were given to the Controller on duty, who numbered the message, and then entered such on the log. These messages were filed in a daily file, and this file was kept in the Control Room for a 30 day period. After this period, messages were placed in a permanent file.
(2) Verbal Message Log - This log was kept in the Control Room. All important verbal messages were kept on this log. Air-ground communications, such as messages from aircraft of sighting reports, attack reports, position reports, and emergency landing reports were kept in this log. This was

Cont'd

a permanent file handled by the Controller on duty, who entered the message he sent out and received, what action was taken and the time. This form was kept in daily file for 30 days, then went to the permanent file.

E. Handbook of Controller's Information.
A standard operating procedure for the Control Section was established and in this file was the following information:
(1) Handling of messages - both written and verbal.
(2) Information on available communications.
(3) Notes on procedures to be followed.
(4) Rating of intelligence going through the office.
(5) Turning points and coordinates of courses flown.
(6) Plans of cooperation with the 69th Wing and their anti-shipping capabilities.
(7) Notes on Shadow Tactics.
(8) Cruise control chart.
(9) Procedure for plotting our planes and enemy shipping.
(10) Code names used in messages.

IV. Duties of Controller

A. The Controller was responsible for the direction of air effort against enemy shipping. He evaluated, plotted and relayed all air-ground communications, and took such immediate action as was warranted by the situation to get the most effective results. For example: Upon receiving a sighting report or attack report the following steps were taken:
(1) The report was first entered upon the Verbal Message Log.
(2) The sighting or attack was plotted. This information was sent immediately to the 373rd Bomb Squadron for their information.
(3) The report was given immediately to the Navy Communications Section for retransmission to the Fleet.
(4) The report was given to the 69th Wing provided it was within their limits of operations.
(5) The weather was given to the Navy Weather Section, and also to Base Weather at Kunming.
(6) If the situation was appropriate, the Controller would order additional striking forces off Luliang.
(7) The Controller analyzed the situation by checking his plotting map for plane positions and position of the sighting. He sent the necessary information to planes within striking distances to go to the sighting.
(8) In cases where it was practical for the plane to shadow the sighting, the Controller ordered the plane to shadow and turn on his IFF. He then contacted other planes which could reach the sighting and told them there was a plane shadowing and they could "home in" by using IFF as a beacon.

V. Evaluation of System

A. The following excerpt has been taken from a statement by Lt. Cmdr. S. S. Savage, Commander, U.S. Naval Unit, Hdqtrs., 14th Air Force:

Cont'd

"The benefits mutually accuring are many. In my opinion, the combined operations from a Joint Operations Headquarters is the practical and ideal solution to the problem of coordinating 308th Bomb Group operations with Pacific Naval Commands."

He further indicated that some of the advantages derived were as follows:

(1) Advantages to Navy
(a) Receipt, generally within a few minutes of time of sighting, of enemy shipping contact reports, sightings are passed through U.S. Naval Group. China communications to U.S. submarines and Philippines based aircraft have resulted in the destruction of many Japanese ships in the South China Sea.
(b) The results of strikes against enemy shipping in the Tonkin Gulf area by 308th planes are immediately passed to the fleet.
(c) Evaluation of enemy shipping losses due to 308th Bomb Group activity is more accurately assessed in view of the use of Naval Photo Interpretation Officers specially trained in shipping.
(d) Prompt interchange of information between U.S. submarines and 308th strike planes. In one instance, 308th planes were able to destroy a large ship damaged by submarine attack.
(e) Navy is kept currently and promptly informed on 308th Bomb Group mining missions.

(2) Advantages to 308th Bomb Group
(a) Centralization of operational shipping reports from all China Theater sources at one point where they are filtered by trained Naval shipping officers. Sources include: U.S. Naval Group China, coastwatchers, OSS agents, AGAS agents, French sources, British sources, intercepts of submarine and Philippine based planes sightings reports. From the various reports, enemy shipping positions are predicted for 308th strikes.
(b) Availability of Naval Ordnance Officers in connection with mining activity.
(c) Daily weather reports and predictions by Naval Aerological Officers based on Naval weather stations in China.
(d) Availability of Naval Photo Interpretation Officers.
(e) Availability of Naval Recognition Officers for training of crews in JMST system of ship identification.
(f) The benefit of U.S. Naval Group China's communication with the fleet.
(g) Instant contact with Naval rescue facilities.

B. An analysis of the system was made by the Operational Analysis Section of 14th Air Force Headquarters, and is attached at Tab A.

William D. Hopson,
Lt. Col. Air Corps,
Commanding

ANALYSIS OF THE OPERATIONS OF THE 308TH BOMB GROUP RADAR CONTROL CENTER BY THE OPERATIONAL ANALYSIS SECTION, FOURTEENTH AIR FORCE HEADQUARTERS, KUNMING CHINA, FEBRUARY 23–APRIL 5, 1945.

B-24 LAB OPERATIONS

Table of Contents

I. SUMMARY AND RECOMMENDATIONS

1. The Kunming control system now used to direct LAB operations originating from Luliang is analyzed for the six-week period from February 23 through April 5. It is shown that to accomplish a given result approximately 30 percent more sorties would be required if the system did not operate than if the system did operate.

2. Sorties acting on intelligence data regarding specific targets should take preference over sorties which are sent out to search. The former sorties should be armed reconnaissance sorties unless information dictates the use of a striker. Search sorties should be sent out in accordance with the remaining available force according to the following:

a. One search sortie available per day. Armed reconnaissance sortie timed so as to arrive and be able to sweep within blind bomb line just after dark.

b. Two search sorties available per day. One sortie as above; the other sortie should sweep a complimentary area outside the blind bomb area, and it should be timed so as to complete sweep just after dark so that if a ship is being "shadowed," it can be attacked.

c. Three search sorties available per day. Two sorties as above; third sortie should be striker over area within blind bomb line. These recommendations are based on the assumption that obtaining intelligence is relatively unimportant compared with sinking shipping.

3. The number of sea targets is rapidly decreasing in the area being swept, and the effectiveness of the sorties is diminishing correspondingly. This trend should continue to be studied during the next few months, and if it persists, the LAB forces should be otherwise deployed.

II. Effectiveness of the control system

1. To analyze the effectiveness of the control system, the sorties were divided into two classes:

a. "Briefed sorties" - those which were directed as a consequence of the control system.

b. "Unbriefed sorties" - those which were not directed as a consequence of the control system.

Source: Courtesy Simpson Historical Center, Maxwell Air Force Base, Alabama. This document is declassified in accordance with DOD DIR. 5200.30.

If a sortie was briefed but did not find the briefed target, but did find another target for which it was not briefed, it was placed in the class with the "unbriefed sorties." This tends to make an evaluation of the control system conservative. Abortive sorties were not considered in either class.

2. For all sorties, it was then determined whether the sorties did or did not find sufficient sea targets to use all their bombs. These data are tabulated in Table I.

3. Of a total of 134 sorties, 67 sorties found targets for their bombs. This is one out of 2.0 sorties which found targets. Of the sorties which were not briefed, 29 out of 76 sorties found targets, or one out of 2.6. If it is assumed that this same latter ratio would have held if the control system was not in operation and none of the sorties briefed, it follows that to accomplish a given result 30 percent more sorties would be required if the control system did not operate than if the control system did operate.

4. While the value of 39 percent can not be considered exact, due to the sparcity of data, it is at the same time clear that a significant improvement results from the use of the control. The value of 30 percent tends to be conservative since all sorties not finding a briefed target, but finding another target, were put in the "unbriefed sortie" class. It is probably significant, also, that for each individual week, with the exception of the week of March 30 - April 5, the briefed missions were more effective than those which were not briefed.

III. STRAIGHT RECONNAISSANCE SORTIES VERSUS ARMED RECONNAISSANCE SORTIES

1. Information on the desirable proportion of straight reconnaissance and armed reconnaissance sorties may be derived from Table I. Most of the unbriefed sorties are armed reconnaissance planes. If these had been straight reconnaissance planes, the number of ships finding targets would be 29 x (7/5) or 40. This assumes the time over water to be 7 hours and 5 hours for straight reconnaissance and armed reconnaissance sorties respectively, and that the number of targets found is proportional to the time over water. If sorties were sent out to attack these 40 vessels they would have found (38/50) 40 or 30 of them. This is essentially the same as the number of unbriefed armed reconnaissance sorties finding targets (namely, 29). From this it follows that if all the unbriefed sorties were unarmed, even though an additional 40 sorties were sent out to attack the ships found by them, the number of targets attacked would not have increased. The inadvisability of straight reconnaissance sorties is thus obvious. The argument is even stronger when applied to the latter part of the selected period during which time the number of targets found per sortie are less than for the first part of the period.

2. Added to this is the fact that straight reconnaissance sorties are not able to attack secondary targets.

IV. ARMED RECONNAISSANCE SORTIES VERSUS STRIKERS

1. The decision between strikers and armed reconnaissance sorties is less obvious and requires a knowledge of the number of ships sighted by sorties on various missions. During the periods in question, the frequency with which no ships were sighted by a sortie, one ship was sighted, etc., is given in column 2 of Table II.

2. Suppose a sufficient number of armed reconnaissance sorties to observe this number of ships were sent out as shown in column 3. Assuming strikers can be over the water 3 hours and armed reconnaissance sorties can be over water 5 hours, the number of ships sighted by strikers would be 3/5 of the number sighted by an equal number of armed reconnaissance sorties. These values are given in column 4 of Table II. Assuming that a striker can attack 3 ships, and an armed reconnaissance sortie can attack 2 ships, the last two columns in Table II give the number of ships which can be attacked by armed reconnaissance sorties and by strikers. The total number is 20 percent greater for armed reconnaissance sorties than for strikers. This indicates the inadvisability of using strikers except where a particular target dictates their use.

TABLE I

Week	Briefed Sorties		Unbriefed Sorties	
	Total No. of briefed sorties	No. of sorties finding target	Total No. of unbriefed sorties	No. of sorties finding target
Feb 23 Mar 1	13	11	8	5
Mar 2 Mar 8	9	9	8	5
Mar 9 Mar 15	12	9	12	8
Mar 16 Mar 22	7	3	24	9
Mar 23 Mar 29	6	4	18	0
Mar 30 Apr 5	11	2	6	2
TOTAL	58	38	76	29

TABLE II

Number of ships sighted by sortie	No. of times given number of ships were sighted by sortie	Assumed No. of times number of ships would have been sighted by armed recon	No. of times given number of ships would have been sighted by strikers	No. of ships which could have been attacked by armed recon	No. of ships which could have been attacked by strikers
0	63	63			
1	16	16	10	16	10
2	10	10	6	20	12
3	10	10	6	20	18
4	6	6	4	12	12
5	3	3	2	6	6
6	6	6	4	12	12
Greater than 6	17	17	20	34	30
			Total	120	100

Glossary

ASV	air surface vessel.
ATC	air transport command.
CBI	China-Burma-India theater.
drift meter	device mounted in aircraft to determine the amount of drift caused by wind on any given compass heading by using a ground reference point.
ETA	estimated time of arrival.
H2X	radar-equipped aircraft for high-altitude bombing.
IFF	identification friend or foe.
LAB	radar-equipped aircraft for low-altitude bombing.
Lister bag	a portable bag of rubberized cloth or canvas used for carrying disinfected drinking water.
MAD	magnetic anomaly detection.
on the step	flight attitude of aircraft to achieve maximum airspeed and eliminate drag by adjusting trim tabs to get plane in a balanced and level flight position.
prop feathering	flight procedure that involves rotating propeller blades to the vertical position in order to eliminate drag.
straight B-24	B-24 without radar capabilities.
trimming the plane	flight procedure that involves moving trim tabs on vertical and horizontal surfaces so as to correct for directional and vertical stability.

Index

ABOUT THE AUTHOR

A. B. FEUER is a military historian and freelance newspaper and magazine journalist. The author of *Bilibid Diary: The Secret Notebooks of Commander Thomas Hayes* (1987), *Combat Diary: Episodes from the History of the Twenty-Second Regiment, 1866–1905* (Praeger, 1991), and *Coast Watching in the Solomon Islands: The Bougainville Reports, December 1941–July 1943* (Praeger, 1992), he has also published articles in numerous journals, including *Military History Magazine*, *Sea Classics*, *Civil War Quarterly*, and *World War II* and is a book reviewer for *Military Review*.